MULTICULTURAL AND GENDER EQUITY

IN THE MATHEMATICS CLASSROOM

THE GIFT OF DIVERSITY

1997 YEARBOOK

Janet Trentacosta

1997 Yearbook Editor
San Diego City Schools (Retired)

Margaret J. Kenney

General Yearbook Editor
Boston College

NATIONAL COUNCIL OF TEACHERS OF MATHEMATICS

Library of Congress Cataloging-in-Publication Data:

Multicultural and gender equity in the mathematics classroom : the gift of
    diversity / Janet Trentacosta, Margaret J. Kenney [editors].
        p.   cm. — (Yearbook ; 1997)
    Includes bibliographical references.
    ISBN 0-87353-432-8 (hardcover)
    1. Minority students—United States—Education—Mathematics.
2. Mathematical ability—Sex differences.   3. Multicultural
education—United States.   4. Sex differences in education.
I. Trentacosta, Janet.   II. Kenney, Margaret J.   III. Series:
Yearbook (National Council of Teachers of Mathematics) ; 1997.
QA1.N3   1997
[QA13]
370.117—dc21   97-658
                                                                 CIP

Printed in the United States of America

Contents

PART 3: CURRICULUM, INSTRUCTION, AND ASSESSMENT

PART 4: PROFESSIONAL DEVELOPMENT

PART 5: FUTURE DIRECTIONS

Preface

The demographics of our mathematics classrooms are changing and reflect more diversity—in cultures, ethnic groups, and languages. At the same time, mathematics education is changing as teachers emphasize more problem solving, hands-on activities, interactive learning experiences, the use of a variety of technological tools, and new kinds of assessments such as portfolios and open-ended questions. The NCTM *Curriculum and Evaluation Standards* calls for an "opportunity for all students" to learn mathematics. The 1992 Mathematics Framework for California Public Schools pointed out that "instead of diversity being viewed as a challenge, it can now be seen as a gift.... Along with the gift of diversity come responsibilities. Empowering mathematics programs are inclusive; they use nonracist and nonsexist language, culturally diverse situations, and teaching materials that make mathematics accessible."

This NCTM 1997 Yearbook presents a vision of how research and classroom practices related to multicultural diversity and gender equity can reinforce each other to ensure a powerful mathematics program for all students regardless of their gender, race, ethnicity, or socioeconomic situation. It is designed to furnish a variety of perspectives and diverse voices that address relevant issues and suggest possible models that exemplify the vision. Special care was taken to ensure that each paper would reflect the voice of the author, even when that voice may differ from the views of others.

Although the yearbook is organized into five parts, the placement of an article into a specific area was sometimes arbitrary, since articles may overlap the content of several sections. Part 1, articles 1 through 5, address general issues and perspectives related to multicultural and gender equity that will be addressed in more depth in later papers. Papers in Part 2, articles 6 through 12, give some insights into classroom cultures that capitalize on the rich gift of diversity that is available in every classroom. They afford a look into a variety of classrooms and attempt to show how classrooms can offer mathematically powerful mathematical programs for all students, regardless of their race, ethnicity, language, or gender. Papers in Part 3, articles 13 through 21, focus on curriculum, instruction, and assessment and how these influence equity in the mathematics classroom. Examples of curriculum, instructional strategies, and assessment practices that promote equity in the classroom for all students are included. Part 4, articles 22 through 26, addresses some specific professional development activities, including one involving preservice teachers and two others related to increasing family involvement. Finally, papers in Part 5, articles 27 and 28, present two challenges for the future.

The production of this yearbook represents the commitment of many people over a three-year period. Close to seventy manuscripts were submitted to the Editorial Panel for review, and this final publication includes twenty-eight papers from forty-five authors. The Editorial Panel developed the guidelines for this yearbook, reviewed all the submitted papers, selected those to be included, and made valuable suggestions for improving manuscripts. My sincere thanks and appreciation go to these outstanding people:

Gerlena Clark	Los Angeles County Office of Education (retired)
Kay Gilliland	EQUALS, Lawrence Hall of Science (retired), Berkeley, California
Clo Mingo	New Mexico Highlands University, Las Vegas, New Mexico
Rick Scott	University of New Mexico, Albuquerque, New Mexico

I also want to thank those people who assisted the Editorial Panel in reviewing some of the manuscripts. I especially want to thank Margaret Kenney, General Editor for the 1996 through 1998 Yearbooks, who was very generous in providing support and guidance. My thanks, as well, go to the editorial and production staff at the NCTM Headquarters Office, who turned a collection of manuscripts into a finished yearbook.

The writers of the papers in this yearbook have proposed a variety of questions from different points of view and have shared examples of high-quality mathematics programs that show that all students can succeed. It is our hope that all teachers will reflect on the ideas presented in this publication and will commit themselves to mathematics programs that truly address the diversity found in their classrooms and ensure a powerful mathematics program for all our students.

Janet Trentacosta
1997 Yearbook Editor

1

Mathematics for All Students
Access, Excellence, and Equity

Lucille Croom

DURING the 1980s, numerous national reports documented the underachievement in mathematics of students in American schools. The general sentiment shared by most of these reports was a call for change. In 1989, the National Council of Teachers of Mathematics (NCTM) published its *Curriculum and Evaluation Standards,* which included a new vision for mathematics education. The underlying assumption on which this new vision was based is that changes and improvements in teaching and learning will afford every child equal access to a substantive mathematics education. As NCTM (1989, p. 4) concludes:

> The social injustices of past schooling practices can no longer be tolerated.... Mathematics has become a critical filter for employment and full participation in our society. We cannot afford to have the majority of our population mathematically illiterate: Equity has become an economic necessity.

A proliferation of research documents the lack of achievement in mathematics by disproportionate numbers of African American, Hispanic, Native American, and female students (National Research Council [NRC] 1990, 1989; Secada 1992; Oakes 1990).

As we approach the next century, the mathematics education community is making dramatic changes in curriculum, instruction, and assessment. These changes are the principal components of a concerted effort to create equitable and high-quality learning opportunities for all students, including those groups whose achievement has been impeded because of social injustices in school practices and policies. Both minorities and females must be provided an equal opportunity to acquire the mathematical literacy essential for employment, leadership positions, and social and economic advancement in an increasingly technological society (Oakes 1990). The economic and scientific viability of this nation is influenced by the extent to which all students are empowered with the quantitative literacy required for full participation in today's society (NRC 1989).

1

A VIEW TOWARD EQUITY

The workforce of the future will be expected to deal with the complexities of the workplace through teamwork, logical reasoning, and the use of problem-solving skills. Underachievement in mathematics must not represent the norm for the majority of students in American schools (NRC 1989). According to Secada (1990), "students from diverse backgrounds are not well served in the mathematics that they are taught" (p. 354). This article examines the critical changes needed in curriculum, pedagogy, policies, and beliefs to promote equity in mathematics education for all students in the nation's schools. Equity in mathematics education implies fairness, justice, and equality for all students so that they may achieve their full potential, regardless of race, ethnicity, gender, or socioeconomic status.

The mathematics education community must help parents and the larger community understand how implementing the *Standards* promotes equity for all students. Furthermore, the general public must know about the new directions currently under way in school mathematics designed to increase students' achievement. The National Research Council (1989, p. 14) warns that if not corrected, innumeracy and illiteracy will increase the likelihood of the United States

> becoming a divided nation in which knowledge of mathematics supports a productive, technologically powerful elite while a dependent, semiliterate majority, disproportionately Hispanic and Black, find economic and political power beyond reach.

Policymakers, administrators, teachers, researchers, parents, and students themselves must not only verbalize but actually believe that it is possible to instill quantitative literacy in every student in the nation's schools.

CULTURAL DIVERSITY IN THE CLASSROOM

Providing student populations that differ in culture, race, gender, and socioeconomic background with an equitable learning environment must become a high priority. In 1990, Steen reported that more than 50 percent of the students enrolled in twenty-three of the twenty-five largest public school systems were minority (p. 130). Demographic trends indicate that by the turn of the century the majority of those persons entering the workforce will be female or from an ethnic-minority group and that half of the students in our nation's schools will come from non-European-American backgrounds (Hodgkinson 1994, 1988).

Beginning in elementary school, policies that track students into low-level classes on the basis of their perceived abilities serve only to diminish students' opportunities to learn and develop higher-order thinking skills (Oakes 1986). The inequitable practice of tracking students affects minority and economically disadvantaged students adversely (Jones 1993; Oakes 1985). As Jones (1993, p. 1) reminds us, if we eliminate tracking and create a level playing field—and then provide the support system for *all* students—then all students can succeed.

Students' achievement in mathematics is related to high expectations for educational attainment. Schools and teachers must implement research-based strategies that increase achievement and access, thereby enabling every student to develop mathematical power. Black and Hispanic students' achievement in mathematics in elementary school lags behind that of white children (Dossey et al. 1988). A disproportionate number of students from underrepresented groups drop out of mathematics. Encouragement by teachers, guidance counselors, and parents is essential if African American, Hispanic, Native American, and female students are to remain in mathematics throughout their school experience.

PROMOTING GENDER EQUITY

An increasing number of educators, researchers, and social critics assert that girls and minorities have been shortchanged in school, receive less encouragement, and have fewer opportunities to learn challenging mathematics and science than white males (American Association of University Women [AAUW] 1992; Oakes 1990; National Research Council 1989; National Science Foundation [NSF] 1994). In recent studies, researchers have found that gender differences in mathematics achievement have declined (AAUW 1995; Lee, Bryk, and Smith 1993). However, gender differences still appear in enrollment in upper-level, college-preparatory courses that are considered essential to acquiring the foundation for further study of advanced mathematics (Campbell 1995; Burton 1995; NRC 1989; NSF 1994). Women as well as minorities are underrepresented among those preparing to pursue mathematics- and science-related careers (AMS 1995; NSF 1994; NRC 1989).

Research shows that gender differences related to ability in mathematics persist in girls' and boys' perceptions throughout their schooling. Females reported more often than males that they had less confidence in their ability to do mathematics and expressed feelings of dislike for the subject as they got older (Hyde et al. 1990). The differential treatment females and minorities experience in the mathematics classroom may account for their lack of interest in, and understanding of, mathematics (Campbell 1995; Secada 1992; Oakes 1990). Researchers stress the importance of offering early intervention programs for underrepresented groups. These programs would emphasize career preparation, improve mathematical skills, and develop interest and positive attitudes (Oakes 1990).

Teachers and educators face a formidable challenge: to increase female and minority students' continuance in mathematics and science. This will require (1) modifying deep-rooted beliefs about who can learn mathematics, (2) making mathematics and science instruction more attractive, and (3) developing effective strategies to stimulate students' interest in these areas as college majors or as career choices.

EXPLORING A MULTICULTURAL PERSPECTIVE

An equitable learning environment affirms the richness of cultural diversity and creates an opportunity to engage all students in an interactive learning process. Efforts to introduce higher-level concepts must emanate from an appropriate cultural context or experience in which the student has some familiarity. In line with this belief, NCTM (1989) urges integrating students' cultural experiences into the learning process (p. 68). Banks (1989) reminds us that multicultural education is an ongoing process whose major goal is to improve the academic achievement of students from all racial, gender, cultural, and social-class groups (p. 3).

The curriculum for a multicultural approach to teaching mathematics should be organized around historical and cultural perspectives. This approach allows students to connect the historical sequence of mathematical developments with varied contributions of ancient civilizations. When teachers emphasize the roles different cultures have played in the evolution of mathematics, students' pride in the accomplishments of their people is enhanced and they begin to value mathematics as a human activity (Ascher 1991).

A multicultural mathematics curriculum emphasizes both the mathematical and the sociocultural aspects of the topics under consideration. The link between a concept and how it is used in the student's culture is an important part of learning mathematics. Equally important is how mathematics is perceived in that culture (NCTM 1991).

CREATING OPPORTUNITIES TO LEARN

An equitable learning environment engages students as active participants in mathematics instruction. Research shows that students cannot learn mathematics effectively by passively listening, disengaged from the learning process. Teachers must provide opportunities for students to construct their own understanding of mathematical concepts (NCTM 1989). Multiple learning situations must be provided that build on students' prior knowledge and cultural backgrounds.

Mathematical World Views

Diverse student populations have diverse world views of mathematics. Linguistic, cultural, and environmental factors determine a person's mathematical world view; "vestiges of other world views persist in some families for several generations" (Council of Chief State School Officers [CCSSO] 1995). Teachers' awareness of differences in students' mathematical world views enables them to develop strategies for dealing effectively with students' multiple perspectives of mathematics. The Council of Chief State School Officers (1995, p. 32), in its resource document for teacher licensing and development in mathematics, contrasts the mathematical world views used by other cultures with those found in the United States:

> The United States uses base ten counting ... but some societies use base-20 or base-60.... Many others incorporate place value into their counting (5234 is read five thousands two hundreds three tens four) ... the United States views fractions through a part-whole lens. A whole is divided into equal parts.... However, some languages do not even contain words for dividing things up ... they build fractions up (take one object, quadruple it, and then take three of the resultant objects).

In order to create an equitable learning environment among a growing diverse student population, it is important for teachers to understand the relationship between learning mathematics and the linguistic and cultural backgrounds of the students (CCSSO 1995; NCTM 1991). Teachers who understand the interrelatedness among topics in mathematics and acquire the facility to operate using different mathematical world views can help students develop their ability to understand mathematics and to build on their own mathematical world views (CCSSO 1995).

Opportunity to Learn

Diverse ethnic groups and females must be afforded the same chance to learn higher-level mathematical concepts as their upper- and middle-class white male counterparts. It is imperative that classroom teachers examine their own assumptions and beliefs about who can learn mathematics. Mathematics should not be considered valuable only for those students who will pursue careers in science, engineering, or technology. Mathematics affects every aspect of life; therefore, all students deserve an opportunity to develop their reasoning and analytical skills and to achieve their full potential. The classroom should be a nonthreatening, supportive place that encourages students to explore, conjecture, reason, and make decisions. Learning activities should present mathematics as alive, exciting, and a useful human endeavor in society, using pedagogical approaches that build on the full range of students' prior knowledge and understanding of mathematical ideas. Classroom teachers must use a variety of teaching and assessment strategies to promote the development of reasoning and problem-solving skills. Teachers need support, however, through professional development workshops on how to link these strategies with content and how to organize instruction in a way that promotes the learning of higher-level mathematical concepts for all students.

In addition, equitable treatment of all students requires that schools and teachers devise strategies that support and encourage family involvement in school matters as well as in mathematics instruction. When teachers form partnerships with families and their communities, mathematics education becomes more meaningful.

Promoting Equity through Professional Development

Improving the opportunity to learn, along with higher teacher expectations, improves student learning and achievement in mathematics (Oakes 1995). In its *Professional Standards for Teaching Mathematics,* the National Council of Teachers of Mathematics (1991) urges mathematics teachers and schools to focus on new ways for improving the quality of mathematics instruction. Therefore, schools and teachers must organize instruction to accommodate diversity in ways that are beneficial to students and compatible with their interests and needs. To help schools and teachers accomplish this goal, the following issues must be considered:

- *Is the curriculum organized to accommodate the learning styles of culturally diverse students?* Are students assigned to work cooperatively in groups using the students' own cultural or personal experiences? Does the classroom environment generate complex problem-solving situations that promote active engagement and improve motivation?
- *Are professional development activities organized to enhance teachers' knowledge of different mathematical world views and cultural perspectives?* Are teachers helped to understand how learning mathematics is influenced by the students' ethnic, cultural, socioeconomic, and linguistic backgrounds and gender?
- *Is equity in mathematics education promoted by ensuring that minority and female students have an equal opportunity to learn substantive mathematics?* Is there an attempt to end the sorting of elementary school students into low-level tracks? At the secondary school level, are minorities and females encouraged to enroll in upper-level, college-preparatory mathematics courses?
- *Is the achievement of limited-language-proficiency students promoted?* Are language-based barriers to learning mathematics removed from the curriculum? Is support provided to teachers who offer instruction to second-language learners?
- *Have strategies been devised to form partnerships with families?* Have families been helped to understand the critical role they can play in influencing their children's mathematics achievement, through such things as participating in school-sponsored family activities and offering support to their children in developing thinking skills in the home?
- *Are the richness and strength of cultural diversity affirmed?* Is a climate created that encourages sensitivity and respect for oneself and others?

Changing Pedagogical Practices

Lee and Smith (1995), using the results from the National Assessment of Educational Progress (NAEP), found that in schools that implemented nontraditional "restructuring" practices—including interdisciplinary teaching teams, mixed-ability classes in mathematics and science, and co-operative learning—students had higher achievement scores in mathematics than students in more traditional schools. Integrating such restructured practices into a multicultural curriculum promotes the student's total development by providing learning opportunities that support the belief that all students are expected to learn and achieve their human potential (Banks 1989).

Cooperative Learning

Small-group, cooperative-learning experiences help students explore mathematical concepts in an interactive problem-solving setting. Research reveals that group interaction or cooperative learning promotes female and minority students' self-esteem, motivation, and achievement. Group interaction also promotes the development of mental operations or processes in children, since children tend to internalize the talk heard in the group (Vygotsky 1978). Research shows that when students participate in cooperative learning, their attitudes toward their classmates, particularly those from different ethnic backgrounds, improve (Slavin 1986). Students learn to respect other students' points of view and differences.

CONCLUSION

NCTM notes that equity is a critical factor in the nation's economic viability. By the year 2000, the workplace will require all Americans, including minorities and women, to have the mathematical skills needed to meet the demands of the global marketplace. Eliminating the social injustices of past schooling practices will require the support of policymakers, administrators, teachers, parents, and others concerned about excellence and equity in mathematics education. The ideals of a democratic society require that all students be given an equal opportunity to acquire the quantitative literacy essential to compete for employment and leadership positions in today's society. The mathematics education community must expand its efforts to galvanize broad-based support for changing school mathematics in ways that increase opportunities to learn challenging mathematics and, in turn, increase the achievement of minority and female students. All children can learn challenging mathematics with appropriate support and an equitable learning environment, irrespective of ethnicity, race, gender, or social class.

A multicultural approach to mathematics instruction builds a foundation for promoting academic excellence and equity for all students. The challenge to change confronts all of us. Effective innovations in mathematics education require extensive modification of practices, school structures, policies, curriculum, pedagogy, and assessment in order to deal with the rigorous demands of a technologically advanced society.

REFERENCES

American Association of University Women. *Growing Smart: What's Working for Girls in School.* Washington, D.C.: AAUW Educational Foundation, 1995.

————.*How Schools Shortchange Girls.* Washington, D.C.: AAUW Educational Foundation, 1992.

American Mathematical Society. "A Report on the 1995 Survey of New Doctoral Recipients, Salary Survey for New Doctoral Recipients, and Faculty Salary Survey." *Notices of the AMS* 42 (1995):1504–12.

Ascher, Marcia. *Ethnomathematics: A Multicultural View of Mathematical Ideas.* Belmont, Calif.: Brooks/Cole Publishing Co., 1991.

Banks, James A. "Multicultural Education: Characteristics and Goals." In *Multicultural Education: Issues and Perspectives,* edited by James A. Banks and Cherry A. McGee Banks, pp. 2–26. Boston: Allyn & Bacon, 1989.

Burton, Nancy. "Trends in Mathematics Achievement for Young Men and Women." In *Prospects for School Mathematics,* edited by Iris M. Carl, pp. 115–27. Reston, Va.: Mathematics Education Trust, National Council of Teachers of Mathematics, 1995.

Campbell, Patricia B. "Redefining the 'Girl Problem in Mathematics.' " In *New Directions for Equity in Mathematics Education,* edited by Walter G. Secada, Elizabeth Fennema, and Lisa Byrd Adajian, pp. 225–41. New York: Cambridge University Press, 1995.

Council of Chief State School Officers. *Model Standards in Mathematics for Beginning Teacher Licensing and Development: A Resource for State Dialogue.* Draft. Washington, D.C.: Council of Chief State School Officers, 1995.

Dossey, John A., Ina V. S. Mullis, Mary M. Lindquist, and Donald L. Chambers. *The Mathematics Report Card: Are We Measuring Up?* Report no. 17-M-01. Princeton, N.J.: Educational Testing Service, 1988.

Hodgkinson, Harold. "How We're Changing: The Demographic State of the Nation." *Demographics for Decision Makers* 2 (Winter 1994): 1–3. [Washington, D.C.: Center for Demographic Policy, Institute for Educational Leadership]

———— ."An Interview with Harold Hodgkinson: Using Demographic Data for Long-Range Planning." *Phi Delta Kappan* 70 (October 1988): 166–70.

Hyde, Janet S., Elizabeth Fennema, Marilyn Ryan, Laurie Frost, and Carolyn Hopp. "Gender Comparisons of Mathematics Attitudes and Affect: A Meta-analysis." *Psychology of Women Quarterly* 14 (1990): 299–324.

Jones, Vinetta. "Views on the State of Public Schools." Paper presented at the Conference on the State of American Public Education, sponsored by the Phi Delta Kappa Institute on Education Leadership, 4–5 February, 1993.

Lee, Valerie, Anthony S. Bryk, and Julia B. Smith. "The Organization of Effective Secondary Schools." *Review of Research in Education* 19 (1993): 171–267.

Lee, Valerie, and Julia Smith. "Teaming and Mixed-Ability Classes Linked to Higher Achievement." *Harvard Education Letter* 11 (May/June 1995): 8.

National Council of Teachers of Mathematics. *Curriculum and Evaluation Standards for School Mathematics.* Reston, Va.: National Council of Teachers of Mathematics, 1989.

————.*Professional Standards for Teaching Mathematics.* Reston, Va.: National Council of Teachers of Mathematics, 1991.

National Research Council. *Everybody Counts: A Report to the Nation on the Future of Mathematics Education.* Washington, D.C.: National Research Council, 1989.

————.*Reshaping School Mathematics: A Philosophy and Framework for Curriculum.* Washington, D.C.: National Academy Press, 1990.

National Science Foundation. *Women, Minorities, and Persons with Disabilities in Science and Engineering.* NSF 94-333. Washington, D.C.: National Science Foundation, 1994.

Oakes, Jeannie. *Keeping Track: How Schools Structure Inequality.* New Haven, Conn.: Yale University Press, 1985.

————."Opportunities, Achievement, and Choice: Women and Minority Students in Science and Mathematics." *Review of Research in Education* 16 (1990): 153–222.

————."Opportunity to Learn: Can Standards-Based Reform Be Equity-Based Reform?" In *Prospects for School Mathematics,* edited by Iris M. Carl, pp. 78–98. Reston, Va.: Mathematics Education Trust, National Council of Teachers of Mathematics, 1995.

————."Tracking, Inequality, and the Rhetoric of Reform: Why Schools Don't Change." *Journal of Education* 168 (1986): 60–78.

Secada, Walter G. "Needed: An Agenda for Equity in Mathematics Education." *Journal for Research in Mathematics Education* 21 (November 1990): 354–55.

————."Race, Ethnicity, Social Class, Language, and Achievement in Mathematics." In *Handbook of Research on Mathematics Teaching and Learning,* edited by Douglas Grouws, pp. 623–60. New York: Macmillan Publishing Co., 1992.

Slavin, Robert E. "Learning Together: Cooperative Groups and Peer Tutoring Produce Significant Academic Gains." *American Educator* 10 (Summer 1986): 6–11.

Steen, Lynn Arthur. "Mathematics for All Americans." In *Teaching and Learning Mathematics in the 1990s,* 1990 Yearbook of the National Council of Teachers of Mathematics, edited by Thomas J. Cooney, pp. 130–34. Reston, Va.: National Council of Teachers of Mathematics, 1990.

Vygotsky, Lev S. *Mind in Society: The Development of Higher Psychological Processes.* Cambridge, Mass.: Harvard University Press, 1978.

2

In Addition to the Mathematics
Including Equity Issues
in the Curriculum

Marilyn Frankenstein

THE first learning experience with which I start my criticalmathematical[1] literacy curriculum involves students' considering the advertisement shown in figure 2.1. They conclude that Poluhoff's main message is that "with proper resources all people can learn mathematics and science," and I always add that "with enough time and hard work, I guarantee that everyone in the class will learn the mathematics." In addition, this

---

WITH APOLOGIES TO PYGMALION

Give me the price of one aircraft carrier group
plus
10,000 little black misfits from the ghetto sewer
and
in 30 years I will bring you:
1,000 Einsteins and 9 Nobel Laureates
Guaranteed! No ifs, ands or buts

—Nicholas Stephen Poluhoff

P.S. $C_{77}H_{98}O_{33}N_{14}S$
P.P.S. Too low they build who build beneath the stars

Fig. 2.1. Reprinted with permission (*Nation,* 18 June 1990, p. 855).

---

1. The term *criticalmathematics* was coined by Professor Arthur B. Powell of Rutgers University, Professor John Volmink of the University of Natal in Durban, South Africa, and the author to name a group of mathematics educators that we organized in 1990. See page 12 for a brief definition; in essence, this article in its entirety illustrates the meaning of the term applied to mathematical literacy. Contact the author for a broader definition and information about the group.

ad provokes many other discussions. Students reflect on their prior mathematics learning experiences and begin the process of analyzing the real reasons why they haven't yet learned basic mathematics—maybe it wasn't because of their "lack of mathematical ability," a reason they have often internalized from bad schooling and from the stereotypical assumptions prevalent in U.S. society about who can do mathematics. Students also begin the process—a process reinforced throughout the curriculum—of building self-confidence in their intellectual abilities. When someone inevitably asks who Pygmalion was, we discuss the importance of background information and how not knowing this fact does not mean you are "stupid"—it just means you need to find it out. This turns our reflections to the ways in which so many students' prior mathematics learning experiences involved "getting by," avoiding asking for missing information, and cleverly pretending to know, so that it has become hard for some people to figure out what they actually do understand in depth and what new mathematics learning they need. Further, we brainstorm how one goes about finding information. The "P.S." chemical formula is an additional ideal learning experience: I relate how none of the three chemistry professors I asked could help me do this research, and how I then called the magazine to put me in touch with Poluhoff. He told me it was the formula for melanin, the chemical that determines the shade of our skin color. Students learn that no one knows everything, and everyone can learn through research. Usually, some students express disagreement and anger at his phrases "black misfits" and "ghetto sewer," but sometimes I need to bring this up. Northeastern University Professor Robin Chandler pointed out that students' avoidance of that language reflects a "conspiracy of silence" about racism in our society. We discuss how those offensive phrases contradict his message of respect for those children's intellectual abilities. We look at how placing quotes around those phrases completely changes their meaning (just as small visual changes can completely change the meaning of mathematical expressions), making their meaning consistent with the rest of Poluhoff's message. With quotes it means "*society* thinks these children are misfits who live in a sewer, but give me the proper resources and I'll guarantee you brilliant scientists, and so on." Finally, in some classes we return to the content of the Pygmalion story and discuss issues of cultural hegemony: do people deserve respect only if they can be Nobel laureates? When women, for example, participate in mathematics fields, does their presence change the discipline?

This learning activity illustrates one of the ways in which I integrate equity issues into the content of my mathematics curriculum. Further, the meanings in this advertisement touch on themes that underlie my entire curriculum and could underlie other mathematics and other learning experiences: interdisciplinarity, ethnomathematics, and the politics of knowledge.

THE CONTEXT OF THE CURRICULUM

My students at the College of Public & Community Service (University of Massachusetts at Boston) are mainly working class, urban adults aged thirty to fifty and older who had not been "tracked" for college; many of them were labeled failures in secondary school. Most have internalized negative self-images about their knowledge and ability in "academic" disciplines. Approximately 60 percent are women; 30 percent, people of color. Most work (or are looking for work) full-time, have families, and attend school full-time. Most work in public and community service jobs; many have been involved in organizing for social change. Students can work toward their degree using prior learning from work or community organizing, new learning in classes, or new learning from community service. The faculty are activists as well as intellectuals; approximately 50 percent are women, 30 percent people of color. Teachers have less institutional power over students than in most universities because we don't give grades, and students can choose another faculty member to evaluate their work if they are dissatisfied with the first evaluation. We cannot require attendance or any other work that is not clearly discussed in the competency statement, which details the criteria and standards for demonstrating knowledge of the topic that students are studying.

MY CRITICALMATHEMATICAL LITERACY CURRICULUM

Criticalmathematics literacy involves both the ability to ask basic statistical questions in order to deepen one's appreciation of particular issues and the ability to present data to change people's perceptions of those issues. A critical understanding of numerical data prompts one to question taken-for-granted assumptions about how a society is structured, enabling us to act from a more informed position on societal structures and processes (Frankenstein and Powell 1989). The themes in my criticalmathematics literacy curriculum range from demystifying the structures of mathematics to using numerical data for demystifying the structures of society. Almost all my students have some knowledge of the basic operations, although many would have trouble adding fractions or doing long division. All can decode in reading English, but many have trouble succinctly expressing the main idea of a reading. Almost all have trouble with basic word problems. Most have internalized negative self-images about their knowledge and ability in mathematics. I start lessons with a graph or chart or short reading that requires some knowledge of the scheduled mathematics skill to understand. When the discussion runs into a skill question, we take time out and I teach that skill. This is a nonlinear way of learning basic numeracy because questions often arise that involve future topics. I handle this by "previewing": the scheduled topic is "formally" taught and other topics are discussed so that students' immediate

questions are answered and so that when the "formal" time for these topics comes in the syllabus, the students will already have some familiarity
with them. The theory and practice of this curriculum are discussed in
depth in Frankenstein (1987, 1989, 1990).

INTERDISCIPLINARITY: MATHEMATICS INTEGRATED WITH OTHER LEARNING

Not only is learning not linear, but knowledge is not created and re-
created in the fragmented forms in which most school subjects are presented. Mathematics occurs in contexts, integrated with other knowledge
of the world. Further, mathematics problems that use real-life numerical
data can hide the data's real significance if the numerical information is
used only as "window dressing" to practice a particular mathematics skill.
When no better understanding of the data is gleaned through solving the
mathematics problem created from the data, using real-life data masks
how other mathematical operations could be performed that would illuminate that same data. It gives a "hidden curriculum" message that using
mathematics is not useful in understanding the world; rather, mathematics
is just pushing around numbers, writing them in different ways depending
on what the teacher wants. In addition, real-life data used out of context
can wind up reinforcing stereotypes and myths about institutional structures. For example, many U.S. textbooks use charts of population statistics
in different countries to create problems like "How many people per
square foot does each country have?" or "If the birthrate is x, what will
the population of country y be next year?" Without any context, using
these numbers will reinforce many people's stereotypes that countries in
Africa, Asia, and Latin America are depleting our resources and that their
people have no "self-control"—no sense that having so many children
makes them poor—and so on. Adding some context reveals that historically the richer countries like the United States are the ones using the
most resources (Vail 1994):

> There are roughly 250 million people in the United States and roughly 1 bil-
> lion people in India, and the average U.S. per capita resource consumption is
> roughly 20 times what it is in India. 20 times 250 million is 5 billion "Indian
> equivalents" in the United States. The United States thus has five times the
> impact on the global ecosystem that India has. Another way of looking at the
> current situation is that about 5 billion people can be added to the current
> population if the resources consumed in the United States were evenly dis-
> tributed among them."

Adding more context supports an argument Commoner (1980) makes
that poverty causes high birthrates. He shows that as the standard of living
rises and infant mortality declines, the birthrate drops. He presents both
an ethnographic study and a theoretical analysis to support his position.

In the following examples concerning equity issues, solving the mathematics problems deepens one's understandings of the situation on which the problem is centered.

Example 1. I ask the students what the poster in figure 2.2 means to them.

Used with permission from AP/WORLD WIDE PHOTOS

Fig. 2.2

This activity leads to a discussion about how percents start as fractions, as comparisons between two groups (and, of course, we show how the fraction is then written as a decimal and then as a percent). We then look at how the percents of Latinos differ according to the base—Los Angeles, the United States, the world.... We also discuss how often numbers are behind economic, political, or social issues even if there are no numbers "visible" in the picture. Then we discuss the other learning integrated with the mathematics: How effective is this political art? How do we know it refers to Latinos? Is it a powerful visual image? Why or why not? Finally we look at the politics of knowledge, where Latinos and other people of color are referred to as "minorities" when in 1986 the population of Africa and Asia alone made up 70 percent of the world's population.

Example 2. I ask students to discuss what conclusions they can draw from the results of the following study (Sklar 1993, p. 53) and what other information they would want in order to clarify or deepen their analysis of the data:

66 student teachers were told to teach a math concept to four pupils—two white and two black. All of the pupils were of equal, average intelligence. The student teachers were told that in each set of four, one white and one black student was intellectually gifted, the others were labeled as average. The student teachers were monitored through a one-way mirror to see how they reinforced their students' efforts. The "superior" white pupils received two positive reinforcements for every negative one. The "average" white students received one positive reinforcement for every negative reinforcement. The "average" black students received one positive reinforcement for every 1.5 negative reinforcements, while the "superior" black students received one positive response for every 3.5 negative ones.

One of the first things students realize is that a chart is a better way of sorting out the data; we then discuss the possible types of charts and the concept of ratios, and we notice the different treatment based on race and supposed intelligence. Students ask many questions about the study, such as how do they measure positive and negative reinforcements and were the student-teachers black or white. We also discuss the ethics of these kinds of studies. I cannot answer many of their questions, since my source is not the original research, so students learn that teachers don't know everything. We then discuss how we could find the answers to their questions. I ask my students to consider their prior schooling, reflect on similar or different experiences they have had, and review how those experiences might have formed the negative judgments that they have internalized about their mathematics abilities. We speculate about reasons for the student-teachers' interactions with their pupils and discuss the role of racism in both the different treatment of black and white students and the more negative treatment of supposedly intellectually gifted blacks than supposedly intellectually average blacks. This example does more than integrate learning how to create tables from numerical data with the results of educational research studies—it also breaks the fragmentation between learning and teaching. By reading about mathematics education studies, students learn the mathematics more deeply because they are continually reflecting on the learning process and what impediments interfered with their mathematics learning. Further, they learn about a variety of strategies they can use to overcome those blocks (Frankenstein in press).

Ethnomathematics: Mathematics Interacting with Culture and History

For D'Ambrosio (1985, p. 45), ethnomathematics, existing at the crossroads of the history of mathematics and cultural anthropology, is "the mathematics which is practised among identifiable cultural groups, such as national-tribal societies, labor groups, children of a certain age bracket, professional classes, and so on." D'Ambrosio views mathematical knowledge as dynamic and the result of human activity, not as static and ordained. Necessarily, this conception of ethnomathematics admits a critique of the historiography of mathematics (D'Ambrosio 1988). That is, there are mathematical notions of peoples that written history has hidden, frozen, or stolen. Including these ideas makes it clear that what is labeled "Western" mathematics is more accurately called "world mathematics" (Anderson 1990). Frankenstein and Powell (1994) and Powell and Frankenstein (in press) argue that ethnomathematics includes reconsidering what counts as mathematical knowledge, considering the interactions of culture and mathematical knowledge, and uncovering the hidden and distorted history of the development of mathematical knowledge. Illustrations of these aspects can be found in Ascher (1983), Harris (1987), and Joseph (1991).

The following examples from my criticalmathematical literacy curriculum illustrate how the interactions of culture and mathematical knowledge, as well as the hidden history of mathematical knowledge, can be used to deepen one's understanding of mathematical concepts and introduce equity issues.

> *Example 1.* When we are learning the algorithm for comparing the size of numbers, I ask my students to think about how culture interacts with mathematical knowledge in the following situation: Steve Lerman (1993) was working with two five-year-olds in a London classroom. He recounts how they
>
>> were happy to compare two objects put in front of them and tell me why they had chosen the one they had [as bigger]. However, when I allocated the multilinks to them (the girl had 8 and the boy had 5) to make a tower... and I asked them who had the taller one, the girl answered correctly but the boy insisted that he did. Up to this point the boy had been putting the objects together and comparing them. He would not do so on this occasion and when I asked him how we could find out whose tower was the taller he became very angry. I asked him why he thought that his tower was taller and he just replied "Because IT IS!" He would go no further than this and seemed to be almost on the verge of tears.

At first students try to explain the boy's answer by hypothesizing that each of the girl's links was smaller than each of the boy's or that she built a wider, shorter tower. But after rereading the information, they see that this could not be so, since the girl's answer was correct. We speculate about how the culture of sexism, the culture that boys always do better or have more than girls, blocked the knowledge of comparing sizes that the boy clearly understood in a different situation.

> *Example 2.* In the following discussion of how I use a "hidden" mathematical contribution of the Incas when we're learning the meaning of place value, I also illustrate my general philosophy behind constructing such examples: the hidden contributions should *not* be presented as a kind of "folkloristic" five-minute introduction to the "real" mathematics

lesson; rather, these hidden contributions should be presented in their material context, connected to the situations and cultures in which they were developed, "showing the necessity of any given piece of calculation, measure or pattern for the particular society of which it was a part" (Singh 1991, p. 21). Further, the reasons *why* these contributions have been hidden—reasons that involve equity issues such as racism, sexism, and imperialism—should be part of the context in which the problem is presented.

I use the Inca quipu, a knotted place-value system for recording numbers, so students can gain a deeper understanding of place value. I first show pictures of actual quipus and ask them to look at the schematic in figure 2.3, which shows part of a quipu (Ascher 1983, p. 274), and figure out how that place-value system works. Then we discuss more information about quipus, such as the fact that the "colors of the cords, the way the cords are connected together, the relative placement of the cords, the spaces between the cords, the knots on the individual cords, and the relative placement of the knots are all part of the logical-numerical recording" that can communicate complicated records such as data in multilayered matrix charts (Ascher 1983, p. 269). We discuss how the Incas had no writing as we think of that form of communication and how the quipu challenges the ways in which we think of that form of communication. Next, we show how the quipu played a decisive role in the very methodical, data-organized Inca civilization. The Incas kept track of resources, taxes, and other data in the vast territory under their control through the messages encoded in the quipu. A runner would tie the quipu around his waist and carry the message to another place, where the next runner took the quipu, and so on. The quipu developed in an ideal way for the needs of the Inca civilization— portable, compact, clear, and not likely to be destroyed along the strenuous journey. Finally, we look more broadly at the larger picture of the Inca civilization of three to five million people, which existed from about A.D. 1400 to 1560 in Latin America. They built extensive road and irrigation systems; imposed a system of taxation involving agricultural products, labor, cloths, and other "finished" products; and built storehouses to hold and redistribute

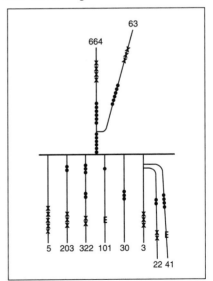

Fig. 2.3. A schematic of part of an Inca quipu. © American Federation of Information Processing Societies, Inc. Used with permission.

agricultural products as well as to feed the army as it moved. We discuss the idea that imperialism is a probable reason the mathematics of the quipu is not more extensively known: "Within about 30 years after the Europeans reached the Andes and 'discovered' the Incas, the Inca culture was destroyed" (Ascher 1983, p. 269).

THE POLITICS OF KNOWLEDGE: MATHEMATICS CONCEALING POLITICAL STRUGGLES AND CHOICES

Perhaps the most dramatic example of the politics involved in seemingly neutral mathematical descriptions of our world concerns the choice of a map to visualize that world. Any two-dimensional map of our three-dimensional earth will, of course, contain mathematical distortions. The political struggle or choice centers on which of these distortions are acceptable to us and what other understandings of ours are distorted by these false pictures. For example, the map with which most people are familiar greatly enlarges the size of "Europe." As Grossman (1994) discusses, "Europe has always been a political and cultural definition. Geographically, Europe does not exist, since it is only a peninsula on the vast Eurasian continent." He further discusses the history and various contradictions of geographers' attempts to "draw the eastern limits of 'western civilization' and the white race" (p. 39). That map also shrinks the size of Africa; most people do not realize that the area of what is commonly referred to as Europe is smaller than 20 percent of the area of Africa, and that the area of the United States is about 31 percent of the area of Africa. That common Mercator map, created in 1569, highly distorts land areas but preserves compass direction, making it very helpful to navigators who sailed from "Europe" in the sixteenth century. However, when used in textbooks and other media, combined with the general (mis)perception that size relates to various measures of so-called significance (Kaiser 1991, p. 12), the Mercator map distorts popular perceptions of the relative "importance" of various areas of the world. As Wood (1992, pp. 78–79) emphasizes, "The map is not an innocent witness … silently recording what would otherwise take place without it, but a committed participant, as often as not driving the very acts of identifying and naming, bounding and inventorying it pretends to no more than observe."

In a variety of situations, statistical descriptions don't simply, neutrally record what's out there (Frankenstein 1994). The following examples illustrate some other ways in which political struggle and choice are involved in supposedly neutral mathematical descriptions of our world. Through considering these examples, students gain experience asking questions about what is behind the surface numerical data, about how different categories for reporting data are defined, about how different categories for disaggregating data are determined, about what additional data could be collected to clarify or refute the data, and about how these decisions have an impact on analyzing equity issues.

Example 1. The U.S. government rarely collects health data broken down by social class. When it did do this in 1986 for heart and cerebrovascular disease, enormous gaps were found: "The death rate from heart disease, for example, was 2.3 times higher among unskilled blue-collar operators than among managers and professionals. By contrast, the mortality rate from heart disease in 1986 for blacks was 1.3 times higher than for whites.... The way in which statistics are kept does not help to make white and black workers aware of the commonality of their predicament" (Navarro 1991, p. 436).

Example 2. A University of Massachusetts at Amherst study, researching possible bias in the location of toxic-waste plants, examined census-tract data and "concluded that facilities are concentrated in industrial areas but are no more likely to be in areas with large black and Hispanic populations than elsewhere." Critics argued that census-tract units, about 0.74 square miles in area and having 4000 people on average, are "too large for meaningful analysis and ignore smaller communities with large minority [*sic*] populations where waste facilities are concentrated.... [Further] the study covered only 36,423 of 61,258 tracts, omitting more rural, largely white areas [thereby] skewing the results.... In addition... the focus on incinerators and similar facilities ignores [a] broad range of injustices" such as the contamination of the Penobscot people's river in Maine by upstream paper mills and the lead-painted houses in which disproportionately many children of color live (Braile 1994b). A subsequent study, sponsored by the NAACP and the United Church of Christ Commission for Racial Justice, took these factors into account. It found that 31 percent of people of color shared a ZIP code with one of the 530 waste facilities surveyed in the University of Massachusetts at Amherst report (compared to 25 percent in 1980), and that people of color were 47 percent more likely than whites to live near such a facility (Braile 1994a).

CRITICALMATHEMATICAL LITERACY:
COMPLEXITY AND CONFIDENCE

The learning that occurs through solving and posing mathematics problems related to all these themes—interdisciplinarity, ethnomathematics, and the politics of knowledge—involves two curricular goals that I think can be generalized to other learning situations. The first is that critical, in-depth learning involves thinking through intellectually challenging, complicated material. Clarity comes through complexity.

The second is that critical learning is in a dialectical relationship with developing deep self-confidence and respect for the varieties of intellectual activity.

Most educational materials and learning environments in the United States, especially those labeled "developmental" or "remedial," consist of superficial, "easy" work. They involve rote or formulaic problem-solving experiences. I argue that this is a major reason that learning is not retained and not used. Further, making the curriculum more complicated, where each problem contains a variety of learning experiences packed in together, teaches in the kind of nonlinear, holistic way in which knowledge is developed in context. So, for example, a discussion about the politics of language that grows out of fraction and percent problems that grow out of considering the meaning of a political protest poster involves the kind of learning that is a foundation to build on for in-depth understandings.

In all these themes, mathematics algorithms are presented as part of a larger intellectual project that involves making meaning of our world, using mathematical knowledge as part of what Freire calls "reading the world." In order to teach basic mathematics concepts this way, we must develop the kind of deep self-confidence that seriously considers Freire's (1982) framework on how "our task is not to teach students to think—they can already think—but to exchange our ways of thinking with each other and look together for better ways of approaching the decodification of an object." This idea is so important because it implies a completely different set of assumptions about people, pedagogy, and the creation of knowledge. Because some people in the United States, for example, need to learn to write in "standard" English, *it does not follow* that they cannot express very complex analyses of social, political, economic, ethical, and other issues. And many people with an excellent grasp of reading, writing, and mathematics skills need to learn much about the world, about philosophy, about psychology, about justice, and about many other areas in order to deepen their understandings. In order to study basic mathematics concepts this way, we must develop the kind of deep self-confidence that respects how, in a nontrivial way, we can learn a great deal from "intellectual diversity." Most of the burning social, political, economic, and ethical questions of our time remain unanswered: in the United States we live in a society of enormous wealth and yet have significant hunger and homelessness; although we have engaged in medical and scientific research for scores of years, we are not any closer to changing the prognosis for most cancers (*Health Facts* 1987, 1995). Currently "the intellectual activity of those without power is always labeled non-intellectual" (Freire and Macedo 1987). When we see this as a political situation, what Michel Foucault calls our "regime of truth," we can realize that all people have knowledge, all people are continually creating knowledge, doing intellectual work, and all of us have a lot to learn.

Criticalmathematical Literacy: Connections Between Curricular and Concrete Change?

The underlying focus throughout my criticalmathematical literacy curriculum is how to connect the intellectual activities in the classroom to the economic and political activities needed to resolve what Paulo Freire has identified as the fundamental concern of our epoch—the struggle for liberation against domination. My practice confirms that the criticalmathematical literacy class changes students' perceptions of mathematics and of their ability to understand mathematics. But will including equity issues in the curriculum in addition to the mathematics have an impact on the inequities? The research and activities that many criticalmathematics educators are pursuing involve the dialectics between knowledge and action for change. Arthur B. Powell, John Volmink, and I have organized an international Criticalmathematics Educators Group to share information. Clearly we haven't eliminated societal inequities—yet. With hope, study, and persistence, we continue, trying to connect our work to the struggle for justice, against inequities.

References

Anderson, Sam E. "Worldmath Curriculum: Fighting Eurocentrism in Mathematics." *Journal of Negro Education* 59 (Summer 1990): 348–59.

Ascher, Marcia. "The Logical-Numerical System of Inca Quipus." *Annals of the History of Computing* 5 (1983): 268–78.

Braile, Robert. "Minority Risk of Living Near Waste Sites Is Affirmed." *Boston Globe,* 25 August 1994a.

———."No Pattern of Bias Found in Locating Toxic Waste Plants." *Boston Globe,* 10 May 1994b.

Commoner, Barry. "How Poverty Breeds Overpopulation." In *Science and Liberation,* edited by Rita Arditti, Pat Brennan, and Steve Cavrak, pp. 76–89. Boston: South End Press, 1980.

D'Ambrosio, Ubiratan. "Ethnomathematics and Its Place in the History and Pedagogy of Mathematics." *For the Learning of Mathematics* 5 (1985): 44–48.

———."Ethnomathematics: A Research Program in the History of Ideas and in Cognition." *International Study Group on Ethnomathematics Newsletter* 4, no. 1 (1988): 5–8.

Frankenstein, Marilyn. "Breaking Down the Dichotomy between Teaching and Learning Mathematics." In *Mentoring the Mentor: Dialogues with Paulo Freire,* edited by James Fraser and Donaldo Macedo. Albany, N.Y.: State University of New York, in press.

———."Critical Mathematics Education: An Application of Paulo Freire's Epistemology." In *Freire for the Classroom,* edited by Ira Shor, pp. 180–210. Portsmouth, N.H.: Boynton/Cook, 1987.

————. "Incorporating Race, Class, and Gender Issues into a Criticalmathematical Literacy Curriculum." *Journal of Negro Education* 59 (Summer 1990): 336–47.

————. *Relearning Mathematics: A Different Third R—Radical Maths.* London: Free Association Books, 1989.

————. "Understanding the Politics of Mathematical Knowledge as an Integral Part of Becoming Critically Numerate." *Radical Statistics* 56 (Spring 1994): 22–40.

Frankenstein, Marilyn, and Arthur B. Powell. "Empowering Non-traditional College Students: On Social Ideology and Mathematics Education." *Science & Nature* (1989): 100–12.

————. "Toward Liberatory Mathematics: Paulo Freire's Epistemology and Ethnomathematics." In *Politics of Liberation: Paths from Freire,* edited by Peter McLaren and Colin Lankshear, pp. 74–99. London: Routledge, 1994.

Freire, Paulo. "Education for Critical Consciousness." Unpublished Boston College course notes taken by Marilyn Frankenstein, 5–15 July 1982.

Freire, Paulo, and Donaldo Macedo. *Literacy: Reading the Word and the World.* South Hadley, Mass.: Bergen & Garvey, 1987.

Grossman, Zoltan. "Erecting the New Wall: Geopolitics and the Restructuring of Europe." *Z Magazine*, March 1994, pp. 39–45.

Harris, Mary. "An Example of Traditional Women's Work as a Mathematics Resource." *For the Learning of Mathematics* 7 (1987): 26–28.

Health Facts. "The Latest Cancer Statistics." February 1987, pp. 1–2.

————. "Mammography Screening: No Proof Yet That It Saves Lives." August 1995, pp. 1, 4–5.

Joseph, George G. *The Crest of the Peacock.* London: I. B. Tauris, 1991.

Kaiser, Ward L. "New Global Map Presents Accurate View of the World." *Rethinking Schools* (May/June 1991): 12–13.

Lerman, Steven. Personal communication with the author, 26 March 1993.

Navarro, Vicente. "The Class Gap." *The Nation,* 8 April 1991, pp. 436–37.

Powell, Arthur B., and Marilyn Frankenstein. *Ethnomathematics: Challenging Eurocentrism in Mathematics Education.* Albany, N.Y.: State University of New York, in press.

Singh, Europe. "Classroom Practice: Anti-Racist Mathematics." Unpublished manuscript, 1991.

Sklar, Holly. "Young and Guilty by Stereotype." *Z Magazine,* July/August 1993, pp. 52–61.

Vail, Chris. "Nixing Nixon." *In These Times,* 3 October 1994, p. 4.

Wood, Denis. *The Power of Maps.* New York: Guilford Press, 1992.

3

Including African American Students in the Mathematics Community

Carol E. Malloy

Mathematics classrooms include students from diverse cultures and ethnic groups, students with diverse achievement levels, and students with diverse opportunities to participate fully in the mathematics community. African American students' performance and participation in higher-level mathematics classes has not been equal to that of the total population. Individual teachers, schools, school districts, and national organizations such as the National Council of Teachers of Mathematics have established strategies to address the lack of parity. Although the results from the 1992 National Assessment of Educational Progress show that African American students improved in computational skills, their overall performance was still not comparable with that of the general population. Their performance also did not substantially improve in mathematical problem solving—applying computational skills to problems (Dossey, Mullis, and Jones 1993).

Unfortunately, African American students' mathematical learning is an untold story. Mathematics educators have little knowledge of how African American students perceive themselves as mathematics students, how they approach mathematics, or the role of culture in their perception and mathematics performance. Questions such as the following still remain:

- How do we proactively include African American students in the mathematics community?
- What changes in teaching could make a difference in their understanding and achievement?
- Are we teaching them from their vantage point or from where we think their vantage point should be?

Many mathematics educators believe that students' enculturation into the mathematics community is significantly related to their mathematical-strategy building and achievement (Suydam 1980). Students' engagement in mathematics necessitates their becoming part of the mathematics culture. In this process students must actively construct knowledge and problem-solving skills. Students must experience an enculturation process—assuming the values of the mathematics community—in order to learn to think mathematically. In this process they develop a mathematical point of view, develop competence with the tools of the trade, and use those tools to understand the structure of mathematics (Schoenfeld 1992).

Before we can make instructional recommendations to improve the mathematics understanding and achievement of African American students, it is important to examine some of the factors that affect their enculturation into the mathematics community.

AFRICAN AMERICAN STUDENTS' PREFERENCES FOR LEARNING MATHEMATICS

In the past two decades, numerous studies have investigated the skills students need in mathematics—specifically, problem solving. These studies have traditionally examined majority students and typically excluded data for African American students. Two metaanalyses established basic skills, analytical-reasoning ability, the use of strategy, verification, confidence, field independence, and self-esteem as factors that contribute to higher levels of success in mathematical problem solving (Hembree 1992; Suydam 1980).

Some research on learning preferences suggests that African American students, however, tend to be field dependent and do not prefer to use analytical reasoning. African American students are flexible and open minded rather than structured in their perceptions of ideas, and they use cultural interpretations of visual and pictorial images (Shade 1992). African American students generally learn in ways characterized by social and affective emphases, harmony with the community, holistic perspectives, field dependence, expressive creativity, and nonverbal communication (Stiff 1990; Willis 1992).

Harmony within the community and a holistic perspective provide a basis for social interaction, which seems to be crucial in African American culture. The African American community focuses more on people and their activities than on things, and the interdependence of people and their environment is respected and encouraged (Shade 1989; Willis 1992). One instructional application of interdependence is cooperative learning. It is instrumental in improving the achievement of most students, especially minority students (Slavin 1991). Social learning is an integral part of the school experience for many African American students. Lubeck (1988) found that teachers in the Head Start preschool program reenacted patterns of interaction that prevail within extended-family networks. Teachers structured classwork so that students worked closely together and shared tasks, decisions, and resources. Head Start teachers "appeared to socialize the children to the preeminent values of a society in which the needs of the group prevailed over the needs of individuals, thereby to extend a collective orientation that has had both historic roots and contemporary efficacy" (p. 51).

African American students' use of verbal expression and holistic approaches and their tendency toward field dependency may influence how they solve mathematical problems (Stiff 1990). For instance, African Americans tend to be creative, adaptive, variable, novel, stylistic, and intuitive, and they prefer simultaneous stimulation that contains verve and animated oral expression (Solomon 1992). Thus, African American students may incorporate elaborate verbal and motor skills to communicate mathematical ideas and relationships. They may use creative stories or verbal elaboration to convey specific mathematical meanings.

African American students often use holistic reasoning in mathematical problems in which synthesis is important as a strategy in finding the solution (Malloy 1994). Consequently, they respond in terms of the whole picture instead of its parts, prefer inferential reasoning to deductive reasoning, and approximate space, numbers, and time rather than use exact calculations (Willis 1992). For example, consider the approach of African American middle school students in a recent study (Malloy 1994) as they solved the pattern problem shown in figure 3.1.

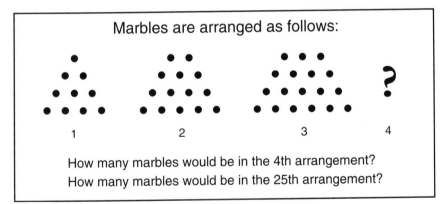

Fig. 3.1. A pattern problem given to African American middle school students

Using an analytical approach, a student might count the marbles in each arrangement to reveal that the number in successive arrangements increases by four and then apply this increasing pattern to find the fourth and twenty-fifth arrangements. The majority of successful students, however, used a holistic approach. They looked at all the arrangements and saw that the number of marbles in each first row was the same as the number of the arrangement and that each succeeding row increased by one marble.

These approaches have strong underlying influences from African heritage and culture. They reflect preferences for students' interaction with the environment; affect cognition, attitude, behavior, and personality; and differ from approaches favored by the majority population. However, not all African American students demonstrate all these characteristics. Socialization in families and schools and students' bicultural experiences influence how they integrate and adapt their learning approaches.

UNDERPINNINGS OF THE ENCULTURATION PROCESS

Culture is acquired knowledge transmitted among groups. It is shared meaning (but not necessarily consensus)—the taken-for-granted values and beliefs that are seen in what people do, what they know, and the tools they use (Bogdan and Biklen 1992; Eisenhart 1989). Culture related to mathematics learning affects African American students in two ways: culture shapes students' perceptions of themselves as members of the mathematics community, and students' indigenous skills are not valued because cultural and academic knowledge are oppositional.

Cultural Shaping

The social, cultural, and historical context in which students live defines and shapes the students and their experience. Students are active participants in their environment—they learn from their cultural experiences. This learning takes place first in the social plane and then derivatively in the inner plane of the students' development (Vygotsky and Luria 1993). In other words, learning occurs first in experiences with other people and then on the individual level, where it is internalized.

Students also internalize the expectations of external sources. Social cognitive theory suggests that initially behavior is self-regulated on the basis of an anticipated outcome mediated by the social environment. The way students perceive their capabilities depends on the environment in which they are socialized (Gergen 1977). If the social environment continues to define students in a specified way without intervening information, they will come to accept the publicly provided definition as their own. "In the course of development, the regulation of behavior shifts from predominately external sanctions and direction to gradual substitution of internal sanctions and mandates rooted in personal standards" (Bussey and Bandura 1992, p. 1238). For example, many African Americans are recognized to have superior athletic ability in basketball. Because students can see the social reinforcement given to African Americans through scholarships to college and large professional basketball contracts, they internalize the social acceptance of basketball proficiency and are motivated to achieve in this area.

Just as students identify with society's positive appraisal of their capabilities, so they identify with negative judgments about their abilities. Many African American students choose to avoid mathematics and mathematical success for several reasons. The media continually provide schools, homes, parents, and teachers with information about the achievement gap between African American students and the majority population. Such a focus leads to stereotypes of poor achievement among African Americans. When schools track students into lower-level groupings in the early grades, their mathematics preparation suffers. Institutional, parental, and peer expectations for their achievement are low, so the students achieve at the expected lower levels. More profoundly, students internalize the external expectations of the broader society, which exclude the possibility of mathematics-related careers, mathematics achievement, and recognition for mathematical skills (Bussey and Bandura 1992). African American students become vulnerable to the stereotypes and internalize expectations of failure in mathematics, so they dissociate from the learning process (Steele 1992).

Oppositional Cultures

Cultural knowledge and academic knowledge sometimes oppose each other. Banks (1993) states, "The assumptions, perspectives, and insights that students derive from their experiences in their homes and community cultures are used as screens to view and interpret the knowledge and experiences that they encounter in the school and in other institutions within the larger society" (p. 7). Banks posited an interrelationship among five types of knowledge: personal-cultural, popular, mainstream academic, transformative academic, and school. He defined personal-cultural knowledge as the concepts, explanations, and interpretations students derive from personal experiences in their homes, families, and community cultures. Academic knowledge consists of concepts, paradigms, theories, and explanations that constitute traditional and established knowledge in Western history and the behavioral and social sciences. Personal and cultural knowledge can be problematic in three instances: when it conflicts with scientific ways of validating knowledge, when it opposes the culture of the school, and when it challenges the main tenets and assumptions of mainstream academic knowledge. The failure of many educators in general, and mathematics educators specifically, to recognize, understand, and use the African American students' culture in instruction results in many African American students' finding the school culture alienating and inconsistent with their cultural experiences, hopes, dreams, and struggles.

Students develop on the basis of their experiences different models for understanding mathematics (Tate 1994). Tate demonstrated how a school system's test designers used their personal assumptions based on their experiences to design test items. On one test item students whose experiences were different from those of the designers found an answer that was correct for the students' experiences but was judged incorrect on the test battery. The problem is as follows:

> It costs $1.50 each way to ride the bus between home and work. A weekly bus pass is $16. Which is the better deal, paying the daily fare or buying the weekly pass?

Urban students' personal-cultural knowledge would include the awareness that in some urban families three or four people may use the same
bus pass at different times of the day or on weekends or that if one person
is using the bus pass, he or she could have two jobs. Tate explains that the
test designers seemed to assume that only one person would be using the
bus pass, that the bus pass would not be used on weekends, and that the
person had only one job.

In summary, African American students often have difficulties in school
because cultural knowledge within their community conflicts with school
knowledge, norms, and expectations (Fordham and Ogbu 1986). Differences pose obstacles to the students' adjustment and achievement and
could result from curricula and teaching practices that do not recognize,
or have not been modified to respond to, the way African American students learn (Stiff 1990). Unfortunately, little research is available on
African American learning and less on African American learning in
mathematics or mathematical problem solving. But recommendations can
be made for modifications in practice based on students' culture and
learning preferences.

SUGGESTED PRACTICES

How do we teach mathematics to African American students on the
basis of what is known about their culture and preferences for learning?
African American students learn from direct contact with teachers and
peers and take a holistic, relational, and intuitive stance. Mathematics
generally is taught using an expository method in a linear, rigorous, and
analytical manner. Schools should offer multicultural educational programs taught by effective teachers. These programs should provide an
academic environment that relies on students' cultural backgrounds and
experiences as the foundation for teaching and learning.

Affective interaction between, and the engagement of, teacher and students is fundamental to the teaching and learning of African American
students. Apart from affective interaction, trust, engagement, and a culturally congruent atmosphere, no special pedagogy needs to be developed
for African American students. Their learning and achievement depends
on solid, existing pedagogy that addresses the cognitive, cultural, and affective development of students.

Solid, culturally responsive mathematics pedagogy is predicated on the
teacher's interpreting, understanding, and recognizing the students' culture and integrating it into the learning process; the teacher's allowing
students to construct mathematical knowledge on the basis of their experiences; and effective classroom practice. The teacher must respect and
have knowledge about students' lives, culture, and experiences in order to
use the students' life experiences in instruction. Multicultural teaching
helps students understand how knowledge is constructed. It gives students

opportunities to investigate and determine how cultural assumptions, frames of reference, perspectives, and biases within a discipline influence the ways its knowledge is constructed (Banks 1993). Teachers should be sensitive to the motivations, conversations, social preferences, and thought patterns of their students. They should emphasize language development and take care to contextualize instruction in the meaningful experiences of their students (Tharp 1989).

Irvine (1992) indicates that effective teachers of minority students share some characteristics and teaching behaviors with all other effective teachers. Effective teachers (1) are competent in the subject matter, (2) provide all students with high-level knowledge regardless of the students' previous categorization or labeling, and (3) have appropriately high standards and expectations for their students. Teachers of African American students need to be more than effective teachers. They need to be "culturally responsive teachers who contextualize teaching by giving attention to immediate needs and cultural experiences of their students" (p. 83).

Teachers can make mathematics classrooms culturally responsive by establishing educational programs that are culturally compatible and congruent. "This means that education practices must mesh with the students' culture in ways that ensure the generations of academically important behaviors. It does not mean that all school practices need to be completely congruent with their cultural practices, in the sense of exactly matching or agreeing with them" (Jordan 1985, p. 110). Teachers should initiate instruction in the areas in which students exhibit strengths and then stretch students into thinking in ways that are culturally familiar and unfamiliar. For instance, if students are more comfortable with divergent thinking, teachers should use divergence to introduce mathematical topics. Then they should teach students to use convergence in reaching conclusions.

The development of educational practices that lead to culturally compatible classrooms requires the expansion and use of mathematics curricular materials and instructional models that lend themselves to the holistic approaches of intuition, synthesis, and divergence. Instructional models that permit students to participate in cooperative rather than competitive learning activities will allow students to take advantage of their community focus and interdependence as well as their preference for learning through social and affective emphases. Students also must have opportunities to use their unique expressiveness through writing and oral presentations in mathematics.

Teachers can create a classroom atmosphere that reflects the community by using visual aids and classroom exhibits that represent the students and the community in which they live. Teachers should allow students to be active in their learning, encourage high levels of peer interaction, encourage group decision making, and avoid judging students both verbally and nonverbally on the basis of their own biases. Teachers should encourage students' expressiveness through appropriate wait time, physical closeness, acknowledgment, feedback, probing, and listening. Teachers should involve themselves in the experiences of their students by attending community events and extending these events into classroom mathematics projects and activities. Moreover, teachers must frequently acknowledge, respect, and use students' cultural heritage in classroom activities.

Culturally responsive classroom practice can reach beyond the classroom into the home and community to give students, especially African American students, a resilient attitude about life and learning. Schools can form formal or informal student-centered partnerships with parents and community organizations. For decades, research on African American students' achievement relied primarily on cultural-deviance theories; however, recent research (Nettles and Pleck 1993) has explored the resources and mechanisms that develop competent students. Nettles and Pleck examined the resilient behaviors rooted in overcoming odds and found that resilience results from students' use of protective factors to reduce individual, community, and societal impediments that place them at risk. Many African American families and communities encourage resilience through a positive sense of self reflected in positive self-talk, a sense of academic competence, an appropriate attribution of failure, a sense of responsibility, and the determination to overcome obstacles.

African American parents and students believe that education is a means to improve their condition in life (Ogbu 1988). Parents teach their children to have high self-esteem, pride in racial heritage, positive attitudes about being African American, and racial-social awareness (Bright 1994). Many parents believe that although hard work and talent are important to success, it takes more to get to the top in mainstream society. They understand that academic enlightenment comes through eschewing the deficit model and focusing on internal strengths and the strengths of the community. Parents and the broader African American community teach their children how to use the cultural and intellectual strengths they bring to school and to deal with obstacles they may encounter in their lives.

In a recent study, African American students manifested protective behaviors such as high self-esteem and self-efficacy and a desire for mathematics achievement that enabled them to reduce their risk factors and thus achieve in mathematics (Malloy 1994). These students were generally achieving in a community where African American students' achievement, as a whole, falls well below the achievement of the general population. They overcame the impediments to African American students' achievement by (1) reducing their exposure to risk through positive family, school, and community interaction; (2) reducing negative academic chain reactions through their help-seeking behaviors when they encountered difficulties; (3) developing high self-esteem and self-efficacy in their academic ability; and (4) participating in activities that opened up opportunities.

Along with the support afforded the students in their community, schools can help students develop resilience in the face of low expectations for their academic achievement. They can (1) provide teachers with training to develop positive student-teacher interactions and student trust; (2) facilitate positive peer interactions in multiracial settings that promote communication and the acknowledgment of the "pluralistic ignorance" of all students; (3) include mentoring for students and social support systems that foster academic behaviors; (4) provide extracurricular activities that make students feel connected to the school and environment; (5) offer career exploration, appropriate course selections, and adequate preparation for postsecondary schooling; (6) collaborate with community-based agencies to provide opportunities for students to discover and develop their interests and talents; and (7) stress acceleration with a challenge over remediation (Steele 1992; Winfield 1992). These recommendations can be implemented for all students; however, they are particularly important to the mathematically underserved and underrepresented African American student population.

CONCLUSION

Change begins with hypothesized modifications to classroom practice based on empirical findings, and then research to measure the success of the changes. A first step is suggested here. This paper has recommended culturally responsive educational practices to improve African American students' mathematics achievement. Culturally responsive teaching and materials are tools to counteract the opposition many African American students experience between the cultures of the school and the community. We can make a difference in how African American students perceive themselves and in how they learn mathematics. We can include them in the mathematics community.

A pivotal step in change is to expand educational research to give prominence to factors that contribute to mathematics achievement in diverse populations. Reform in mathematics education is predicated on research and interventions that address populations that historically have had low achievement and that have learned in spite of social forces, reduced opportunity, and low expectations (Secada 1991). The current reform movement must include similar research on African American students. Research is almost nonexistent about the effect of culturally compatible classrooms on the mathematics learning of African American students. To recommend empirically based changes in mathematics instruction for African American students, further research is needed into the attributes and impact of culturally responsive instruction and the cultural context of teaching (Irvine 1992). Change in educational practice to include all students in the mathematics community depends on this proactive research and on implementating its findings in the mathematics classroom.

REFERENCES

Banks, James A. "The Canon Debate: Knowledge Construction and Multicultural Education." *Educational Researcher* 22 (June–July 1993): 4–14.

Bogdan, Robert, and Sari Biklen. *Qualitative Research for Education: An Introduction to Theory and Methods.* Boston: Allyn & Bacon, 1992.

Bright, Josephine A. "Beliefs in Action: Family Contributions to African-American Student Success." *Equity and Choice* 10 (Winter 1994): 5–13.

Bussey, Kay, and Albert Bandura. "Self-Regulatory Mechanisms Governing Gender Development." *Child Development* 63 (October 1992): 1236–50.

Dossey, John A., Ina V. S. Mullis, and Chancey O. Jones. *Can Students Do Mathematical Problem Solving?* Washington, D.C.: U.S. Department of Education and National Center for Education Statistics, 1993.

Eisenhart, Margaret. "Reconsidering Cultural Differences in American Schools." *Educational Foundations* 3 (Summer 1989): 51–68.

Fordham, Signithia, and John Ogbu. "Black Students' School Success: Coping with the Burden of Acting White." *Urban Review* 18 (September 1986): 176–206.

Gergen, Kenneth J. "The Social Construction of Self-Knowledge." In *The Self: Psychological and Philosophical Issues,* edited by Theodore Mischel, pp. 139–69. Totowa, N.J.: Rowman & Littlefield, 1977.

Hembree, Ray. "Experiments and Relational Studies in Problem Solving: A Meta-Analysis." *Journal for Research in Mathematics Education* 23 (May 1992): 242–73.

Irvine, Jacqueline J. "Making Teacher Education Culturally Responsive." In *Diversity in Teacher Education,* edited by Mary E. Dilworth, pp. 79–92. San Francisco: Jossey-Bass Publishers, 1992.

Jordan, Cathie. "Translating Culture: From Ethnographic Information to Educational Program." *Anthropology and Education Quarterly* 16 (Summer 1985): 103–23.

Lubeck, Sally. "Nested Contexts." In *Class, Race, and Gender: American Education,* edited by Lois Weis, pp. 43–62. Albany, N.Y.: State University of New York Press, 1988.

Malloy, Carol E. "African-American Eighth Grade Students' Mathematics Problem Solving: Characteristics, Strategies, and Success." Ph.D. diss., University of North Carolina at Chapel Hill, 1994.

Nettles, Saundra M., and Joseph H. Pleck. *Risk, Resilience, and Development: The Multiple Ecologies of Black Adolescents.* Baltimore: Center for Research on Effective Schooling for Disadvantaged Students, 1993. (ERIC Document Reproduction Service no. ED 362607)

Ogbu, John U. "Class Stratification, Racial Stratification, and Schooling." In *Class, Race, and Gender: American Education,* edited by Lois Weis, pp. 163–82. Albany, N.Y.: State University of New York Press, 1988.

Schoenfeld, Alan H. "Learning to Think Mathematically: Problem Solving, Metacognition, and Sense Making in Mathematics." In *Handbook of Research on Mathematics Teaching and Learning,* edited by Douglas A. Grouws, pp. 334–70. New York: Macmillan, 1992.

Secada, Walter G. "Diversity, Equity, and Cognitivist Research." In *Integrating Research on Teaching and Learning,* edited by Elizabeth Fennema, Thomas Carpenter, and Susan J. Lamon, pp. 17–53. Albany, N.Y.: State University of New York Press, 1991.

Shade, Barbara. "The Influence of Perceptual Development on Cognitive Style: Cross-Ethnic Comparisons." *Early Child Development and Care* 51 (October 1989): 137–55.

————."Is There an Afro-American Cognitive Style? An Exploratory Study." In *African-American Psychology,* edited by A. Kathleen H. Burlew, W. Curtis Banks, Harriette P. McAdoo, and Daudi A. Azibo. Newbury Park, Calif.: Sage Publications, 1992.

Slavin, Robert. "Synthesis of Research on Cooperative Learning." *Educational Leadership* 48 (February 1991): 71–82.

Solomon, Patrick. *African-American Resistance in High School: Forging a Separatist Culture.* Albany, N.Y.: State University of New York Press, 1992.

Steele, Claude M. "Race and the Schooling of African-Americans." *Atlantic Monthly,* April 1992, pp. 68–78.

Stiff, Lee V. "African-American Students and the Promise of the *Curriculum and Evaluation Standards.*" In *Teaching and Learning Mathematics in the 1990s,* 1990 Yearbook of the National Council of Teachers of Mathematics, edited by Thomas J. Cooney, pp. 152–58. Reston, Va.: National Council of Teachers of Mathematics, 1990.

Suydam, Marilyn N. "Untangling Clues from Research on Problem Solving." In *Problem Solving in School Mathematics,* 1980 Yearbook of the National Council of Teachers of Mathematics, edited by Stephen Krulik, pp. 34–50. Reston, Va.: National Council of Teachers of Mathematics, 1980.

Tate, William. "Race, Retrenchment, and the Reform of School Mathematics." *Phi Delta Kappan* 57 (February 1994): 477–84.

Tharp, Roland G. "Culturally Compatible Education: A Formula for Designing Effective Classrooms." In *What Do Anthropologists Have to Say about Dropouts?* edited by Henry T. Trueba, George Spindler, and Louise Spindler, pp. 51–66. Bristol, Pa.: Falmer Press, 1989.

Vygotsky, L. S., and A. R. Luria. *Studies on the History of Behavior: Ape, Primitive, and Child.* Translated by Victor I. Golod and Jane E. Knox. Hillsdale, N.J.: Lawrence Erlbaum Associates, 1993.

Willis, Marge G. "Learning Styles of African-American Children: Review of the Literature and Interventions." In *African-American Psychology,* edited by A. Kathleen H. Burlew, W. Curtis Banks, Harriette P. McAdoo, and Daudi A. Azibo. Newbury Park, Calif.: Sage Publications, 1992.

Winfield, Linda F. "Developing Resilience in Youth in Urban America." Paper presented at the Restructuring to Educate the Urban Learner seminar, 5–6 November 1992, Research for Better Schools, Philadelphia.

4

Teaching Mathematics in a Multicultural Classroom
Lessons from Australia

Jan Thomas

MY PROFESSIONAL career as a fully qualified teacher of mathematics began in an inner-city school in Melbourne in 1976. As in many similar schools in Australia, the majority of the students were from a non-English-speaking background (NESB). NESB is used in Australia to describe students who speak a language other than English at home. It describes students who have skills in a language other than English but may need additional help with English. (The expression Limited English Proficiency [LEP] is not used in Australia.)

I soon found that I was not "fully qualified" to teach these students. When I started searching for more appropriate teaching strategies and a more suitable curriculum, I found that little was available. I originally concentrated on language and mathematics learning but soon realized the issues were more complex, involving both language and culture, and were not isolated from gender and socioeconomic factors. Twenty years later I believe we still have a long way to go before there is an appropriate curriculum for students learning mathematics in a second language.

Many Australian schools have significant numbers of NESB students. The ethnic mix may vary, but commonly two or three languages will be spoken by a significant number of students, with many more languages spoken by smaller groups. Bilingual education is usually not an option, because of the number of languages involved. Some support may be available in the form of bilingual aides, but usually the only language support lies with English as a second language (ESL) instruction. Australia has a very strong reputation in ESL curricula, but it took time for this expertise to find its way to the mathematics classroom.

On the day I started teaching in 1976, I was asked what I was going to teach. When I said mathematics and science, the response was, "Oh, aren't you lucky—it doesn't matter if they can't speak English." There are still vestiges of this notion that mathematics and science are really about symbols and therefore students do not need English to study these subjects in schools today. Newly arrived immigrants are often still encouraged to pursue careers in mathematics and science because "language won't be such a problem."

My teaching career also began a few months after East Timor became part of Indonesia, which provided my first encounter, as a teacher, with refugees. After the first Timorese student was placed in one of my mathematics classes, each subsequent arrival was also put there until about a third of that class was composed of recent Timorese refugees. I learned from experience that anything that reminded them of gunfire terrified them.

Some years later the Ministry of Education was about to publish a book of mathematics activities that included one based on the game of hangman. I pointed out an article where a teacher in an American school had found herself with a distraught Cambodian student when using this activity (Olsen 1988) and that a judicial inquiry had just been made into Aboriginal deaths while in custody, many by hanging. The activities book was still published with this activity. Mathematics materials in Australia occasionally still show cultural and social insensitivity.

The mathematics classroom is not immune to racism. It is the unexpected that is most difficult to manage. At another school where I taught, a mathematics question on whether a particular number was a reasonable estimate for the population of Australia caused a tirade of abuse from a student with an English-speaking background (ESB) toward the Vietnamese in the class: "It was a reasonable estimate until ..."

These and other instances made me feel inadequate as a teacher; I felt that little in my preservice education had prepared me for teaching mathematics to NESB students. Consequently, I acquired a further degree in ESL teaching so that I could teach mathematics more effectively. I am still learning about language and culture and their effects on mathematics learning. As a mathematics education lecturer, I make sure the beginning teachers I teach are better prepared than I was, but teaching mathematics is never easy. Linguistic and cultural diversity presents additional challenges.

Considerable literature is now available to help teachers develop a theoretical framework for the linguistic and cultural aspects of mathematics education. A reading list would include Secada (1992), Tate (1994), Bishop (1988), Mellin-Olsen (1987), Stigler and Baranes (1989), Cocking and Mestre (1988), and Nunes (1992). Australian authors would include Ellerton and Clarkson (1992), Dawe (1983), Clarkson (1991), and Harris (1992). Far less is available when it comes to strategies and materials for use in the classroom.

Many, but certainly not all, mathematics educators in Australia now accept that teaching mathematics in Australia means teaching a culturally bound subject in a multicultural society. Evidence abounds that understanding the social context of mathematics teaching and learning is essential if the needs of all students are to be met. Conveying this to a public that believes mathematics both is culturally neutral and has very little to do with language is a major task. It means that as mathematics educators, we need to write about these aspects of mathematics education in many journals and newspapers. Greater community understanding of these factors is essential if the resources are to be made available for catering to the diversity within our classrooms.

Although mathematics teachers may feel frustrated by the lack of understanding of the complexity of their task, there are many things they can do to assist students learning in a second language. In the following sections, the focus is on NESB students learning mathematics in English. I will discuss some of the principles, teaching strategies, and resources I consider important in teaching mathematics to NESB students. Although the emphasis is placed on language issues, these cannot be divorced from cultural effects. I have tried to draw on examples where links with language and cultural background can be made.

PRINCIPLES

Language is learned in context. If students are going to learn the language associated with mathematics, it has to be done as they engage in learning mathematics. In the early days of mass immigration to Australia, textbooks were chosen because they had plenty of what I have described as symbol manipulation (Thomas 1983). Hard-working, conscientious NESB students learned by rote how to move the symbols around and apparently did quite well in mathematics. When they reached senior high school and had to solve word problems and read textbooks, they found they were failing because their development of the language skills required for mathematics had been ignored.

Sensitivity to cultural and social issues is important. In the schools where I have taught, the following considerations have had to be considered:

- Refugee students need to feel safe before they can learn and may not be familiar with school and classroom routines.
- Beacause of family religious and cultural values, some students may feel very uncomfortable if, for example, they are asked to calculate the cost of a meal involving pork or solve probability questions involving an understanding of gambling games.
- School attendance can be affected by, for example, Ramadan, Greek Orthodox Easter, or students being needed away from classes to act as interpreters for adults in their families. Girls may be kept at home to look after younger siblings. Sometimes girls have even been sent back to the country of origin because the only high school available was coeducational.

Students need good models. Students, particularly those coming from NESB or lower socioeconomic backgrounds, may not have access to examples of what I call "excellence." They can confuse being able to get the right answer on symbol manipulations with being good at mathematics. This may be compounded by a curriculum, frequently encouraged by state and national testing schemes, that stresses symbol manipulations. Moves to establish assessment practices that are criteria-based and that clearly demonstrate to students where their work meets standards of excellence and where it could be improved seem to be a step in the right direction (for example, see Taylor [1994]).

Good mathematics teaching for NESB students is good teaching for all students. The principles above apply to all students. Teachers can feel overwhelmed when they are confronted with separate policies suggesting special strategies to deal with NESB students, girls, students with disabilities, indigenous students, and other groups. This diversity of need is not going to be met until teachers are supported as they tackle the factors affecting participation in mathematics in a more holistic way.

There is an issue of equal rights for mathematics teachers in this—mathematics teachers have a right to expect that they will receive the same amount of support from the ESL and other support staff as teachers in the humanities and other areas. In this regard it is important, particularly at the high school level, that schools select ESL staff who can provide support across all curriculum areas.

TEACHING STRATEGIES

Some general factors that can affect NESB students' learning of mathematics will be considered first. Teaching the four language skills of speaking, listening, reading, and writing will follow.

NESB students need time. NESB students are likely to need more time learning mathematics than those from an ESB. For most NESB students the mathematics classroom is the only place for them to learn both mathematics and the appropriate language. In discussing young people's need to be constructive, inventive, and forceful when faced with difficult life situations, Mellin-Olsen (1987, p. 17) made the following argument:

> They should be able to document and contribute to the solution of their problems.... Language education is probably the most important subject in this respect. It is my conviction, however, that mathematics education can be as important. Mathematics is also a structure of thinking-tools appropriate for understanding, building, or changing society.

Any consideration of equity must include structuring the school curriculum so that the issue of time is addressed for students needing additional language or mathematics instruction. In Australia, extra classes for English are common; for mathematics, they are rare.

Mathematics symbols are not universal. Not all students are familiar with the Hindu-Arabic numerals, and there are many different ways of expressing standard algorithms (Thomas 1986). In the United States there is the added difficulty of a nonmetric measurement system, which many students will not have encountered before. The different symbol systems are not a major problem, provided that teachers recognize that NESB students may not be familiar with the systems being used in their classrooms. Sharing different ways of recording from different cultures can be a useful teaching strategy. If students use a comma for a decimal point, it may be something with which they grew up; it can lead to a class discussion on place value.

Develop concepts before language. Because it is much easier to learn the language relating to a concept if one understands the concept, the use of demonstrations, photographs, models, and so on is important in ESL teaching. Concepts are also much easier to learn if they can be discussed in familiar language. There are two important implications for mathematics classrooms having NESB students: (1) The use of concrete materials and diagrams is even more important than with ESB students, and (2) letting students talk about the ideas in their first language often helps them learn the concepts, so they can then learn the English. It is another aspect that requires sensitive classroom management—teachers do not want ghettos in their classrooms, but allowing children of the same language background to work together can be very beneficial for the students.

Mathematical language has different forms. A simple mathematical statement can be written in three distinct forms: the informal vernacular, the technical subject-specific language, and in mathematical symbols:

1. Three apples and two apples is five apples.
2. The sum of three and two is five.
3. $3 + 2 = 5$

Students need to be able to use all three forms. There is little understanding of (3) if students can not relate it to (1). Without (2) students will eventually be excluded from the study of mathematics.

Speaking and Listening

NESB students need to practice both speaking and listening in English. However, they may come from a school culture where discussion has not been encouraged and listening in English is a demanding task. They will recognize the need to learn English, so discuss the importance of speaking and listening with them.

NESB students tend to take longer to process information. Dawe (1983) found that even students who had all their education in English may translate a problem into their first language and then back into English. Students tended to do this more when under stress. Allowing plenty of time for students to think about an answer, known as wait time, is very important. It is also important to use open-ended questions requiring more than a single-word response. These students are not only learning mathematics but learning English as well.

Many students in my classes in Australia had very poor listening skills. After years of understanding very little of what the teacher was saying, they had stopped trying to listen. After the introduction to the lesson was finished, their hands would go up for help; they would want me to show them how to manipulate the symbols to get the right answer. I found it useful to use short oral tests that focused on mathematical language and kept the mathematics simple. If I had been teaching prime numbers, for example, the test would include items like "What is the next prime number after 3?" Students soon found that they could do very well on these tests if they learned what the words meant and listened carefully.

These students need encouragement, motivation, and rewards for the effort it takes to try and understand mathematics in a difficult and confusing language. One Greek-background student's mathematics improved dramatically after he asked how he could help his classmate and friend who had severe learning difficulties as a result of a childhood illness. I suggested that by listening carefully he would be able to show his friend what to do.

Reading

To encourage students to read mathematics embedded in text—

1. choose familiar contexts;
2. avoid difficult linguistic constructions;
3. help students develop reading strategies.

Reading in mathematics is a complex task. It requires readers to use their general comprehension skills to understand the context and to extract meaning from the text. They then have to use their mathematical knowledge to extract—and comprehend—the mathematics embedded in the text. It requires that comprehension and mathematical skills be brought together, and many students find it extremely difficult.

In spite of this, research in reading and mathematics continues to attract little attention. An Australian publication (Stephens et al. 1993) on mathematics and language issues had no contributions that specifically considered the skills required for reading mathematical text. In 1989, Siegel, Borasi, and Smith called for a new synthesis of reading and mathematics instruction. A subsequent paper (Borasi and Siegel 1992) dealt extensively with the need for transmission models in both language and mathematics teaching to be replaced by a process of inquiry based on the construction of meaning. It failed, however, to address the fundamental issues of what is different about reading in mathematics compared to reading ordinary prose and what the implications are for helping children in mathematics classrooms.

Culture is important in reading mathematics because if the mathematics is embedded in a context that bears no relationship to anything in the student's experience, it is a barrier to comprehension. Some years ago the term "galvanized iron" was used in a mathematics examination in Australia and caused considerable consternation for the many NESB students for whom the term was completely unfamiliar. Knowing the term was not essential to solving the problem, but without knowing what was meant, the students did not know this.

Prior knowledge is very important in reading comprehension in mathematics. A child in a Catholic school, confronted with a multiple-choice question about "which angle was the right angle" interpreted "angle" as "angel." She was then able to apply this to the diagrams and interpret the examples of angles as "wings of angels." This is a powerful example of the way in which a child's view of the world can impinge on comprehension (Clements 1980).

The complexity of reading comprehension behaviors was demonstrated by Casteel and Rider (1994) in a study where Caucasian children were given reading passages depicting characters from either Caucasian or African American background. Fifty-five of the fifty-seven students scored higher when a Caucasian was the protagonist. Findings of this type pose interesting research questions concerning comprehension when mathematics is embedded in text, especially for students who are also finding mathematics difficult.

I like the story I was told about a test item that involved moving cattle from one part of a farm to another along a road. Cattle were added and subtracted as some wandered off into trees and strays were found along the way. I am told that the children from the wheat-farming areas happily arrived at a number that was less than the number of cattle they started with. The children from the dairy-farming areas seldom did. Sometimes they had more—but very rarely fewer. Now I grew up on a farm, and I have a certain empathy with the children from the dairy farms. Losing animals for which you have responsibility is not something even the most tolerant father takes lightly, but picking up strays along the way is another matter altogether.

If children are going to learn to read mathematics, context is important. It also makes culturally unbiased national and state testing extremely difficult. It is unlikely that standard readability formulas will ever be able to offer real help in coming to understand what it is about mathematics embedded in text that makes it difficult to read. A far more important task is identifying areas of difficulty. One is context, as discussed above; another is linguistic difficulty. Consider this apparently simple question:

> If a man takes three minutes to run 500 meters, how long will he take to run a kilometer?

This superficially simple question requires that the student assume the man runs at a constant rate, recognize that *long* refers to time and not length in this context, and know the connection between meters and kilometers. It also assumes that the student can use logical connectives, a rather dubious assumption for the level of mathematics involved. Logical connectives (*if, then,* etc.) are used extensively in mathematics and have to be learned. If they are used with young children or poor readers, they can be a real barrier to understanding. Gardner (1977) showed that extreme care should be taken with logical connectives until children are in at least middle high school even if they are ESB. The question above could be reworded to something like this:

> A man took three minutes to run 500 meters. He kept running at the same speed. How long did he take to run a kilometer?

It now has no logical connectives and contains only one piece of information in each sentence. Although students do have to read more linguistically complex questions eventually, we often ask them to do the equivalent of running before crawling when reading mathematics.

Newman (1977) found that NESB students were much more likely to be able to sound out the words correctly but unable to restate the question in their own words. The implications of this finding are very important. It is not sufficient to ask students to read a problem aloud when looking for possible language problems. The student may still have major difficulties with comprehension. A kit developed by Newman (1983) is one of the few resources available to teachers that can help them identify comprehension problems in mathematics and suggest strategies for improving comprehension. Although directed at primary schools, the strategies are also useful for high school students. They are quite simple and include having students highlight words they do not understand and find out what they mean from a teacher or a friend, draw a diagram of the problem, and so on.

Writing

In contrast to reading, writing in mathematics has attracted considerable attention. It is very important to remember that writing in mathematics should involve learning mathematics. The student who knows that 2 + 5 = 7 and writes, "I had two apples and I was given another five. Now I have seven apples altogether" has not learned any new mathematics. Winograd and Higgins (1995) show that writing problems to be solved by other members of the class can, however, help students consolidate mathematical concepts and improve their writing in mathematics.

When students are asked to write in mathematics, it should be a task that is cognitively challenging, related to mathematical language, or related to learning to write mathematically. Some of the best examples I have encountered have involved ESL teachers. In one instance an ESL teacher with a strong interest in mathematics teaching was working in a center for newly arrived immigrants. I arrived one day after the teacher had given a lesson on the Pythagorean theorem. For homework the students had been given the task of writing a lie about the theorem. This is what I mean by a cognitively challenging task—students with very little English had been asked to come up with a counterexample.

Journal writing can also be useful for NESB students, but it needs to be structured. Norwood and Carter (1994) have documented some very practical suggestions for journal writing that would be applicable with ESB and NESB students. In all aspects of language, mathematics teachers need to realize that it is often necessary to be very explicit with some students. Very few ESB or NESB students come from homes where mathematical ideas are commonly discussed. They need good models and explicit instruction.

RESOURCES

Remember that ESL teachers should be in schools to help teachers and students in all areas where ESL expertise is required, including mathematics. In Australian schools there are sometimes bilingual teacher aides who can help students develop concepts in their first language. Often these aides have taught in other countries; their help in the mathematics classroom, or in helping parents understand a new curriculum, can be invaluable.

Very few resources have been specifically developed for teaching NESB students. Some good materials have been published that have addressed mathematics in different cultural settings. There are also two useful publications for teachers that address language teaching in mathematics. Both were developed by people with considerable ESL and mathematics teaching experience. *Mathematical Literacy* (Ballagh and Moore 1987) consists of a book and a video and shows how a variety of ESL techniques can be used to teach mathematical language to students. Although directed at senior high school students, many of the strategies have much wider application. *Teaching Mathematics in the Multicultural Classroom* (MacGregor and Moore 1991) is a resource for teachers and teacher educators that in my opinion is the best currently available anywhere. My high school student-teachers have found it very useful.

The development of specific textbooks for NESB students would be a retrograde step. All students need textbooks that are well written and that encourage them to learn the language of mathematics. In 1988 I looked at the glossaries in some textbooks in use in the United States at the time. They would have been of little use to any student, since they frequently used technical language to describe technical terms and seldom used diagrams. Many dictionaries of mathematics are also very inadequate, although there are exceptions (Thomas 1992).

As a consultant with the Ministry of Education, I developed a checklist to help teachers analyze the linguistic difficulty of mathematics textbooks (Thomas 1986). What became apparent from this work was that many commonly used textbooks were too difficult to read for most students. They had additional problems for NESB students relating to layout, linguistic features, and cultural background. I have suggested to the Australian Mathematical Society that many students beginning first-year university mathematics courses do not have the reading skills to access prescribed texts because they gave up trying to read mathematical textbooks early in secondary school. NESB—and ESB—students need textbooks. They are something concrete with which students can work using dictionaries, friends, and any other resources at their disposal to try and make sense of what is happening in the classroom. They need to learn to read them before they get to university. They also need better textbooks.

It is essential that publishers move beyond some of the rather trivial attempts to make their books more inclusive and make them genuine tools for learning. Such textbooks will be developed only with the help of ESL specialists to get the language right and people with cultural sensitivity to get the contexts right. Cultural sensitivity must be sensitivity in its broadest sense. There is a wonderful English publication, *Everyone Counts: Looking for Bias and Insensitivity in Primary Mathematics Materials* (Mosley 1985). Ignore the "primary mathematics" in the title—this is a book every publisher should have regardless of what they are publishing, and so should every school community or government agency responsible for choosing textbooks.

CONCLUDING REMARKS

Teaching mathematics in a multicultural classroom is not easy, but the challenge brings its own rewards. Sharing different experiences, beliefs, and values, seeing traumatized refugee children realize they are safe and start to smile again, meeting the parents who have such high expectations and are prepared to do so much to ensure the success of their children—these things are especially rewarding.

There is also something special about some of our Australian schools and the way they are accepting cultural and linguistic diversity and making it a strength. I was visiting an elementary school to see one of my student-teachers. As the end of the day approached, the classroom teacher picked up a guitar and the children gathered on the floor in the front of the room. I do not remember what the song was, but it had numbers in it. They sang the numbers in English. Then the children from different language backgrounds helped so they could sing it using the numbers in Portuguese, Vietnamese, and several other languages. There was no rush for the door when the bell rang for the end of the day—they were all having too much fun sharing and accepting the many cultures represented in the classroom.

These children may not have understood the meaning of "the gift of diversity" in the title of this book. They were, however, a wonderful example of the idea that diversity *is* a gift, a gift that can enrich our mathematics classrooms. In sharing some of my perspectives from Australia, I hope I have also given a small gift to my colleagues in other parts of the world.

REFERENCES

Ballagh, Alan, and Robert Moore. *Mathematical Literacy.* Melbourne, Victoria: Footscray College of Technical and Further Education, 1987.

Bishop, Alan. *Mathematical Enculturation.* Dordrecht, Netherlands: Kluwer Academic Publishers, 1988.

Borasi, Raffaella, and Marjorie Siegel. "Reading, Writing and Mathematics: Rethinking the 'Basics' and Their Relationship." In *Selected Lectures from the Seventh International Congress on Mathematical Education,* edited by David F. Robitaille, David H. Wheeler, and Carolyn Kieran, pp. 35–48. Sainte-Foy, Quebec: Les Presses de l'Université Laval, 1994.

Casteel, Clifton A., and David P. Rider. "Reading Comprehension in Caucasian Middle School Students: Effects of the Race of the Protagonists." *British Journal of Educational Psychology* 64 (February 1994): 19–27.

Clarkson, Philip C. *Bilingualism and Mathematics Learning.* Geelong, Victoria: Deakin University Press, 1991.

Clements, M. A. (Ken). "Analyzing Children's Errors on Written Mathematical Tasks." *Educational Studies in Mathematics* 11 (February 1980):1–21.

Cocking, Rodney R., and Jose P. Mestre, eds. *Linguistic and Cultural Influences on Learning Mathematics.* Hillsdale, N.J.: Lawrence Erlbaum Associates, 1988.

Dawe, Lloyd. "Bilingualism and Mathematical Reasoning in English as a Second Language." *Educational Studies in Mathematics* 14 (November 1983): 325–53.

Ellerton, Nerida F., and Philip C. Clarkson. "Language Factors in Mathematics Learning." In *Research in Mathematics Education in Australasia: 1988–1991,* edited by Bill Atweh and Jane Watson, pp. 153–78. Brisbane: Queensland University of Technology, Mathematics Education Research Group of Australasia, 1992.

Gardner, Paul. "Logical Connectives in Science: A Summary of the Findings." *Research in Science Education* 7 (February 1977): 9–24.

Harris, Pam. "Contexts for Change in Cross-Cultural Classrooms." In *School Mathematics: The Challenge to Change,* edited by Nerida F. Ellerton and M. A. (Ken) Clements, pp. 79–95. Geelong, Victoria: Deakin University Press, 1989.

MacGregor, Mollie, and Robert Moore. *Teaching Mathematics in the Multicultural Classroom.* Melbourne, Victoria: University of Melbourne, Institute of Education, 1991.

Mellin-Olsen, Stieg. *The Politics of Mathematics Education.* Dordrecht, Netherlands: D. Reidel, 1987.

Mosley, Fran. *Everyone Counts: Looking for Bias and Insensitivity in Primary Mathematics Materials.* London: Inner London Education Authority, 1985.

Newman, M. Anne. "An Analysis of Sixth Grade Pupils' Errors on Written Mathematical Tasks." *Victorian Institute for Educational Research Bulletin* 39 (December 1977): 31–43.

——— . *The Newman Language of Mathematics Kit*. Sydney: Harcourt Brace Jovanovich, 1983.

Norwood, Karen S., and Glenda Carter. "Journal Writing: An Insight into Students' Understanding." *Teaching Children Mathematics* 1 (November 1994): 146–48.

Nunes, Terezinha. "Ethnomathematics and Everyday Cognition." In *Handbook of Research on Mathematics Teaching and Learning,* edited by Douglas A. Grouws, pp. 557–74. New York: Macmillan Publishing Co., 1992.

Olsen, Laurie. "Crossing the Schoolhouse Border: Immigrant Children in California." *Phi Delta Kappan* 70 (November 1988): 212–18.

Secada, Walter G. "Race, Ethnicity, Social Class, Language, and Achievement in Mathematics." In *Handbook of Research on Mathematics Teaching and Learning,* edited by Douglas A. Grouws, pp. 623–60. New York: Macmillan Publishing Co., 1992.

Siegel, Marjorie, Raffaella Borasi, and Constance Smith. "A Critical Review of Reading in Mathematics Instruction: The Need for a New Synthesis." In *Cognitive and Social Perspectives for Literacy Research and Instruction,* edited by Sandra McCormick and Jerry Zutell, pp. 269–77. Chicago: National Reading Conference, 1989.

Stephens, Max, Andrew Wayward, David Clarke, and John Izard, eds. *Communicating Mathematics: Perspectives from Classroom Practice and Current Research.* Melbourne, Victoria: Australian Council for Education Research, 1993.

Stigler, James W., and Ruth Baranes. "Culture and Mathematics Learning." In *Review of Research in Education* 15 (1988–89): 253–306.

Tate, William F. "Diversity, Reform, and Professional Knowledge: The Need for Multicultural Clarity." In *Professional Development for Teachers of Mathematics,* 1994 Yearbook of the National Council of Teachers of Mathematics, edited by Douglas B. Aichele, pp. 55–66. Reston, Va.: National Council of Teachers of Mathematics, 1994.

Taylor, Catherine. "Assessment for Measurement or Standards: The Peril and Promise of Large-Scale Assessment Reform." *American Educational Research Journal* 31 (Summer 1994): 231–62.

Thomas, Jan. "Dictionaries of Mathematics." *Australian Mathematics Teacher* 48 (October 1992): 8–9.

——— . *Number ≠ Maths.* Melbourne, Victoria: Child Migrant Education Services, 1986.

——— . "Real Maths or Symbol Manipulation?" In *The Essentials of Mathematics Education,* edited by Dudley Blane, pp. 309–14. Melbourne, Victoria: Mathematical Association of Victoria, 1983.

Winograd, Ken, and Karen M. Higgins. "Writing, Reading, and Talking Mathematics: One Interdisciplinary Possibility." *Reading Teacher* 48 (December 1994/January 1995): 310–18.

5

Class Matters
A Preliminary Excursion

Sarah Theule Lubienski

Diversity and equity are popular topics in the mathematics education community today amidst reforms intended to empower "all students." But as Secada (1992, p. 640) notes, social class is rarely focal in our discussions:

> Social class differences are not as problematic in the literature as are racial, ethnic, or other disparities. For example, while the research literature and mathematics-education reform documents (for example, NCTM, 1989; NRC, 1989) at least mention women and minorities, issues of poverty and social class are absent from their discussions. Frankly, the literature does not bristle with the same sense of outrage that the poor do not do as well in mathematics as their middle-class peers as it does with similar findings along other groupings.

Granted, we can find statistics about poor children and their relatively low achievement in mathematics. For example, we know that roughly 23 percent of persons under age eighteen live in poverty and that a strong correlation exists between socioeconomic status (SES) and mathematics achievement (Rechin 1994; Secada 1992). But we lack qualitative explorations of how and why this correlation occurs (Reyes and Stanic 1988). As Secada (1992) argues, we tend to see SES as the explanation for the correlation instead of looking for underlying causes.

I have been concerned about issues of class for some time. My concerns are rooted in my own history; they stem, in part, from my own lower-SES family. For example, family members occasionally seek my advice (or receive it anyway) about their finances. They tend to pay for purchases in very costly ways—with credit cards or rent-to-own options—and generally make the lowest monthly payment possible. Only the present costs seem to matter. Experiences such as these led me to wonder about ways

The author would like to thank Deborah Loewenberg Ball, Suzanne Wilson, Jennifer Borman, Kathy Burgis, and Chris Lubienski for their helpful encouragement and critiques of this work.

to help lower-SES people become more critical of schemes designed to persuade them to part with scarce resources.

Additionally, while teaching seventh graders, I have had many concerns about my students: their self-concepts, intellectual abilities, hormone levels, gender, race, and class, to name just a few. Although I could find helpful research on how some of these variables—gender, for example—might influence the way my students think and learn about mathematics, I had difficulty finding similar discussions about class.

I wonder why the issue is ignored. Perhaps it is because we in the United States cling to a belief in equal opportunity for all and we are not as ready to admit the existence of classes as those in other countries. Or perhaps it is simply difficult to get the research ball rolling. When we wish to study how gender might affect mathematical thinking and learning, we have little difficulty in defining who is male or female. But when trying to explore class, one can easily be attacked for defining class categories in problematic ways and for insulting students by "labeling" them as lower class. Moreover, when discussing differences between the cultures of *upper* and *lower* classes, we run the risk of sounding like a proponent of deficit theory. Perhaps to avoid these accusations, we tend to limit our talk to the positive aspects of diversity. But what positive things can we say about large disparities of wealth and social status? Hence, although deficit theory is certainly problematic, the strictly positive rhetoric restricting current discussions of diversity is potentially more devastating to low-SES children, who tend to be ignored in these discussions.

AN EXPLORATION

Curious, I set out to explore how students' class backgrounds might influence their mathematical thinking and learning. To define a manageable task, I chose to focus on the students' thinking about mathematical claims in the media. I think it is essential that students develop the ability and inclination to critically analyze mathematical claims in the everyday world, such as those that fill newspapers, magazines, and television. I am particularly concerned about this skill for lower-SES students, since they can least afford to be manipulated by others.

During the 1993–94 school year, I conducted a one-year research project as I taught seventh graders in a socioeconomically diverse school. My role was that of a "test teacher" for the Connected Mathematics Project (CMP), funded by the National Science Foundation to create a middle school curriculum aligned with the NCTM *Standards*. (See Fitzgerald et al. [1990] for more information.) Although developing students' understanding of mathematics as used in the media was not a primary focus of the curriculum I was testing, I wondered if students who have been encouraged to reach and justify their own understandings of important mathematical ideas would be able and inclined to make thoughtful interpretations of mathematical claims in the media.

To get a sense of students' class backgrounds, I surveyed their parents, focusing on occupation, education, income, number of books in the home, and newspapers read regularly. Although there is disagreement about which indicators should be used to categorize students by SES (Banks 1988; Duberman 1976), I chose these indicators because they have face validity and are similar to those used by others (e.g., Kohr et al. [1989]). I used the survey data to place the eighteen participating students into two admittedly rough categories: lower and higher SES. The lower-SES students were primarily lower or working class (e.g., the students' parents have little or no college education and are unemployed or hold factory or service jobs). The higher-SES students were what most Americans would call middle or upper-middle class (e.g., college-educated parents in professional careers, such as engineering or teaching).

I would like to note two caveats. First, I am not making careful distinctions between SES and social class in this article. (In relation to SES, class can be thought of as connoting more permanence and shared group values about roles in society. See Secada [1992] for more information.) Second, placing students into these two SES categories makes many people uncomfortable—myself included. But although the categories are rough and might cause some discomfort, they are useful as a starting point for comparing the mathematical cultures and needs of lower- and higher-SES students.

UNCOVERING FAULTY ASSUMPTIONS

Several times throughout the year, I used written surveys and interviews to assess the students' understanding of, and attitudes toward, mathematical claims taken from newspapers and magazines. As I conducted this inquiry, I began to uncover my own assumptions about what "all children" need to become critical consumers and citizens. I believed that all students were like me: they would think it is fun and fruitful to analyze mathematical claims in the world around them. I assumed that all students *would* be critical if they *could*.

Contrary to my initial assumptions, all the students displayed more skepticism than I anticipated, but the reasoning behind the skepticism seemed subtly different for lower-SES than for higher-SES students. Generally speaking, the lower- and higher-SES students tended to hold different beliefs about the processes by which data are collected and reported in the media. These beliefs seemed to influence how students interpreted and used mathematical claims in the media. Hence, my discussion of the data is organized around three investigations: students' beliefs about the nature of research, students' interpretation of claims, and the influence of claims. To help the reader distinguish between the two groups of students, I use one-syllable pseudonyms for the lower-SES students and two-syllable pseudonyms for the higher-SES students.

The Nature of Research

The higher-SES students were more familiar with our "mainstream" society's research practices than the lower-SES students. These differences in familiarity seemed to influence students' beliefs about the validity of reported information and the intentions of those reporting it. I now illustrate these differences, using three categories: familiarity, validity, and purposes of research.

Familiarity with research methods

The higher-SES students were more familiar with the common business practices of collecting and reporting data than the lower-SES students. For example, James, an African American student of lower SES, believed that to collect simple numerical data about another country, you would actually need to go to that country. Additionally, I interviewed the students about the graph in figure 5.1, which shows our city's water use over the past twenty years.

Ken was one of the many lower-SES students who revealed that he was not aware of common record-keeping practices:

Interviewer: What decisions did they need to make when they made the graph?

Ken: They probably didn't collect all this information, they probably did it in a couple days, you know. So they probably had it so they could have it down right there and then up and then down for 1992. (*He follows the line of the graph with his finger as he talked about its going up and down.*)

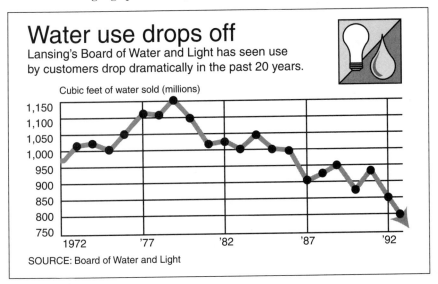

Fig. 5.1. A graph of water use in Lansing, Michigan. From an article by Paul Souhrada in the *Lansing State Journal*, 12 August 1993. ©*Lansing State Journal.* Used with permission.

Interviewer: You think they made up these numbers? Just made them up?

Ken: Yep.

Interviewer: How could they do that?

Ken: I don't think they worried about it in 1972. I think they probably worried about it like 1990 to 1996.

Lynn, another lower-SES student, answered in much the same way:

Interviewer: Do you think all of the information on the graph is accurate and exact?

Lynn: No. Maybe this one is, but I think these over here, unless they keep records or something, I don't think they are. (*She points to the dot for 1993 and then to the dots for the 1970s and 1980s.*) Because that was a long time ago. That's like twenty years ago.

These responses stand in stark contrast to those of the higher-SES students, who assumed that the information was recorded over time and was essentially correct. For them, any inaccuracies were a matter of data representation. When I asked Mollie, Gerrit, and Jason if the information on the water graph was accurate and exact, they responded in these ways:

Mollie: All the dots are really big, so you can't pinpoint them at all.

Gerrit: Yes ... 'cause it's not like saying anything like wrong. Well, it shows like the right amounts, but it shows you in a way that makes people think of something like they're not selling barely any water in 1992, but they're selling a lot of water in 1979.

Jason: You can't really see because every space in here is worth ... 50 million, so they aren't that accurate.

Hence, the higher- and lower-SES students held different assumptions about the ways in which data are collected and recorded in our society. Their beliefs about the research process seemed to affect their views on data validity.

Validity of research

Both groups of students displayed more skepticism than I had anticipated, but the two groups differed in the nature of their skepticism. As mentioned previously, some lower-SES students did not believe that companies keep records of their transactions, so they thought historical data were simply made up. Another view offered by lower-SES students was that information in the media might be faulty because the person who represents the data might choose to do what is easiest:

Interviewer: Do you think all of the information on the graph is accurate and exact?

Sue: Probably not. I mean, they might have like skipped some people or something.

Interviewer: Why would they do that?

Sue :   To make it like shorter.

Interviewer: What do you mean?

Sue: Like so they wouldn't have to like plot—like figure out less numbers and stuff.

The higher-SES students tended to believe that the information in the ads was based on some truth but that companies could try to manipulate people by the way in which they collected or reported the data. Gerrit's response, given above, is one example. David's response is another:

David: I guess they [ads] all tell the truth, but they kind of—there's always a way in math to like fool somebody. Like you could ask ten people, and three of them said it was bad, and seven people said it's good. But then what if you ask 2 million people, what happens then? 'Cause maybe you just asked the seven people who didn't like it.

Thus, both groups of students were skeptical of the validity of mathematical claims. Many lower-SES students did not assume there was a valid basis for claims; they talked about people guessing, simplifying, or lying about the data. In contrast, the higher-SES students assumed that some data were in fact collected that served as the basis of the claims but that the truth was sometimes stretched by manipulating data collection or reporting methods.

Purposes of research

Because the CMP curriculum emphasized statistics, almost all the students were familiar with various ways to represent data. Still, as exemplified by some of the responses above, the higher-SES students tended to reveal a greater understanding of how data collection and reporting methods could promote an agenda. Probing further into students' understandings of the purposes of those reporting data, I found that lower-SES students were more likely than higher-SES students to equate persuasion with lying. Also, although both groups were aware of economic motives, the higher-SES students seemed slightly more aware of political ones.

I asked students why advertisements and news stories might be intended to persuade people to believe something. Lower-SES students talked about lying to sell products:

Chris: Not a lot of them do tell the truth because they're all trying to sell something.

When I asked them specifically why news stories might persuade people to believe something, they again translated *persuade* into *lie*. Some thought that the news did lie at times:

Ken: Sometimes they tell the truth, and most of the times they might make up something—just to persuade kids to stop violence or something.

Meanwhile, higher-SES students were less likely to equate persuasion with lying. They also gave a slightly wider variety of answers—as opposed to a strict economic focus—when asked about persuasion in advertisements. Mollie, for example, suggested two types:

> Mollie: If they're a product, they want you to use that. If they're an organization, then they want you to like them.

When I asked higher-SES students about persuasive news stories, some thought the news was objective and "gave both sides of the story," as Leanne remarked. But others said writers try to persuade readers to adopt their own perspectives.

On the whole, both groups tended to say that advertisers have a greater incentive to persuade people than news reporters. I saw evidence across the year that a meaningful, personal experience helped some of the students realize how news writers can also use research findings to further their agenda. Chris, referring to a graph from *Newsweek* he had recently shared with the class, explained in a later interview how news writers try to get their point across:

> Chris: Yeah [the news can be dishonest], if they're trying to get a point across like that *Beavis and Butthead* one. They started real high up so it would look like it goes real far down...

I had asked students to look for coordinate graphs that did not begin at 0, and Chris found an example in an article about the perils of today's television shows. The visible part of the y-axis did not start at 0. This omission visually exaggerated the author's point, which, as Chris explained to us, was that students are "brainwashed" by watching shows like *Beavis and Butthead*. This example stuck with Chris the remainder of the year, as demonstrated by his always remembering to check the y-axis scale.

Overall, although both higher- and lower-SES students were more skeptical about information presented in the media (especially advertisements) than I had anticipated, they held different beliefs about the nature of research. The lower-SES students were less familiar with data-collection practices common in the business world. They were more likely to think that mathematical claims in the media were simply made up for the sake of convenience or making money. They did not make fine distinctions between persuasion and lying. For them, lying is the means to persuasion. The higher-SES students assumed that mathematical claims had some basis in research and that people carefully selected their data-collection and -representation methods to get their point across. Hence, for the higher-SES students, thoughtful research is the means to persuasion.

The Interpretation of Claims

I asked students to interpret several advertisements and news stories. I found that lower-SES students tended to ignore the data provided in the media. They tended to reason about the questions I asked using the picture provided in the ad, personal stories about friends and family that had tried various products, and other "common sense" means of reasoning.

Higher-SES students sometimes drew from personal experiences but also tended to scrutinize and search for a loophole in the data provided.

For example, in a written survey, I showed them statistics about male and female drivers (Shook and Shook 1991):

- In 1988, there were 47 093 people killed in car crashes and 3 486 people killed in motorcycle crashes in the United States.
- About 40% of all deaths of 15-to-19-year-olds result from motor-vehicle crashes. Alcohol is involved in about half of these crashes.
- Males outnumber females as fatal-crash victims (people who die in car crashes) by an average of 2 to 1.

I then asked, "Are males worse drivers than females?" All students said no to the question, but the ways they justified their answers were very different. The lower-SES students tended to ignore the information provided and reason about the question in other ways:

> No, because anything can happen at anytime sometimes they can die from something that can't control. (Chris)
>
> No. Some women don't watch the road or get scared all the time. (Ken)
>
> No, they probably just try to show off in their car, then crash. (Lynn)

The higher-SES students based their reasoning on the information provided (or not provided):

> There is not enough info because it doesn't say if the women caused the crashes or if a man did, or even if the woman was driving the car. (Mollie)
>
> No, because it never said anything about the drivers. A female could be driving with 2 other guys, so if they all die in a crash, more males would die than females. (Shelley)
>
> No! Just because they crash more doesn't mean that they can't drive as well! Maybe a female driver had a hit and run on a male. (Jason)
>
> No, because there may be more male drivers. Females may get in more car crashes and not die than males. (Gerrit)

I saw similar patterns in virtually every question I asked requiring students to interpret data. The lower-SES students were much more likely to ignore the mathematical information and use pictures, personal stories, and "common sense" reasoning when they responded to my questions. Higher-SES students tended to use the information in their interpretations, scrutinizing it carefully. (It is important to note that this approach did not always result in the "best" mathematical explanation, as evidenced by some of the responses above.) Additionally, higher-SES students would often combine their scrutiny with "common sense" reasoning, especially on items that seemed to interest the students personally.

The Influence of Claims

It is difficult to know how mathematical information would truly affect students' decisions. As Crossen (1994, p. 17) writes, "We are skeptical about statistical and factual information, but not as skeptical as we think." The higher-SES students in my study tended to say that advertisements would not persuade them to buy a product but they might provide ideas about what to consider. To my surprise, although the lower-SES students tended to be very skeptical of information in advertisements, often saying that the statements were probably outright lies or guesses, they were more likely than the higher-SES students to say that they would be persuaded to buy products on the basis of advertisements.

For example, I asked students about a truck advertisement that makes a 3 percent difference look very large because the *y*-axis begins at 95 percent (see fig. 5.2). I asked students the following questions:

1. The bar for Company A is about six times as tall as the bar for Company D. Does this mean that the chances of one of Company A's trucks lasting 10 years are about six times as great as the chances for one of Company D's trucks?

2. If you wanted to buy a truck, would this graph convince you to buy a truck from Company A?

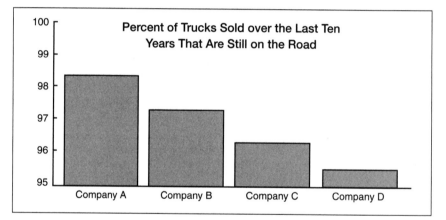

Fig. 5.2. A graph used in a truck advertisement

The responses to the first question (see fig. 5.3) followed the pattern mentioned in the previous section: higher-SES students tended to scrutinize the mathematical basis of the graph more than the lower-SES students, and most of the higher-SES students found a mathematical loophole with which to justify their skepticism. Lower-SES students tended to use "common sense" reasoning, but those who referred to the graph (or perhaps just to the information I gave in the question) were persuaded that Company A is much better. Regardless of their answer to the first question, the lower-SES students tended to say that the graph *would* convince them to buy a truck from Company A, whereas higher-SES students said they were not convinced.

Hence, the higher-SES students tended to scrutinize the mathematical

Name	Does this mean a Company A truck is six times as likely to last 10 years?	Does the graph convince you to buy a truck from Company A?
Lower-SES Students		
Dawn	No, because maybe the other company is just having a bad year, so there they can't keep the rate up.	Yes, because it said the most trucks are still on the road.
Ken	No, because it depends on the inside by the engine and also by outside body and standard performance.	Yes, because it tells you of the high quality and power of a car.
Chris	Yes, because if the bar is six times greater than that is how much more trucks are still on the road compared to other companies.	Yes, I would buy a truck from Company A because they last alot longer than any other company's trucks.
Higher-SES Students		
Shelly	No, it means that about 3% of all of Company A's trucks that were bought 10 years ago are still on the road today, not 6 times more.	No, because if I bought a truck today, then it might be gone in 10 years while a Company D truck would still be here, even though now there are more Company A trucks.
Jason	No, the graph starts at 95%, therefore, Company D's bar isn't really 6 times as low, therefore making everything think that A is 6 times better but really it's not!!!	No, because maybe the owners of Company A's trucks are too cheap to get a new truck, so they spend a fortune on maintenance and keep their Company A trucks.
Leanne	No, the graph does not mean Company A's trucks are 6 times greater because they could have sold all their trucks in the last year, while Company D sold theirs 10 years ago.	No, this graph would not convince me, because I would have to know how well they work. Company A trucks could break down all the time, but it would be fixable, which would make Company A trucks more expensive.

Fig. 5.3. Students' responses to two questions about the truck advertisement

basis for ads and say they would use the information more cautiously in decision making than the lower-SES students.

Perhaps the lower-SES students did not see any contradiction between thinking that ads are often lies and being influenced by them. In an interview, James was asked to give examples of dishonest news stories. He responded, "How would I know if it wasn't true?" Perhaps, as Crossen (1994) argues, when people feel powerless to judge the truthfulness of information, they do not attempt to make rational decisions on the basis of that information. Bruner (1975, p. 36) argues that poverty produces "a sense of powerlessness [that] alters goal striving and problem solving in those it affects." Hence, the lower-SES students might be more easily persuaded by information in the media because they may not feel they have the power to scrutinize and judge it and because they believe all possible influences on their opinion are equally suspect.

OBSERVATIONS AND CONVICTIONS

The higher- and lower-SES students in my study tended to hold different beliefs about the nature of research. These differences seemed to influence the ways in which they interpreted and said they would use mathematical claims in the media. Of course, these differences were not without counterexample. For instance, I categorized Mark as being of lower SES, but his thinking usually aligned closely with that of the higher-SES students. Mark's case raises two points.

First, although categorizing students by a single variable can be useful for some purposes, Mark reminds us of the dangers of stereotyping.

Second, carefully examining Mark's counterexample can lead us to reexamine how we define SES or class. Mark lived with his mother, a secretary. Thinking about why Mark's responses seemed so different from those of the lower-SES students whose parents worked in factories or were unemployed, I began to reconsider how I was determining SES. Mark's mother's experience in the mainstream business world might have helped Mark become more aware of the norms of the "culture of power."

I did not expect that students coming into my classroom would think so differently about mathematics in the media. But that I found otherwise is important not only for teaching students about mathematics in the media but also for thinking more generally about the educational needs of "all students." I initially believed that, as a teacher, I should try to make students more skeptical of mathematical information in the media. But when I looked carefully at my students' thinking, I found plenty of skepticism. My experience raises the questions, What should be the role of mathematics educators in this area? and What should our goals be?

My study included a small number of students, so any conclusions I make about differences between groups of students are tentative. Still, my excursion has helped me develop three convictions:

First, Crossen (1994) argues that we need to "clean up the information industry" because people have become accepting of the lies in the media and, therefore, powerless consumers in their relationship with the information givers. I believe that those involved with mathematics education need to work from both ends—helping promote honest uses of mathematics in the media and helping students, particularly students who are already relatively powerless in our society, develop the ability and inclination to use information critically.

Acquainting students with the processes by which data are collected and reported in the real world and helping them understand how one's intentions can affect the decisions made in these processes might be fruitful ways to begin. I saw some evidence over the course of the year that a meaningful, personal experience with an item in the media could challenge students' assumptions and help them feel more powerful as consumers. For example, Chris scrutinized graphs more closely and said he would use the information more cautiously after his experience with the *Beavis and Butthead* graph.

Second, our approach to the study of statistics should be guided by the differing needs of our students, especially those who are already relatively powerless in our society. In my situation, instead of assuming that I should help students become more skeptical, I should have tried to familiarize students with the processes and intentions behind data gathering, analysis, and reporting. I should have spent time looking at more credible sources, such as *Consumer Reports,* to help my students understand that they do not have to be powerless consumers of information. I should have spent more time talking about consumers' rights and ways to take action when presented with questionable information. I had assumed that the lower-SES students should become more skeptical when, in fact, many already distrusted mathematical claims to the point of feeling powerless to use information to their advantage. But the point is not simply that I should or should not have taught my students differently. The point is that an understanding of the types of diversity that existed in my classroom was needed in order to educate my students effectively and equitably.

This leads me to my third conviction. This exploration focused on students' understandings of mathematical claims in the media. Through it, I found just one possible area of overlap between what is important in mathematics and the cultures of various groups of differing SES. Although one interpretation of my data is that the lower-SES students were just lacking in mathematical abilities or intelligence, I would like to discourage this interpretation. The two groups of students had different beliefs about research and how it is used. As Harrigan (1993) argues, what might appear as irrational reasoning might, in fact, be a very rational response to the alienation pervasive in lower-class culture. I believe we need to further explore ways in which lower-SES students' cultures might affect their beliefs about, and learning in, mathematics, as well as ways to address their specific educational needs.

In reading current reform documents, one can be swept away amidst the "mathematics for all" rhetoric and conclude that constructivist-inspired pedagogical methods are the solution to our equity problems. But I wonder if some current reform directions might be based on questionable assumptions and limited understandings about the cultures and needs of "all students."

I argued earlier that the lower-SES students equated persuasion with lying, whereas higher-SES students equated persuasion with careful data collection and representation. Although this difference pertained to persuasion in the media, might it also influence or relate to the way students view mathematical arguments in the classroom? Might there be clashes among different views of acceptable mathematical reasoning?

In the beginning of the year, as the middle-class boys tended to dominate our mathematical discussions, I often wondered, "Is it any more empowering for the 'lower status' students to be given ideas or to have their conjectures judged by their 'high status' peers than it would be if I were still the primary authority in this. classroom?" What is to keep society from simply reproducing its inequities in our classrooms when we let students have more freedom of thought and expression? I found myself becoming an "intervener" for the sake of equity. But because of the relatively rich research on gender and mathematics classroom processes with which I was familiar, I found I was more prepared to effectively address gender inequities than racial and SES inequities in my classroom (Lubienski in preparation).

Still, the goals of the current reforms seem promising; it is very important that students learn to think for themselves. But evidence such as that presented in the *NCTM News Bulletin* (1993) article happily entitled "NAEP Results Show Improvement" is quite disturbing. The article quotes Lamar Alexander (former secretary of education) as saying, "It seems reasonable to conclude that the new standards adopted by the National Council of Teachers of Mathematics are having an effect." We also learn, however, that although the overall average proficiency of fourth, eighth, and twelfth graders on the mathematics portion of the 1992 National Assessment of Educational Progress (NAEP) rose 5 points, the average proficiency of disadvantaged, urban eighth graders declined significantly. In fact, the same NAEP data were the basis of an article entitled "Test Gap Widening between Rich and Poor" (Rechin 1994). Although we should be cautious about jumping to conclusions about the causes and effects involved in these statistics, we must also be careful that we do not blindly cheer the reforms on at the expense of the students who most need to become mathematically powerful.

At the very least, the NAEP results should prompt us to learn more about the cultures and needs of our underserved students. But we need to be prepared to face dilemmas about the type of teaching and learning that seems most intrinsically valuable yet might also be more likely to reproduce, if not increase, disparities in our society. We must also continually question our goals for "all students," including pushing all students to learn more mathematics as opposed to pushing for a society in which all students' talents and ways of thinking and knowing are equally valued. Living with these issues, I tend to want to prepare students to become mathematically powerful in our present society so that they might join us in helping make our society more equitable in the future.

REFERENCES

Banks, James A. "Ethnicity, Class, Cognitive, and Motivational Styles: Research and Teaching Implications." *Journal of Negro Education* 57 (1988): 452–66.

Bruner, Jerome S. "Poverty and Childhood." *Oxford Review of Education* 1 (1975): 31–50.

Crossen, Cynthia. *Tainted Truth: The Manipulation of Fact in America.* New York: Simon & Schuster, 1994.

Duberman, Lucile. *Social Inequality: Class and Caste in America.* Philadelphia: J. B. Lippincott Co., 1976.

Fitzgerald, William, Glenda Lappan, Elizabeth Phillips, Susan Friel, and James Fey. *Connected Mathematics: A Proposal Submitted to the National Science Foundation.* East Lansing, Mich.: Michigan State University, 1990.

Harrigan, John J. *Empty Dreams, Empty Pockets: Class and Bias in American Politics.* New York: Macmillan, 1993.

Kohr, Richard L., James R. Masters, J. Robert Coldiron, Ross S. Blust, and Eugene W. Skiffington. "The Relationship of Race, Class, and Gender with Mathematics Achievement for Fifth, Eighth, and Eleventh Grade Students in Pennsylvania Schools." *Peabody Journal of Education* [Special Issue] 66 (Winter 1989): 147–71.

Lubienski, Sarah Theule. *Mathematics for All? Examining Issues of Class in Mathematics Teaching and Learning.* Ph.D. diss., Michigan State University, in preparation.

National Council of Teachers of Mathematics. *Curriculum and Evaluation Standards for School Mathematics.* Reston, Va.: National Council of Teachers of Mathematics, 1989.

———. "NAEP Results Show Improvement." *NCTM News Bulletin,* May 1993, pp. 1, 12.

National Research Council, Mathematical Sciences Education Board. *Everybody Counts: A Report to the Nation on the Future of Mathematics Education.* Washington, D.C.: National Academy Press, 1989.

Rechin, Kevin. "Test Gap Widening between Rich and Poor." *Lansing State Journal,* 4 December 1994, p. 9A.

Reyes, Laurie Hart, and George M. A. Stanic. "Race, Sex, Socioeconomic Status, and Mathematics." *Journal for Research in Mathematics Education* 19 (January 1988): 26–43.

Secada, Walter G. "Race, Ethnicity, Social Class, Language, and Achievement in Mathematics." In *Handbook of Research on Mathematics Teaching and Learning,* edited by Douglas A. Grouws, pp. 623–60. New York: Macmillan Publishing Co., 1992.

Shook, Michael, and Robert Shook. *The Book of Odds.* New York: Penguin Group, 1991.

6

Teacher Questions + Student Language + Diversity = Mathematical Power

Patricia F. Campbell
Thomas E. Rowan

Pᴿᴏᴊᴇᴄᴛ IMPACT (Increasing the Mathematical Power of All Children and Teachers) has been addressing schoolwide reform in elementary school mathematics in predominantly minority urban schools outside Washington, D.C. This project is a National Science Foundation–funded effort to design, implement, and evaluate in schools with predominantly minority student populations a model for elementary school mathematics instruction that is compatible with the NCTM's (1989) *Curriculum and Evaluation Standards for School Mathematics.* The project's focus has been on enhancing students' understanding by supporting changes in teaching practices in a schoolwide effort. The schools in Project IMPACT reflect diversity in the children's racial-ethnic heritage and primary language. Project IMPACT's efforts to support mathematical understanding in the classroom have encompassed language, communication, mathematical content, mathematical connections, decision making, and equity. Teachers and children work together to create a mathematics culture in their classroom. The schools have been encouraged to use instruction to support and foster each child's "making sense" of mathematics without separating students into ability groups that limit access to mathematics.

The research reported in this material was supported in part by the National Science Foundation under Grants Numbers MDR 8954652 and ESI 9454187. The opinions, conclusions, or recommendations expressed in these materials are those of the authors and do not necessarily reflect the views of the National Science Foundation.

A VISION OF TEACHING AND LEARNING

Classroom Environment

"Mathematical power for all" cannot be fully realized if the classroom environment limits any child's access to challenging mathematics instruction. If students are to persist in their efforts to make sense of mathematics, if students are to do the work that is an inevitable aspect of understanding mathematics, if students are to make public their emerging concepts and problem-solving strategies, then each student must feel that his or her response is valued. No student is exempt from participation; no student is allowed to limit another's efforts to participate. Each child is expected to contribute to the problem-solving process.

Challenging Mathematics

If the mathematics addressed in the classroom is trivial or frustrating, then the vision of mathematical understanding for all will not materialize. Mathematics must be challenging to students, without being discouraging, in order to stimulate engagement. If the mathematics is trivial or not meaningful to the students, then it may be boring. If it is boring, then the classroom environment will rapidly disintegrate.

Project IMPACT has found that expectations for urban mathematics students are generally low. Through Project IMPACT we have found that the following approach is workable: Teachers plan a lesson incorporating some meaningful real-life mathematics problems that aim a little higher than usual for their students. They solicit students' ideas about how the problems might be solved and then give the students time to solve the problems. As the teachers reflect on the strengths and ideas offered by their students, their expectations generally change.

Project IMPACT seeks to implement instruction in which each student learns and mathematics is accessible to all. To realize these goals, the classroom must be a place where thoughts are accepted, ideas are investigated, and meaningful problems are solved. The result is an equitable environment for learning.

AN EQUITABLE ENVIRONMENT FOR LEARNING

Language and Communication

The reconceptualization of thinking and learning that is emerging from the body of recent work on the nature of cognition suggests that becoming a good mathematical problem solver—becoming a good thinker in any domain—may be as much a matter of acquiring the habits and dispositions of interpretation and sense-making as of acquiring any particular set of skills, strategies, or knowledge (Resnick 1988).

The proportion of the student population in Project IMPACT schools that speaks other languages or comes from a different cultural heritage is extremely high, so the use of language and of cultural background is especially important in IMPACT schools. Prior to Project IMPACT, the response to this language and cultural diversity was to remove language and context from the mathematics that the students were asked to do. This approach, of course, left the children with only symbol manipulation. Some students were quite proficient at symbol manipulation, so the notion that this practice was appropriate persisted for some time. If, however, we accept Resnick's views, then we must recognize that such a program does not really foster these children's learning of mathematics. It only leads them to acquire that small subset of mathematics called arithmetic.

Will children who lack fluency in English benefit from mathematics discourse in English? Will students who speak some English but exhibit limited oral expression be able to participate in full-class discussions? Or will these students simply observe without understanding or, even worse, develop diminishing self-esteem because of their limited oral proficiency? Consider the following example.

Many children in the IMPACT schools move from one apartment to another. They will transfer from a school, appearing sometimes at another IMPACT school and sometimes at a local school outside the project. One such student left one of our classrooms and went to another school. The child's new teacher telephoned the IMPACT school to ask, "What kind of math program do you have at your school? After he gives an answer, he is always asking me why I didn't ask him to explain how he got that answer."

Once students become accustomed to using language in mathematics, they seem to enjoy it and to realize that they gain from it. In an individual testing session, one fourth-grade student, Darrell, clearly showed how he used language to guide his thinking. This student had not been taught an algorithm for division or multiplication. Darrell had been taught the concepts and typically invented his own procedures. He was accustomed to tackling problems in context, even when he did not have an automatic procedure or routine for solving the problem. Darrell was given the following problem:

> Four children had 3 bags of M & M's. They decided to open all 3 bags of candy and share the M & M's fairly. There were 52 M & M's candies in each bag. How many M & M's candies did each child get?

Darrell asked for the problem to be read aloud to him three times. Then he considered the problem for a moment before he began talking as he wrote (see Darrell's written work in fig. 6.1):

Four people.	(*Writes* $\lfloor 1 \lfloor 2 \lfloor 3 \lfloor 4$)
So I said, uhh.... So I took.... First, I did this.	
I numbered the four people. And then I put,	
then I put 3 times 52.	(*Writes* 3×52)
Then I said equals.	(*Writes* =)

Four children had 3 bags of M & M's. They decided to open all 3 bags of candy and share the M & M's fairly. There were 52 M & M candies in each bag. How many M & M candies did each child get?

Fig. 6.1. Darrell's solution to the problem about sharing M&M's

And that equals ... 3 times 52 equals ... 150 ... 152, 154, 156. And that equals 156.	(*Writes 156*)
So, since there's four children, I split the 156 and I said, 20, 20, 20, 20.	(*Writing 20's as he speaks*)
I said, 20,... so I added all the 20's up. 20, 40, 60, 80.... Then I said, 85, 90, 95, 100.	(*Writing 5's in each column*)
Then I said 10, 20, 30, 40. These are tens.	(*Writing 10's in each column*)
... 141, 142, 143, 144,	(*Writing 1's in each column*)
... 145, 146, 147, 148,	(*Writing 1's in each column*)
... 149, 150, 151, 152,	(*Writing 1's in each column*)
... 153, 154, 155, 156. And so, ... so each, each child got, ... 30, 35. Each child got 20,	(*Pointing to 20 in the first column*)
30,	(*Pointing to 10 in the first column*)
35,	(*Pointing to 5 in the first column*)
36, 37, 38, 39.	(*Pointing to 1's in the first column*)

Each child got 39 M&M's.

As Darrell solved this problem, the language he spoke seemed to give life to the problem and guide his solution strategy. For many children, like Darrell, their quiet vocalizing of the ideas that are leading them to a solution makes clear the powerful role that language plays for them. Other children will sometimes sit quietly and think about such a problem before writing anything. For these children, the vocalizing is not necessary.

Consider another example of the power of oral explanation. A second-grade child was working in a small group on the following problem:

Tiger went to the amusement park. He wanted to ride the Ferris wheel and the minicoaster. It takes 2 tickets to ride the Ferris wheel for 3 minutes. It takes 3 tickets to ride the minicoaster for 4 minutes. Tiger wants to ride the Ferris wheel for 6 minutes and the minicoaster for 8 minutes. How many tickets does Tiger need?

The children had Unifix cubes available. It was obvious to an observer that the children were working industriously because they liked the idea of solving a problem about amusement park rides. After working independently, the children shared within their groups. Sharing enabled them to increase their understanding by hearing the strategies and thinking of the others in their group. By first sharing within their group, the children also gained the confidence they would need to share with the whole class.

After the children had completed their group work, the teacher called on Jose to share. Jose gave his answer, which was correct, and then began to explain his solution process. About halfway through his explanation, it became clear to the observer that this approach was not going to lead to Jose's original answer. Jose also realized this and stopped. How wonderful it was that the teacher simply waited. A full twenty-five seconds of silence elapsed. Then Jose smiled and started over. This time he talked his way flawlessly through to the solution. By the end of this process, two things had become very clear. First, Jose's confidence had grown immeasurably. Second, he understood the problem and his own solution process better than he had before he attempted to verbalize it. When children are expected to explain their strategies, they must reflect on their thinking, which deepens their understanding.

These are only two examples of what has been observed in Project IMPACT classrooms. Language has the power to help children organize and link their partial understandings as they integrate and develop mathematical concepts. In IMPACT classrooms, one child's verbalized solution process frequently enables another child to work through his or her own ideas by relating them to what the first child has done or said. The teacher who listens to these verbal exchanges gains information needed for making decisions about what instructional activities should occur next to ensure that the children have the best possible opportunity to grow mathematically.

Children whose first language is not English also gain from this approach to mathematics instruction. After Project IMPACT's first year, the classroom teachers and the ESOL teachers (English for Speakers of Other Languages) agreed that the children had improved both in mathematics and in language proficiency more than they had under other approaches. The children whose first language was English increased their appreciation of the ESOL students' cultural heritage because both groups were encouraged to express ideas from their backgrounds.

Figure 6.2 describes some of the techniques that Project IMPACT teachers have used to make more effective use of language in their classrooms.

Approaches to Support the Effective Use of Language

- Use mixed-ability groups as often as possible to promote the language growth of students who are less facile.
- Have students write in journals about the mathematics they are learning.
- Have students share their ideas in small groups or pairs before sharing with the entire class.
- Have students write their own story problems using personal experiences, and then expect students to share their problems with the rest of the class.
- Have students explain the information in a word problem or restate the problem in their own words using whole-class sharing before expecting students to work on the problems individually, in pairs, or in groups.
- During class discussions, first call on students with language difficulties or with fewer experiences. Doing so allows these children to share the ideas that are more apparent and challenges those with more experience or language to stretch for ideas.
- Allow students to adjust the numbers in, or the circumstances of, a problem if they are having difficulty understanding the problem or using the numbers given. Always ask the students to explain why they made the adjustments.
- When students with no English fluency come to the classroom, assign them a buddy who can help with translation. If that is not possible, use concrete materials or diagrams and connect them to words so that the students can understand the problem as much as possible without necessarily understanding all the language.

Fig. 6.2

Questioning

In a classroom where the teacher uses language to add power to the children's learning, the teacher is often a facilitator rather than a source of rules and information. The teacher guides the children, often through the use of carefully crafted questions. These questions encourage the children to construct their own mathematical understanding and to determine independently whether they have reached a mathematically valid solution to a problem.

To illustrate the benefits of questioning, consider this event; it occurred in a second-grade classroom in early February. The children were asked to solve this problem:

Pierre (a child in the class) made 41 fuzzballs. He sold 23. How many did he have then?

The children had multilink cubes, base-ten blocks, and place-value mats. The teacher gave the children their choice of how to solve the problem, saying, "Now if you would like, you can use cubes—you *can*. But you can do it any way that you want. You can use the base-ten blocks; you can use the Unifix cubes." Her tone communicated that it was up to each child to decide whether to use the materials.

After a time, the teacher told the children to "whisper your answer to a friend." Most children whispered the answer, 18, but 17 was also stated. The teacher then called on children "to share how they got their answer." After an explanation was offered and clarified, the teacher asked the important question, "Did anyone else do it differently or get a different answer?" When all methods had been stated, the teacher returned to the issue of two different answers and asked the class, "How can we check to see which is the correct answer—17 or 18?" Again, the decision was returned to the class.

At this point, a child named Anthony said that he could write out his method. The teacher later indicated that she had hoped that a manipulative process, not a written procedure, would be offered. However, no other student volunteered, so Anthony's persistent request to contribute was honored. The teacher did not insist on the use of materials; instead she told Anthony to come to the chalkboard and "talk out loud while you write." Anthony's method is shown in figure 6.3.

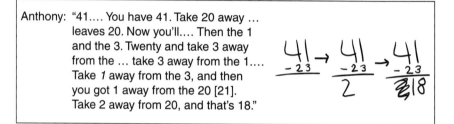

Anthony: "41.... You have 41. Take 20 away ...
leaves 20. Now you'll.... Then the 1
and the 3. Twenty and take 3 away
from the ... take 3 away from the 1....
Take *1* away from the 3, and then
you got 1 away from the 20 [21].
Take 2 away from 20, and that's 18."

Fig. 6.3. Anthony's solution to the fuzzballs problem

When Anthony had finished, the teacher knew that some children in the class did not understand his method. She also knew that although other children had understood the method, it had not verified the correct answer. So the teacher asked, "Does anyone have another way to check?"

Fig. 6.4. Carentha's solution to the fuzzballs problem

Carentha offered to show a way. Her strategy is shown in figure 6.4. It is interesting to note that Carentha's original independent strategy for solving the problem was the traditional regrouping strategy of trading 1 ten for 10 ones, using base-ten blocks. However, the question being resolved in the class was not How many fuzzballs did Pierre have left? but Which answer is correct—17 or 18? The teacher did not decide. Rather, she engaged her class in determining a strategy that would clarify the solution. Carentha indicated that tallying by ones would be a way "to tell for sure."

There are two important points regarding the teacher's use of questions in this lesson. The first is that her questions allowed the students to take control over how to solve the problem rather than just practice a procedure. Second, the teacher accepted and valued both the mathematically astute method offered by Anthony and the more basic method offered by Carentha. The teacher did not devalue any suggestion offered by the class.

Consider the implications of these two strategies. Anthony's invented solution procedure illustrates the kind of mathematical power that children can offer when they are given the opportunity. It is very closely related to the way that children naturally use base-ten blocks when displaying subtraction (noted as follows in brackets). Anthony had recognized that when using the base-ten blocks to subtract from a total, his first step was to remove the indicated number of tens, essentially ignoring the ones [4 tens, 1 one; remove 2 tens; the blocks now display 2 tens, 1 one]. It was then necessary to remove 3 ones, but there was only 1. Subtracting the available one, Anthony noted that he had taken 1 of the 3 ones that he needed to take away. That still left 2 ones to be removed from the remaining 2 tens [2 tens, 1 one; remove 1 one; the mat displays 2 tens]. Finally Anthony subtracted the 2 ones from the 20, leaving 1 ten and 8 ones, or 18, as the solution [2 tens; place tip of finger over 2 ones at the end of one of the tens; count the remainder visible on the mat; 18 remain]. Although this method is a natural use of the base-ten materials, it is obviously not the traditional subtraction algorithm. Carentha, in contrast, turned to the most basic method used by children of this age if they really want to be sure of the solution. She used a counting strategy. Recall that when working independently, Carentha had solved this problem using a regrouping strategy, but the question later changed to verifying the correct answer. Counting is a reliable and understandable way to verify answers that was accepted in Carentha's classroom.

Questions that lead children to develop this kind of mathematical power are used by Project IMPACT teachers in place of telling the children rules and procedures. Figure 6.5 presents typical questions used in Project IMPACT classrooms.

Using questions to promote thinking is not easy if the teacher is used to explaining a procedure, giving an example, and then providing practice. It takes self-discipline and patience to use questions instead of telling children what to do. However, teachers must permit students to solve problems in ways that are meaningful to them. Doing so is especially important when students have diverse understandings and perspectives. Of course, each diverse strategy must be held up to this standard: Is it mathematically valid and generalizable?

The benefit of this approach is clear in the remarks and behaviors of the children. It is evident during an assessment when a fourth grader, having worked for ten minutes on a problem and seeming frustrated, is asked if

---

Questions to Develop Mathematical Power

- How did you get your answer?
- Tell me what you are thinking.
- Is there a pattern?
- How can you check to see for yourself?
- Tell me what to do next. Explain it to me.
- Did anyone get that answer in a different way?
- Did anyone get a different answer? What was your way?
- What is alike (or different) about these two ways of solving this problem?
- I'm confused. I don't understand. Why did you ...? (used to (1) focus attention on an error in reasoning or computation or (2) cause the child to highlight a component of an explanation)
- Will this way work if we use different numbers or a different shape? Try it.
- Make a drawing (or use materials or use symbols) to show me your thinking.
- Find a friend and see if you can work it out together.
- What else could we do or use to help us figure this out?

Fig 6.5

he would like to move on to another problem and replies, "Is it okay if I keep working on this one?" Confidence and perseverance are benefits.

Differentiation Decisions

Research studies suggest that ability grouping in mathematics can amplify differences among students and produce differentiated outcomes in students' achievement (Gamoran 1992; Oakes 1985, 1990), particularly if the group definitions become permanent (Goodlad 1984). The diverse classrooms that characterize Project IMPACT differentiate instruction by often using in-class, flexible groupings. Sometimes these groups are heterogeneous, and sometimes they are homogeneous. In any event, group work is generally followed by whole–class sharing. Sometimes the distinct groups operate for the entire mathematics class with whole-class sharing occurring the next day; at other times they operate for only a portion of the class period and are followed by whole-class engagement. Sometimes the whole class operates as the group. When a student is permitted to hear and question the strategies of the other students, whether they solved a particular problem or not, that student is afforded another opportunity to learn.

How can whole-class sharing be meaningful if a student does not solve every problem being discussed? One approach is for the students to solve similar problems, with different numbers to differentiate for difficulty while maximizing the opportunity for subsequent discussion. Consider the following second-grade scenario. Some children are asked to solve this problem:

> Marissa had some crayons. She gave 7 crayons to her best friend. Now Marissa has 15 crayons. How many crayons did she have to start with?

Other children solve a similar problem in which Marissa has given her best friend 17 crayons. The problem presented to a third group of children has the condition that after Marissa has given away her 17 crayons, she has 45 crayons left. Follow-up sharing may reveal similarities in the strategies used to solve the three problems as well as patterns between the numbers in the problems and the answers. These discoveries can lead to a discussion of place value as children explain their ideas using base-ten blocks and the hundred chart. The result is a lesson that involves each child in grappling with place-value concepts as the children compare their approach and numbers to those of the other children.

Teachers base decisions about whether and how to group on a given day on the mathematics content under study, the observed performance of the students on content of that type, and whether the topic is being introduced, elaborated, or reinforced. In IMPACT classrooms, although groupings may distinguish the level of difficulty or abstraction of the mathematics topic, all students will be studying the same topic. Differentiation is never used to give some children opportunities to address a mathematical topic that other students will not experience.

Where do differentiated problems for a single mathematics topic originate? One approach is for the children to write problems for the class to solve. This approach admits diversity, since each child must interpret the mathematics addressed and then express the mathematical concept in a situation that is meaningful to that child. It also permits the teacher to discern more information about each child's conceptual and contextual understanding of the mathematics. For example, a fourth-grade IMPACT class was studying elapsed time. Consider what the teacher learned as she read the offerings suggested by two children in her class (see fig. 6.6).

Problem 1: Amanda went to the mall. She left her house at 11:00 and went to 6 stores. She spent 20 minutes at each store. Altogether, it took her one hour to get between the bus stop and her house. She spent 15 minutes riding the bus home. What time did she get home?

Problem 2: Mr. Jenkins drives to work every day. The first way takes 15 minutes without traffic lights. The second way takes 18 minutes without traffic lights. There are 10 lights the first way and 3 lights the second way. Each light that is red or yellow will stop him for 1 minute. Assume he would be able to go to work without getting stopped on half of the lights. Which way would be faster? Explain.

Fig. 6.6. Two problems involving elapsed time that were written by fourth-grade students

Communication in the mathematics classroom allows teachers to reflect on students' understandings and to ask questions to stimulate thinking. As children communicate with one another or the teacher, the teacher gains insight into their understanding. This insight can be used to make grouping decisions as well as decisions about the need for further instruction for individuals or the whole class. Thus, the communications by students that build their power over the mathematics also increase the teacher's power to make appropriate instructional decisions.

SCHOOLWIDE REFORM TO SUPPORT THE POTENTIAL OF DIVERSITY

In traditional instruction, diversity may be perceived as an overwhelming challenge. Within Project IMPACT, teachers work in grade-level teams to support one another's efforts to implement differing ideas and approaches, both the ideas of the teachers and the ideas of their students. The result is a mathematics program in which children and teachers work together and share. As teachers focus on each child's need to "make sense" and to participate, diversity is not ignored. Instead, it is used to maximize each child's engagement and learning. The resulting program is naturally more diverse than traditional ones and produces greater understanding in the population that is the source of that diversity.

REFERENCES

Gamoran, Adam. "Is Ability Grouping Equitable?" *Educational Leadership* 50 (October 1992): 11–17.

Goodlad, John J. *A Place Called School: Prospects for the Future.* New York: McGraw-Hill, 1984.

National Council of Teachers of Mathematics. *Curriculum and Evaluation Standards for School Mathematics.* Reston, Va.: National Council of Teachers of Mathematics, 1989.

Oakes, Jeannie. *Keeping Track: How Schools Structure Inequality.* New Haven, Conn.: Yale University Press, 1985.

———. *Multiplying Inequalities: The Effects of Race, Social Class, and Tracking on Opportunities to Learn Mathematics and Science.* Santa Monica, Calif.: Rand Corp., 1990.

Resnick, Lauren. "Treating Mathematics as an Ill-Structured Discipline." In *The Teaching and Assessing of Mathematical Problem Solving,* edited by Randall I. Charles and Edward A. Silver, pp. 32–60. Research Agenda for Mathematical Education, vol 3. Hillsdale, N.J.:. Lawrence Erlbaum Assoicates; Reston, Va.: National Council of Teachers of Mathematics, 1988.

7

Students' Voices
African Americans and Mathematics

Erica N. Walker

Leah P. McCoy

THERE is perhaps no greater problem in American education than the lagging academic achievement of minority students, particularly African Americans. Despite years of "compensatory" education programs spawned by Lyndon B. Johnson's War on Poverty and the 1954 decision in *Brown v. Board of Education* that affirmed that segregated schooling was detrimental to African Americans' achievement, the academic gap between African American and white students in important subjects still exists. Research documents that "the American educational system is differentially effective for students depending on their social class, race, ethnicity, ... and other demographic characteristics" (Secada 1992, p. 623). Numerous studies have been conducted to attempt to explain why the public education system seems to be failing minority students in general and African American students in particular.

Although African American children "bring to the formal classroom setting [in kindergarten] the same basic intellectual competencies in mathematical thought and cognitive processes as their white counterparts" (Stiff and Harvey 1988, p. 191), from age nine African Americans and Hispanics do not perform as well as whites on national surveys of mathematics achievement (Secada 1992; Stiff and Harvey 1988). This gap continues to widen through high school (Oakes 1988; Secada 1992).

We cannot continue to allow a significant number of our population to be innumerate; we must acknowledge that what occurs in school has a detrimental effect on African American students. Reasons for this failure must be explored, and ideas for combating whatever obstacles exist for African American students in mathematics must be implemented.

African American students' perceptions of their mathematics performance and the influence of their teachers, families, and peers on the development of that perception may be important factors that have been

71

overlooked in our quest to determine the reasons for disappointing performances in mathematics.

BACKGROUND

Few studies have investigated African American students' beliefs and ideas about mathematics. To discern those perceptions, the authors conducted an ethnographic study using structured interviews with African American high school students.

The sample was selected from a high school with an enrollment of 1250 students in a small city. Approximately 30 percent of the students are African American, 65 percent are white, and the remaining 5 percent belong to other ethnic groups. The racial makeup of most of the classes followed these proportions. Exceptions were honors classes in algebra 2 and advanced classes in algebra 3 that consisted primarily of white students. The researcher chose the students with the intent of selecting a group of African American students with differing levels of achievement. Seventeen students—nine females and eight males—in grades 9–12 agreed to participate. Four of those students were enrolled in algebra 1, eleven in geometry, one in algebra 3, and one in honors algebra 2.

Interviews were conducted and recorded either during school (during lunch or study halls) or after school. They lasted approximately twenty-five minutes each. All students were asked a series of open-ended questions about their attitudes toward mathematics, for example, "What influences your mathematics performance?" These general questions were based on the related research and were meant to elicit information about students' attitudes toward mathematics, including their future plans and the causes of these attitudes. The students were assigned pseudonyms to ensure confidentiality. The data were analyzed by identifying common responses and comparing different responses.

VOICES OF STUDENTS

The students' perceptions of mathematics were intricately related to their surroundings at home, in school, and in their communities. The results reveal that most students' beliefs about mathematics are not well defined nor do they remain constant. Indeed, their attitudes toward mathematics are easily changed, depending on what aspect of mathematics is being explored.

"Not Saying Nothing"

Some African American students exhibit a disturbing tendency to be silent in the mathematics classroom. Whether the reason is the embarrassment of "not knowing" or knowing too well that one is the only African

American person in the classroom, this silence certainly affects students' interest in mathematics and their productivity. Kesha mentioned that she is often silent in mathematics class, even if she has a question, because she doesn't want to call attention to herself as the only African American in her algebra 3 class.

Rick doesn't speak up in mathematics class because he doesn't really "catch up to" the work. In other words, he doesn't speak because he perceives that everyone else understands what's going on better than he. Although Rick is not confident in his mathematics ability, he reveals that when he was younger, he was "real good" in mathematics. What happened to Rick during his mathematics career remains a mystery but is important for researchers to discover.

Others in the sample who were good mathematics students reflected that in many of their mathematics classes they felt intimidated because they were the "only black student." Consequently, they rarely spoke up in mathematics class unless they were directly asked a question by their teacher. Linda and Theresa mentioned that white students had made fun of their use of "black English" and looked at them as if to say, "Where [did] she get that from?" Kesha talked about being the only black person in her algebra 3 class and wanting never to be wrong because she was "representing her race." These concerns, expressed by several others, are prevalent perceptions among many African American students (Gilbert and Gay 1985; Stiff 1990).

At the time of the interviews, Linda and Theresa were geometry students in Ms. Taylor's class (Ms. Taylor is a pseudonym for an African American teacher). Unlike in some of their white teachers' classrooms, they were an integral part of Ms. Taylor's classroom. With pride, they revealed that Ms. Taylor "sits [them] up front" so that she can keep an eye on them. In short, they felt as though they belonged in her classroom.

The teacher's response can be an important weapon against African American silence in mathematics class. If the teacher is content to allow African American students like Rick, Linda, and Theresa—whether they are mediocre or excellent—to sit in the back of the classroom and "not say nothing" (as Linda puts it), then we can expect African American students to feel as though they do not matter. If, however, the teacher takes measures against voicelessness in his or her classroom, then students will thrive and respond, as Linda and Theresa have done in Ms. Taylor's classroom.

Can You Relate?

Whether their mathematics teachers care or not seems very important to African American students. This caring characteristic appears to transcend race, although African American students often indirectly mentioned the desire for teachers to be able to "relate" to them as African Americans.

Students' views of mathematics teachers are most often directly linked to how the teacher interacts with them on a personal level. Of the students interviewed, those who felt a personal relationship with their teacher felt confident in the classroom and strongly desired to perform well in that teacher's class. Angie's contention that African American students work harder for African American teachers is exemplified by Jeff, who performs academically for Ms. Taylor but not for his other teachers. Other examples make up the steady stream of African American students who are not in Ms. Taylor's classes but stay after school with her, preferring her help to their own teacher's.

It is probable that since African American teachers can relate to the culture of African American students, many of these students feel more comfortable in an African American teacher's classroom. There seems to be more at stake in an African American teacher's class, since most students perceived that these teachers care more about, and have positive influences on, African American students. Although white teachers were not as a group denigrated by these students, research supports Michelle's belief that white teachers are willing to turn a blind eye to African American students as long as they aren't disruptive (Gilbert and Gay 1985; Secada 1992). Some students believed that white teachers care less about their academic performance than African American teachers. It appears to these students that white teachers' interest in African American students is directly related to behavior: good behavior merits nothing whereas bad behavior merits attention (albeit negative) from the teacher.

Gordon, an African American male who comes from a two-parent, upper-middle-class home, believes that white teachers have difficulty relating to African American students because the teachers are from "good" homes. This is quite disturbing but not surprising, given the media's propensity to perpetuate stereotypes about both African Americans and white Americans. It is highly doubtful that all white teachers come from "good" homes and equally doubtful that all African American teachers come from "bad" homes. However, this belief underscores the contention that cultural dissonance between teachers and students plays an important role in the dynamics of the mathematics classroom (Ford and Harris 1992; Gilbert and Gay 1985).

Gordon's view regarding white teachers' inability to relate to students from poor homes stems from his inherent belief that most poor families are African American. His suggestion that social workers help "bad" families (who appear to be all African American) reveals his prejudice toward families of lower socioeconomic status. That Gordon has bought into the myth that "white" is "good" and "black" is "bad" indicates that we have not come very far from the historical stereotypes of African Americans.

Run, Dribble, or Solve Equations?

Although a few students who cited extracurricular activities as obstacles to their mathematics success were working students, many more cited sports as a diversion. Angie, Todd, and Wayne are student-athletes. Sports play a major part in their lives, admittedly more than mathematics. For example, Wayne estimated that 75 percent of his time was spent on sports and did not consider his sports participation as a negative influence on his course grade, which was a C. Todd thought that he was preparing for his future by spending most of his time practicing basketball, even though he realized that he was neglecting his studies. Angie, realizing that her schoolwork was suffering, decided to give up track, although she was a stellar runner. When asked if her coach (a white mathematics teacher) supported her decision, Angie said, "No. He pressured me not to quit ... and after I explained to him that my grades were dropping, he still didn't want me to quit. But I quit anyway...." It appears that this teacher's instincts as a coach outweigh his instincts as a teacher. Is African American students' sole value their sports ability? Are these students being encouraged to excel academically?

Given Angie's, Todd's, and Wayne's attitudes toward schooling—in particular, mathematics—the answers to those questions in their minds are yes and no respectively. Angie and Todd see mathematics as somewhat important to their future careers, but their attention is not focused on it and they do not fully understand its potential impact. Wayne, however, is totally confused about how his school performance relates to what he does later. Todd's and Wayne's dreams are to go to college on sports scholarships rather than doing mathematics, when they both have the full ability to do mathematics. It is their prerogative to want to do something else—Wayne wants to major in political science—but the fact that they are so accepting of society's role for them is disheartening. As Stiff and Harvey (1988) warned, they seem to think that they are valued more for their athletic ability than for their academic prowess, and we apparently have not given them a different message.

"The Easy Way Out"

When asked why more African American students weren't in upper-level mathematics classes, most students said that their peers wanted to take the "easy way out." This statement implies alternatively that students don't want their GPA to drop, they don't want a challenge, or they are scared. Shawn told us after we had stopped recording that he thought a lot of African American students were scared of the standardized tests and didn't perform well because of the fear. This assessment appears to be consistent with the attributes of mathematics anxiety and learned helplessness.

However, the fact that so many African American students were so willing to label their African American peers "lazy" may indicate stereotypical racism. Often their use of the word *lazy* was erroneous; they did not say that the students didn't want to do the work but that their interest was in other things. Apathy toward learning mathematics is perhaps a more accurate description.

Many African American students said that their peers' apathy or laziness was due to not realizing that mathematics was important to achieving their future goals. Not surprisingly, the students in the sample who wanted to be lawyers, accountants, engineers, architects, and computer programmers realized the importance of mathematics and consequently took more mathematics courses—behavior that was also discovered by Matthews (1984) and Reyes and Stanic (1988). Fortunately, these students constitute a majority of the sample. Those students who were somewhat undecided or ambivalent about their careers were the ones who did not see the importance of mathematics. Although they constitute a minority of the sample, it is possible that they may represent the majority of African American students in mathematics. Most students, regardless of their career goals, wanted to take mathematics to get into college and recognized that they needed it for that reason. For the most part, their interest in mathematics did not extend beyond this goal.

"Have You Done Your Math Homework?"

Parents were the most important influence on students' mathematics performance, only slightly ahead of the students' own motivation. Although counselors had been found to be important influences in 1982 (Johnson), no students mentioned counselors as being influential in their taking more mathematics courses; parental encouragement and support appear to have surpassed the influence of counselors. Mothers were most often mentioned as being helpers and instigators, asking, "Have you done your math homework?" or suggesting, "Call Homework Hotline!" Rick, who mentioned that his mother did not play a great role in his life, let alone his mathematics performance, berated her for not making him do his homework and "not being more strict on him" when he was younger. Jeff, whose family problems are the primary reason for his up-and-down performance, did not mention any family member as influential. Todd did not mention any help from home, either. All these African American males were failing at the time of the interview. Lawrence, who is a successful African American male student, mentioned his mother's encouragement and support repeatedly throughout his interview. Other students who were performing well in mathematics class also cited their families as positive influences. These responses support Johnson's (1992) and Ford and Harris's (1992) finding that positive family influences are essential to academic success.

It was clear that successful students' parents would not tolerate less than their children's best. This "do your best" message was repeated over and over again by students who were successful mathematics students.

"Try Harder and Do Better"

Although Ford and Harris (1992) and Ogbu (1988) contend that African Americans may not be performing well in mathematics because of fear of peer reprisal, the students in this study, despite sometimes being teased, try to do well despite their "friends'" attitudes. Parental intervention and influence probably counteract this peer pressure.

Moreover, as discussed by Johnson (1982), students who were successful at mathematics were recruited to help their friends who needed assistance. Their peers were proud of them for being successful. Good students encouraged their friends to "try harder" and "do better."

It appears that positive encouragement from peers is effective and that negative comments from peers might be overrated, at least according to this sample. A combination of factors—teachers, parents, and self-motivation—seems to combat any negativity from small-minded peers.

"You Don't Get Any Experiences, So You Don't Learn"

Although there are many examples to the contrary, students perceived that familial resources such as money and parental education (cultural capital) influenced mathematics achievement. Often mentioned was the belief that "white people ... have more than African American people" and variations on that theme, including Wayne's astute perception that cultural exposure, "seeing and doing things," is integral to school success. Comments like these were made by students regardless of their grade in mathematics or socioeconomic status. Although many students in the sample whose parents would be considered to have little "cultural capital" are successful mathematics students, those students thought that the lack of advantage might be too much for their less-motivated peers to overcome, especially if other positive influences such as parental support and teacher support are not there. Significantly, Kesha was the only student who exemplified Useem's (1990) theory of parental use of cultural capital, mentioning that her mother came to school and insisted on her course placement in advanced mathematics classes. Kesha was in algebra 3—the highest-level course taken by students in the sample.

Recognizing that there is a tremendous societal emphasis on what one has and hasn't, it is not surprising that the students felt that somehow their family's financial offerings were inadequate. Although this feeling of inadequacy is somewhat pervasive because African Americans are disproportionately poor, these students have shown rather definitively that more than money influences their mathematics achievement.

"I Don't Think They Really Want to Take a Higher Math"

Many factors appear to influence students' motivation to take mathematics courses and maintain an interest in mathematics. When asked why their peers did not want to take more mathematics courses, students said that their peers were intimidated by higher-level mathematics. Successful students said that positive influences—teachers, parents, and their own motivation—attracted them to take more mathematics courses. It seems that if we can increase positive parental and peer influences and decrease negative influences, such as marketing high school students as just sports stars, then the students' own motivation could surface and compete with other distractions, a suggestion made by Stiff and Harvey (1988). Students who were self-motivated and had parents and peers to support them tended to do better in mathematics and realized its importance to their future goals.

Ford and Harris's paradox of underachievement (1992) appeared to be all too prevalent among these students, even those who were "good" students. These students were dissatisfied with their mathematics grades and recognized that they needed to work harder but did not put forth the effort to do so. This paradoxical behavior sideswipes many students with low or misplaced motivation because like Wayne and Jeff, they cannot reconcile their actions with their beliefs. Consequently, they espouse the ideal of working hard to achieve and yet continue to act in a manner completely contradictory to that ideal.

"You Need Math Like You Need Air to Breathe"

The fact that a few students have discerned the importance of mathematics and intuitively realize that mathematics leads to many opportunities otherwise unavailable to them is a positive development. However, far too many do not realize the importance of mathematics in preventing their being squeezed out of the mathematics pipeline into a quagmire of limited opportunities.

Students such as Kesha, who perceived that mathematics is as necessary to her future goals as "air to breathe," planned to take more mathematics courses. Despite their feeling that mathematics was integral to their school success, however, few of the students could see themselves as mathematicians. It was clear that some respondents had little idea of what a mathematician is or does and that we have disseminated a very narrow view of mathematicians to high school students. Even students who had been very successful in mathematics resisted the notion that they could like mathematics enough to want to become mathematicians, which supports the findings of Matthews (1984) and Stiff and Harvey (1988). When we pointed out to some students that their planned careers were very mathematical, it was apparent that they had never thought of their careers in quite that light.

This misapprehension may very well be due to students' having very rarely seen mathematicians, except for their mathematics teachers, in action. It is safe to say that if students saw more practical applications of mathematics, and more people using mathematics, they wouldn't have such a mental block against the possibility that they can be mathematicians. There appears to be a greater emphasis on sports and entertainment role models among African American youth (Stiff and Harvey 1988) because the media portray these role models as African American heroes and heroines. Noteworthy examples of contemporary African American mathematicians, finance wizards, scientists, and professors can certainly be cited. We are doing a grave disservice to African American mathematics students when we limit their horizons to jumping and running. We cannot continue to idolize the athletes and not the actuaries.

IMPLICATIONS

Without seriously restructuring how we view African American students, we will continue to channel them through the mathematics pipeline in ways that limit their opportunities. The fact that some African American students have been so negatively affected by the cultural and social dynamics in their mathematics classrooms indicates that a filtering process, as numerically evidenced by gross disparities in achievement, is occurring. Although many students have been positively influenced by their parents and communities, schools must take an active role in broadening students' perceptions of themselves as mathematics students.

This study suggests that teachers can have a profound effect on the self-image of African American mathematics students. If a teacher actively encourages her students, as Ms. Taylor does by seating them in the front of the classroom and frequently calling on them to solve problems, African American students will thrive. When they are neglected by their teacher or disparaged by other students in the class, they will respond by removing themselves mentally from the classroom. Most of the successful students in this study felt welcomed in their mathematics class because they had a strong relationship with their teacher.

The caring environment exemplified in Ms. Taylor's classroom extended to the homes of successful students. Successful students who expressed discomfort in classes because they were the only African Americans had a safety net of parental encouragement and involvement at home. Parents were responsible for the placement in higher mathematics courses in several instances, directing students to tutors if the parents themselves could not provide assistance and motivating students to "do their best." Students who lacked such positive parental intervention suffered low grades in mathematics courses, were in lower-level classes, and were not at all confident about their mathematics ability.

It is imperative that schools and teachers recognize that what occurs in classrooms can negatively affect students' achievement. The mathematics teacher must realize that his or her classroom environment may be damaging to the confidence of African American students. The classroom should be a positive place where students can and are expected to excel. Schools and parents should work together to ensure that nurturing occurs both in the classroom and in the home.

REFERENCES

Ford, Donna Y., and J. John Harris. "The American Achievement Ideology and Achievement Differentials among Preadolescent Gifted and Nongifted African

American Males and Females." *Journal of Negro Education* 61 (Winter 1992): 45–64.

Gilbert, Shirl E., and Geneva Gay. "Improving the Success in School of Poor Black Children." *Phi Delta Kappan* 67 (October 1985): 133–37.

Johnson, Robert C. *Psychosocial Factors Affecting the Mathematical Orientation of Black Americans.* Final Report. St. Louis, Mo.: Institute of Black Studies, 1982. (ERIC Document Reproduction Service no. ED 251 566)

Johnson, Sylvia T. "Extra-School Factors in Achievement, Attainment, and Aspiration among Junior and Senior High School–Age African American Youth." *Journal of Negro Education* 61 (Winter 1992): 99–119.

Matthews, Westina. "Influences on the Learning and Participation of Minorities in Mathematics." *Journal for Research in Mathematics Education* 15 (March 1984): 84–95.

Oakes, Jeannie. "Tracking in Mathematics and Science Education: A Structural Contribution to Unequal Schooling." In *Class, Race, and Gender in American Education,* edited by Lois Weis. Albany, N.Y.: State University of New York Press, 1988.

Ogbu, John. "Class Stratification: Racial Stratification and Schooling." In *Class, Race, and Gender in American Education,* edited by Lois Weis. Albany, N.Y.: State University of New York Press, 1988.

Reyes, Laurie Hart, and George M. A. Stanic. "Race, Sex, Socioeconomic Status, and Mathematics." *Journal for Research in Mathematics Education* 19 (January 1988): 26–43.

Secada, Walter G. "Race, Ethnicity, Social Class, Language, and Achievement in Mathematics." In *Handbook of Research on Mathematics Teaching and Learning: A Project of the National Council of Teachers of Mathematics,* edited by Douglas A. Grouws. New York: Macmillan Publishing Co., 1992.

Steen, Lynn Arthur. "Mathematics for All Americans." In *Teaching and Learning Mathematics in the 1990s,* 1990 Yearbook of the National Council of Teachers of Mathematics, edited by Thomas J. Cooney, pp. 130–43. Reston, Va.: National Council of Teachers of Mathematics, 1990.

Stiff, Lee V. "African-American Students and the Promise of the *Curriculum and Evaluation Standards.*" In *Teaching and Learning Mathematics in the 1990s,* 1990 Yearbook of the National Council of Teachers of Mathematics, edited by Thomas J. Cooney, pp. 152–58. Reston, Va.: National Council of Teachers of Mathematics, 1990.

Stiff, Lee V., and William B. Harvey. "On the Education of Black Children in Mathematics." *Journal of Black Studies* 19 (December 1988): 190–203.

Useem, Elizabeth L. "Social Class and Ability Group Placement in Mathematics in the Transition to Seventh Grade: The Role of Parental Involvement." Paper presented at the annual meeting of the American Educational Research Association, Boston, 1990.

8

Sí Se Puede, "It Can Be Done"
Quality Mathematics in More
than One Language

Alfinio Flores

SPANISH and Native American languages have been spoken for centuries in many regions of the United States. Successive waves of immigrants have brought additional languages. In many regions, speaking multiple languages goes back several generations; in others, it is a recent phenomenon. With today's international competition and global economy, more and more people in this country realize that speaking more than one language is an asset. Of course, learning two languages requires additional effort, but as Leopold (1949, p. 188) states, "education does not make life easier, but better and richer. Few would condemn education for this reason. Bilingualism should be seen in the same light."

Speakers of Other Languages and Their School Experiences

Some adults remember that when they were children they were physically punished in school if they spoke their home language. Although there has certainly been a change, there is still a long way to go. Many schools equate limited proficiency in English with limited proficiency in academics in general. Only a few programs for gifted and talented students are offered in languages other than English. Many school districts do not try to teach in any language other than English. They argue that several languages are used in the schools and that they obviously cannot offer such a variety. Sometimes students who are not proficient in English are not enrolled in necessary content courses, even though language development is attained better when language is used in context. In many classrooms, students are prevented from discussing and explaining to one another in their own language "because they have to learn English." In some schools a disproportionate number of children who do not speak English well are labeled learning disabled and put into special classrooms because of inadequate testing instruments (Spicker and McLeskey 1981).

Tracking and other school practices limit the opportunities of language-minority students to learn mathematics (Oakes 1990). In many classrooms bilingual instruction is left to teacher's aides rather than certified teachers.

Underrepresentation in Mathematics

Students who speak other languages remember overt discrimination in the past. In the present they still experience in many places subtle but pervasive discrimination even by well-meaning individuals. Therefore, it is not surprising that historically in the United States some language-minority groups have been underrepresented in mathematics. There are three related areas of underrepresentation: achievement in mathematics courses, enrollment in mathematics courses, and participation in careers related to mathematics (Valverde 1984). Low achievement can prevent enrollment in higher-level courses, and lack of enrollment in mathematics courses can prevent participation in mathematics-related careers. At the same time, low participation in those careers causes a lack of role models for future generations.

A Shift in Paradigms

In the past the predominant paradigms in research and practice dealing with the low achievement of language-minority students have been deficit models. "Such models concentrate on pinpointing and describing what students do not know, what experiences they presumably do not have, or what language and behavior differences they possess that result in a mismatch with the norms of the school" (Khisty 1995, p. 279). Instead of focusing on changing the student or the family or on remedying the assumed deficiencies, we can look at the problem in a very different way. What we need to change is school practice in order to address the needs of language-minority students. The recommendations given below are already practiced by many teachers in real schools. The implementation of each recommendation is illustrated in the classroom of at least one of the three teachers who are described below.

Three Teachers

Julia teaches a multiaged, bilingual second-and-third-grade class in an urban elementary school where 90 percent of the students qualify for free lunch. Students in her school come from various backgrounds, but in Julia's classroom almost all children are exposed to some Spanish. Julia first studied Spanish in high school and college. However, she acquired Spanish mostly by living in Honduras, by traveling with students' families in Mexico, and by studying in Spain. She occasionally asks students how to say a word in Spanish. Students help her in the same natural way that she helps them with English words.

Renée teaches a combined fourth-and-fifth-grade class in the same school as Julia. Spanish is Renée's second language, and her fluency was improved by teaching in Guatemala.

Julia and Renée have created classroom environments that are full of life. The walls in Renée's classroom are covered with students' work and art, newspaper articles, and art posters (Picasso, Frida Kahlo). Books in English and Spanish on a wide range of topics fill the shelves.

Isabel, whose first language is Spanish, teaches mathematics to bilingual students in an urban high school in Phoenix where students come from a variety of ethnic backgrounds. When she entered school at age five, the teacher told her family that they should speak to her only in English. She developed fluency in English, but her Spanish was frozen and locked for many years. A few years ago she started working with bilingual students. As she helps the students develop their English, they in turn help her develop and unlock her Spanish.

The examples that are used to illustrate the recommendations were observed during visits to each teacher's classroom.

Recommendations and Classroom Examples

Have High Expectations

Students with talent in mathematics can be found in any ethnic group. Language-minority students should be present among future scientists, mathematicians, and engineers in the same proportion as they are in the whole population. Teachers should have the same expectations for all groups to continue advanced studies and learn the necessary mathematics. Schools should make available information about the educational requirements for careers that use advanced mathematics. Students should be encouraged, guided, and prepared to enroll in mathematics courses beyond the minimum requirements.

Gifted and talented students are equally represented in all groups. However, their potential will not develop unless properly nurtured and encouraged. Students who speak languages other than English should be expected to participate in activities that nurture their potential in the same proportion as in other groups.

The school where Isabel teaches used to list the grades of bilingual students separately from those of the other students, even though the courses were exactly the same. The implicit message was that the expectations were not the same for them. Isabel convinced the administration that there should not be a separation. Now the message is that the expectations are the same.

Provide the Same High-Quality Education for Students Who Speak Other Languages

Higher-order thinking is a basic skill for all students (Chancellor 1991). Making conjectures and testing them, making inferences, giving convincing arguments, and generalizing are skills that all students need to practice and develop.

Renée's class conducts a probability experiment in which students simulate a race by tossing two dice and naming the sum. The first sum to appear nine times is the winner. Before beginning, Renée asks students to predict which sum will be the winner and to mark their favorite. Students work in small groups, tossing the dice and marking the outcomes. Some students call the numbers in Spanish. Despite the wide range of skills, all students participate eagerly in the activity when they have to conjecture and experiment.

We need to attract language-minority students to mathematics at an early age and retain them. This goal can best be accomplished by developing higher-order-thinking skills and using teaching and learning approaches that are sensitive to students' learning needs, including their preferred language for learning mathematics. In one session Julia gives each child a different three-dimensional figure: a cylinder, sphere, square pyramid, cube, hexagonal prism, cone, and the like. She does not tell the students anything about the shapes and asks, "¿Cómo puedes describirlo a un amigo?" ("How can you describe it to a friend?") The children describe their shapes in English or Spanish while the other students listen. They use informal language appropriate for their level of development in geometry, such as "un pico y cuatro esquinas" ("one point and four corners"). They use two-dimensional shapes to describe the faces and cross sections of their solids as seen from different angles. They clearly see the difference between two- and three-dimensional shapes.

Students who speak other languages, as any other group, vary widely in their learning styles. For example, some students feel more comfortable learning in an environment where small-group learning encourages cooperation than in an environment that stresses competition. In Julia's class, pairs of children play "circles and stars." They throw one die and draw that number of circles; then they throw the die again and draw that number of stars inside the circles. Students then find the total number of stars by counting. Some write an expression like $2 \times 1 = 2$ for two circles with one star each; others simply write the answer. Students check one another's work. In the meantime, two girls play a form of the game nim in which they take turns removing one or two objects from a collection and the person who takes the last one loses. One of the girls is able to predict the moves required to win, and she wins most of the time. The other girl does not give up but tries different approaches. She seems to enjoy the game even though she has not figured out a winning strategy.

The dramatic improvement in the performance in mathematics of bilingual students has been noticed by Isabel's school. Now she is invited to share with other teachers what she does. After a demonstration of how to teach bilingual students, one teacher said to her, "But you didn't do anything *special*. That was just good teaching." Isabel answered, "That is the whole point."

Provide Multiple Points of Entrance to Higher-Order Thinking in Mathematics

Many times language-minority students get trapped in a vicious cycle of "remedial" courses. They cannot take part in more interesting and challenging courses in mathematics because they lack "basic" skills in English or in mathematics. Acquiring a language takes several years; acquiring mathematical concepts does, too. Concept learning should not be put on hold while students develop proficiency in English.

In Isabel's school, recent immigrants do not have to wait to take mathematics, even if they don't speak English. The school provides bilingual mathematics courses for Spanish speakers and English as a Second Language mathematics sections for students who speak other languages. Isabel also gives her students opportunities to acquire basic mathematics skills in a meaningful context. Her students, recent immigrants, grew up using the metric system, and they need to learn the English system. The students use measuring tapes to measure their wrist, head, arm, and height in inches and fractions of an inch. They work in pairs and help each other; they stay on task, use a variety of methods to measure, and compare measurements with one another. Isabel does not hold them back from learning more advanced material while these basic skills are acquired. In the same session they work with algebraic expressions.

If the students are not proficient with elaborate paper-and-pencil computational skills, they can use a calculator and focus on how to solve a problem. Isabel hands out calculators to every student for an activity involving algebraic expressions. She writes several problems on the board with instructions like "Solve and explain," "Solve for x and explain," and "Simplify." She encourages the students to work in small groups or in pairs. The students work together and explain to one another, mostly in Spanish, the steps that are necessary to do the exercise. The teacher walks around the room, asking and answering questions. When the students have completed the problems, they explain the exercises at the board by writing the steps and briefly jotting down an explanation for each step.

Another tool that provides access to important concepts for students who lack skills in algebraic symbol manipulation is the graphing calculator. Using the calculator, students can connect different representations—graphs, tables, and equations—of functions. Today's technology facilitates the study of probability, statistics, and geometry. The necessary computational skills can then be developed in a meaningful context.

Manipulative materials and concrete representations can furnish another point of entry. In this context, children who have difficulties with traditional instruction can have success and show their talent. Higher-order-thinking skills such as problem solving, reasoning, conjecturing, experimenting, evaluating, and communicating can be developed in the context of using concrete materials.

Fig. 8.1. One child's solution to Julia's problem

Julia has posed the problem of how many tires are needed for 4 bicycles and 3 tricycles (Burns and Tank 1988), which affords an opportunity to deal with multistep problems. A child solves the problem by making a drawing and recording the partial results (fig. 8.1). Then he adds 8 + 9 mentally to obtain the answer.

Isabel lets her students use whatever materials are appropriate. For the Pythagorean theorem, the students used cardboard pieces to form a puzzle (Hall 1974). She spent two sessions guiding the students and helping them figure out the relations among the pieces. She asked a variety of questions rather than tell them the results. On the departmental test all the students in her classroom answered the questions on this theorem correctly.

Do Not Shortchange Students; Emphasize All Aspects of Mathematical Discourse

Manipulative materials are often used in mathematics to circumvent communication problems between students with limited English proficiency and teachers with no proficiency in the student's language. However, it is important to realize that activities with concrete materials are not enough. Students learn not only from experiences with concrete materials but mostly from reflecting on those experiences (Pirie 1988). Talking about the experience provides the opportunity to reflect, as Cazden (1986) highlights. Students should have the opportunity to discuss their mathematical activities and findings in their first language and in English. We therefore need to foster the development of mathematical vocabulary in both languages.

Julia is working primarily with second graders in this activity. She writes addition problems on the chalkboard. Children compute mentally (and with their fingers), using their own strategies. They then take turns giving their answers and explaining their methods. For a problem like 3 + 8, some students use counting on aloud in Spanish, some use fingers, others count in their heads, some count from 3, a girl counts on from 8, another student adds, "8 + 2 = 10, and 1 is 11." Children occasionally disagree on an answer and use mathematical arguments to convince themselves and other students. One student has doubts about the sum of 7 + 7; to convince himself, he says "seven" and then counts by keeping track with his fingers: "Eight, nine, ten, eleven, twelve, thirteen, fourteen." For the problem 3 + 2 + 8 + 7, one student adds 3 + 7 and 2 + 8, and then adds 10 + 10 to get the final answer. This part of the session is a good example of children's reinventing arithmetic (Kamii 1985, 1989).

There is also another reason that makes communication very important in mathematics. Communication of the internal, mental representations of concepts and their connections is essential to see whether the student has attained understanding. Research has shown that students can reach correct answers by using strategies that reflect very little understanding of the problem (Sowder 1988). It is important that students explain how they arrived at the answer in the language with which they feel most comfortable. When a child tries to explain his counting strategy in English, Julia realizes that at this point his counting in English is by rote but that he can count meaningfully in Spanish. She encourages him: "Si quieres contar en español …" ("If you want, count in Spanish").

In Renée's class students work in small groups conducting probability experiments. Each group conducts a slightly different experiment. They use different objects: a plastic cup, a Styrofoam cup, a bottle lid, a cardboard cylinder. In each instance they drop objects fifty times and record how many times they land in a given position. In the meantime the teacher walks around the classroom and interacts with different teams, clarifying, probing, and questioning. The students engage in a whole-class discussion, using both Spanish and English, on how to compute the experimental probability from the ratio of outcomes in fifty tosses. Renée focuses their attention on the fact that outcomes are not equally likely because of the shape of the objects. Renée guides students to use proportional reasoning to figure out the empirical probability, given the outcomes in fifty tosses. After the experiments are over, the whole class forms a circle to share comments about the activities. The teacher probes their thinking with questions like, "¿Por qué piensan que cayó C más?" ("Why do you think C came out more times?") The students use their own language to explain why. One student said that the cylinder was more likely to fall on the side. Her explanation was "Es más fuerte lo del centro que la orilla" ("In the middle it is stronger than on the rim").

Isabel uses a number line to introduce expressions like "x is equal to 12" and the symbolic representation "$x = 12$." The expression "x is less than 6" is also represented on the number line. She provides many opportunities for all students to develop their communications skills in mathematics. Isabel gives them ample time, asks many guiding questions, and lets students formulate their own description of the relations between the numbers. The students use their own words, sometimes using informal expressions like "una cadena de números" ("a chain of numbers") to describe intervals.

Mathematical discourse in small groups also promotes cooperation among students and encourages them to take an active role. Renée encourages students to discuss the outcome of the probability experiment: "Hablen entre ustedes. ¿Por qué pasó así? ¿Qué piensan? Y después escriben." ("Talk among yourselves. Why did it happen this way? What do you think? And then write.")

Use Fair and Meaningful Assessment and Testing Procedures

A person who is not proficient in English will be at a disadvantage if the mathematics test is in English. However, a test written in the language of the student may still not be fair if the students have not been taught the technical vocabulary used in mathematics, if the students did not have the opportunity to learn to write and read in their language, or if the translation of the test is poor.

Isabel's students have learned to read in Spanish in their country of origin, but their level of English proficiency would not allow them to show what they know in mathematics if the test were in English. She provides a Spanish translation of the departmental test.

The assessment of mathematics in other languages should include measures of high-level conceptual knowledge, high-level procedural knowledge, and higher-order-thinking skills.

Develop Language Proficiency Related to Content Learning

Proficiency in a second language is best accomplished when proficiency in the primary language continues to develop. Language development should be related to content (Crandall et al. 1987), and mathematics should not be an exception. At the same time, the mathematics teacher should also be aware that some of the academic language used in materials and discussions in the mathematics class may be especially difficult (Cuevas 1984). The mathematics teacher should also be a teacher of the terminology and language needed to learn concepts and skills in mathematics. A consistent finding reported by Valverde (1984) is "that bilingual students do better in mathematics when taught bilingually than monolingual English-speaking Hispanic students or students with a limited proficiency in English when taught monolingually" (p. 29).

Julia, Renée, and Isabel use both languages to conduct their lessons. Students have the freedom to use either language, but the teachers are very careful that mathematical terms are learned in both. In her lesson on probability Renée writes the following terms on the chalkboard: *proportion, proporción, probability, probabilidad.* Students use their own words to make sense of the new terms and then use the new terms in both languages.

Schools should try to provide high-quality mathematics materials and books in languages other than English. There are Spanish versions of exemplary materials such as the *Estándares curriculares y de evaluación para la educación matemática* (NCTM 1991a) and *Matemática para la familia* (Stenmark, Thompson, and Cossey 1987). However, the lack of enough mathematics materials for bilingual students is still a problem.

Be Proud of the Cultural Heritage

The teaching and learning of mathematics is certainly not a "culture free" endeavor. Teachers and textbooks should provide examples of past and present contributions to mathematics, science, engineering, and other aspects of culture with mathematical elements from people representing many languages. The curriculum should include examples from the rest of the world as well as from people in the United States whose first language is not English. Language is an important part of the culture. For language-minority students, learning the language at school will improve the proficiency of the language spoken at home and help preserve their cultural heritage.

In Isabel's class, many students have learned algorithms in their countries of origin that are different from the algorithms commonly taught in this country. She helps students compare and understand the differences. She uses whatever algorithm is more convenient for a particular situation. She also learns and presents to her class alternative algorithms from books published in her students' countries of origin.

What If the Teacher Is Not Multilingual?

In some schools it would be impossible for any teacher to speak all the languages represented. Nevertheless, the teacher can help children continue to develop proficiency in their first language at the same time that they develop proficiency in English. The basic premises are respect and encouragement. Students should feel free and proud to express their mathematical thinking in their first language.

In my mathematics methods course, I have students that speak Apache or Navajo—languages I do not understand. The following explanation from a portfolio entry reflects how important it is for students to be encouraged to use their language even if the teacher does not understand it:

dii le k i dinldoo Problem Solving

I included this because this was when I first experienced with writing in my Apache language. I have read and seen the Apache language written in short articles and in the dictionary. However, I had never attempted to write until I came to this class. Now that I know its relevancy, I plan to stick with writing in Apache and reading. I will also incorporate the Apache lessons as a teacher.

Schools that have many languages represented also have a wealth of resources available that they can tap. Students can help other students. Students working in small groups that speak the same language can use it as well as English in their discussions. Students with a greater proficiency in both languages can serve as mediators between the teacher and the other students.

Students who prefer to write their reflections about mathematics in their mother language can receive reinforcement and feedback from parents and other community members.

School districts have successfully used magnet schools for different languages and two-way immersion programs in which everybody learns two languages. Some deal with one of the languages first, find what works for them, and then address the other languages. It is possible for schools to group students so that the number of languages in a single classroom is not too high.

CONCLUSION

In the classrooms described above students show many of the traits stated as goals in NCTM's *Curriculum and Evaluation Standards for School Mathematics* (NCTM 1989): they value mathematics, they are confident in their ability to do mathematics, they are mathematical problem solvers, they communicate mathematically, and they reason mathematically. Teachers show many of the traits described in the *Professional Standards for Teaching Mathematics* (NCTM 1991b). As in the case of Isabel, what they practice is "just good teaching" using two languages. In short, recommendations on how language-minority students can best learn mathematics and how they should be taught do not differ significantly from what is best for other groups: students and their teachers should be proud of who they are and should use their cultural heritage, including their language, to their advantage. Teachers should have high expectations and provide high-quality instruction and learning opportunities for their students. Teachers should use teaching styles and approaches to mathematics that fit the needs of their students. Assessment and testing should be unbiased and should include higher-order-thinking skills.

Coordinated and continuous actions are needed to achieve equity. It is not an easy task; it does not make life easier. However, there are many concrete examples of teachers and schools that in their everyday practice implement the pedagogical, curricular, and policy recommendations described above to provide quality mathematics in more than one language and make students' lives richer and better. *Sí se puede.*

REFERENCES

Burns, Marilyn, and Bonnie Tank. *A Collection of Math Lessons from Grades 1 through 3.* White Plains, N.Y.: Cuisenaire Company of America, 1988.

Cazden, Courtney B. "Classroom Discourse." In *Handbook of Research on Teaching,* 3rd ed., edited by Merlin C. Wittrock, pp. 432–63. New York: Macmillan Publishing Co., 1986.

Chancellor, Dinah. "Higher-Order Thinking: A 'Basic' Skill for Everyone." *Arithmetic Teacher* 38 (February 1991): 48–50.

Crandall, Jo Ann, G. Spanos, D. Christian, Carmen Simich-Dudgeon, and Karen Willetts. *Integrating Language and Content Instruction for Language Minority Students.* Silver Spring, Md.: National Clearinghouse for Bilingual Education, 1987.

Cuevas, Gilberto J. "Mathematics Learning in English as a Second Language." *Journal for Research in Mathematics Education* 15 (March 1984): 134–44.

Hall, G. D. "A Pythagorean Puzzle." In *Teacher-Made Aids for Elementary School Mathematics: Readings from the "Arithmetic Teacher,"* edited by Seaton E. Smith, Jr., and Carl A. Backman, pp. 142–45. Reston, Va.: National Council of Teachers of Mathematics, 1974.

Kamii, Constance. *Young Children Continue to Reinvent Arithmetic.* New York: Teachers College Press, 1989.

———. *Young Children Reinvent Arithmetic.* New York: Teachers College Press, 1985.

Khisty, Lena Licón. "Making Inequality: Issues of Language and Meanings in Mathematics Teaching with Hispanic Students." In *New Directions for Equity in Mathematics Education,* edited by Walter G. Secada, Elizabeth Fennema, and Lisa Byrd Adajian, pp. 279–97. New York: Cambridge University Press, 1995.

Leopold, Werner F. *Speech Development of a Bilingual Child.* Vol. 3. Evanston, Ill.: Northwestern University Press, 1949.

National Council of Teachers of Mathematics. *Curriculum and Evaluation Standards for School Mathematics.* Reston, Va.: National Council of Teachers of Mathematics, 1989.

———. *Estándares curriculares y de evaluación para la educación matemática.* Reston, Va.: National Council of Teachers of Mathematics, 1991a.

———. *Professional Standards for Teaching Mathematics.* Reston, Va.: National Council of Teachers of Mathematics, 1991b.

Oakes, Jeannie. *Multiplying Inequalities: The Effects of Race, Social Class, and Tracking on Opportunities to Learn Mathematics and Science.* Santa Monica, Calif.: Rand Corp., 1990.

Pirie, Susan. "Understanding: Instrumental, Relational, Intuitive, Constructed, Formalised...? How Can We Know?" *For the Learning of Mathematics* 8 (November 1988): 2–6.

Sowder, Larry K. "Children's Solutions of Story Problems." *Journal of Mathematical Behavior* 7 (December 1988): 227–38.

Spicker, Howard H., and James McLeskey. "Exceptional Children in Changing Times." In *The Mathematical Education of Exceptional Children and Youth,* edited by Vincent J. Glennon, pp. 1–22. Reston, Va.: National Council of Teachers of Mathematics, 1981.

Stenmark, Jean Kerr, Virginia Thompson, and Ruth Cossey. *Matemática para la familia.* Berkeley, Calif.: EQUALS, Lawrence Hall of Science, 1987.

Valverde, Leonard A. "Underachievement and Underrepresentation of Hispanics in Mathematics and Mathematics-Related Careers." *Journal for Research in Mathematics Education* 15 (March 1984): 123–33.

9

Making Mathematics Accessible to Latino Students
Rethinking Instructional Practice

Lena Licón Khisty

IN THE last twenty-five years, a notable and extensive advancement in educational research in many areas has contributed to major shifts in fundamental views of how learning occurs as well as to developing rich knowledge bases of effective practice. These changes are particularly evident in mathematics education in which mathematics has been reconceptualized, as reflected in the *Curriculum and Evaluation Standards for School Mathematics* (NCTM 1989), to include problem solving, connections, and communication, among other topics. Within this new framework, optimal contexts for learning mathematics include maximum opportunities for students to use higher-order-thinking skills and to engage in communication (both oral and written) as part of reasoning and learning.

Moreover, the goals for mathematics emphasize that the benefits of this new perspective must "reach all students" (NCTM 1989). But what if students in mathematics do not all speak English or are not as proficient in all aspects of the language as their native English-speaking classmates? Can the assumptions about the nature of communicating mathematically (for example, which language is used and the characteristics of discourse) remain the same? What if these same students have an educational history that includes others' lower expectations of their academic capabilities? Can we simply carry on with implementing innovations, such as group work, with faith in the mere intrinsic worth of the approach and its ability to reach all students?

In the present national context in which classrooms are, or are becoming, linguistically and culturally diverse, these questions are highly relevant. Given the current emphasis on language–rich learning environments, the issues surrounding language must be comprehensively included in conversations about, and decision making in, mathematics teaching practice. This paper's purpose is to demonstrate that genuinely effective learning environments in mathematics that include Latinos require the application of bilingual and ESL (English as a Second Language) concepts and practice. This paper will also demonstrate that integrating mathematics education and bilingual education (which includes ESL, particularly content-based methods) is essential to ensuring an agenda for equity for a growing population of students.

The present discussion is not intended to present an extensive and detailed review of bilingual and ESL theory, research, and practice. Rather, the purpose is to point out why it is important for *all* teachers to have a fundamental understanding of what factors contribute to effective learning by Latinos.

The following sections will highlight three concepts from bilingual education, along with examples of their application: (1) reconceptualizing English proficiency and the role of the student's first or home language (L_1); (2) teaching English through the content and the nature of "comprehensible input"; and (3) making group work effective.

BACKGROUND

Bilingual education has developed a rich base of knowledge about what constitutes effective instruction for the general population of language-minority students (Garcia 1991). This knowledge base centers on the unique cultural and linguistic needs of language-minority students and includes practices not only to meet these needs but also to take advantage of students' language and community. It should be noted that the concepts and applications presented here apply equally well to any group of students whose home language is other than English. This discussion, however, will focus on students who are Mexican or of Mexican descent. I will refer to both groups collectively as Latinos.

Latinos are particularly relevant to this discussion because they compose the largest segment of language-minority students in schools (U.S. Bureau of the Census 1991) and because they have a persistent and disproportionate pattern of underachievement in mathematics. They also have the highest dropout rate in the country (Orum 1990). It is interesting that of all the factors that influence Latinos' staying in school, the one with the strongest correlation is their enrollment in advanced mathematics (Cardenas, Robledo, and Waggoner 1988).

One defining characteristic of Latino students is their strong affinity to Spanish irrespective of their ability with the language. This discussion will concern Latinos who are at varying stages of English acquisition, ranging from non–English proficient to seemingly English proficient because of their conversational skills. But, as will be discussed later, even these latter students may still be weak in the language used in the academic arena.

SOME BASIC ASSUMPTIONS

The following discussion is inherently grounded in reconceptualizing many aspects of teaching and learning. It is therefore important to set forth some basic assumptions that guide this rethinking and the relevance of the concepts to be discussed. First, what goes on in the classroom must enable students of diverse social, economic, and ethnolinguistic backgrounds to participate fully in all aspects of learning. These social factors must be as much a part of the instructional considerations as the content is, but they should be made to work for students, not against them. Learning activities should incorporate students' language, culture, and community rather than reflect beliefs that these characteristics are limitations. Second, the teacher is at the center of engineering learning environments to counter inequitable classroom practices (Khisty 1995). Consequently, equity in mathematics rests on the teacher's beliefs and thinking, the character of classroom interactions created, and the deliberately theory-driven practice. Third, cognitive development is inseparable from social and cultural contexts and activities (Moll 1990). This implies that children acquire a way of thinking, knowing, and talking about, in this example, mathematics, through a process that is socially and culturally mediated. This process depends on the interactions among persons that occur specifically to develop and establish shared meanings. Although students can learn much from one another, the teacher is still the more *experienced and enabling other.* It is the teacher who serves to enculturate or draw each student into intended common experiences, meanings, and modes of thinking. Since interaction is at the heart of this process, what the teacher says and her or his mode of talking is strongly linked to what students ultimately come to know and believe about mathematics (Adams and Khisty 1995).

Since cognitive development is very much a language-based activity, dependent on dialogue for newly shared meanings, if Latinos are to be reached, it is only reasonable that improving learning in mathematics must take into account the existing knowledge relevant to language-minority students. Indeed, most teachers cannot provide the native-language support that Latinos would receive in a bilingual context. However, all teachers can provide the same support as an ESL specialist. Milk, Mercado, and Sapiens (1992, p.7) explain:

> What is critical for ESL specialists is not merely to be able to do certain things in the classroom but to understand at a deeper level why certain conditions must exist in the classroom in order for the needs of second language learners to be met.

RETHINKING ENGLISH PROFICIENCY AND THE ROLE OF THE HOME LANGUAGE

It has long been assumed, and unfortunately continues to be accepted in much of educational practice and policy, that acquiring English proficiency is primarily a matter of garnering oral or conversational skills, which can be done in a relatively short time. This assumption has led to the misconception that if a Latino can converse in a social context using English, then no further thought need be given to the student's functioning in a second language. Given this assumption, the Latino students' home or dominant language is defined as irrelevant once they have been identified as having sufficient "communication" proficiency to be placed in an all-English classroom. However, Cummins (1981) offers a different framework that describes English proficiency as more multidimensional and includes what he calls "cognitive academic language proficiency" (CALP). CALP is the ability to comprehend and use complex decontextualized information, as is typically found in content instruction that is heavily verbal and written. Cummins argues that second-language learners can function more quickly and ably with conversational skills because the interaction is face-to-face in a contextually rich environment. This environment inherently provides extralinguistic support and clues for comprehending. Reading a textbook or listening to an explanation of a new mathematical concept, however, can present difficulties because these activities are frequently abstract with little contextual support, and they require more language analysis. Furthermore, academic-language proficiency requires a considerably longer time to acquire—approximately five to seven years (Cummins 1992).

Recognizing the difference between conversational- and academic-language proficiency is necessary because the difference suggests two things. First, it suggests that the home or dominant language (L_1) continues to play an essential role in instruction, even in all-English classrooms. Second, it suggests that since academic-language proficiency is closely linked to how the language is used in the content, it is best developed as an integrated part of the content (Faltis 1993).

A primary factor in effective instruction for Latinos is appreciating L_1 and recognizing the important role it plays in learning. This fundamental principle derives from understanding that the student's L_1 does not interfere with the development of L_2 (the second language, English) and that proficiency in L_1 actually promotes proficiency in L_2 (Cummins 1992). It is beyond the scope of this discussion to elaborate on the research that has led to this conclusion; however, it is clear that students learn best in the language they understand best. Furthermore, language is inseparable from a person's self-identity. If a student is to feel and behave like a valued and full participant in the school, then that student's L_1 must be accepted, especially because it represents one of the strongest connections between the school and the home and community. Scarcella (1990) points out that even though not all teachers can teach in their students' home language, several procedures can be used in the all-English classroom that are still in keeping with this principle of maintaining the first language. Intrinsic to all these procedures is that teachers must set aside the common belief in, and practice of, discouraging their students from using L_1. Instead, "we can create a climate in

our classroom which shows students that their first languages are valued"
(Scarcella 1990, p. 56) and are important channels for learning. In keeping
with this climate, teachers can do the following:

- Encourage students to use their native language at home. For example, students could write their own word problems in L_1 (for Latinos, Spanish) to be worked at home with their parents or write
  problems in L_1 with their parents that will be used in class.
- Assign homework written in L_1, perhaps with the aid of a parent-
  volunteer or another teacher who is fluent in the language.
- Encourage students to use their first language in collaborative activities. In designing activities for groups, teachers can offer some opportunities for Spanish speakers to work together so that they can
  use their L_1. Teachers might also consider matching a less proficient
  student with a more bilingual one who then can both assist in L_1
  and model L_2 (English).
- Plan instruction to include the L_1 version of the lesson's mathematics
  vocabulary.
- Recruit people who can tutor students in L_1.
- Encourage students to use L_1 when reporting to the whole class. If
  necessary, another student can translate for non–L_1 speakers.
- Furnish materials written in the students' L_1. Unfortunately, there
  are very few higher-order, problem-solving materials published in
  Spanish, which makes it necessary for teachers to develop their own.

In essence, it rests on each teacher to decide and plan how to incorporate students' first language into instruction and to establish a climate that
genuinely affirms the value of that language. Khisty (1994) describes one
classroom in which a teacher simply seized every opportunity to communicate to her students that she had something to learn from them. At times
she had students spontaneously teach Spanish words or phrases to her, or
she attempted to speak Spanish and allowed herself to be corrected if
needed.

ENGLISH THROUGH CONTENT AND COMPREHENSIBLE INPUT

The second implication of a broader conception of language proficiency is that instructional planning and practice should incorporate
teaching English along with the mathematics content. It should also incorporate teaching methods that make the lessons as comprehensible as
possible to Latinos. Planning, then, needs to include the analysis of content and new concepts for how complex and cognitively demanding they
are vis-à-vis the language needed by teachers to explain it and by students
to use it. For example, the introduction of fractions, which involves spe-
cialized terminology such as *numerator* and *denominator* or phrases such as

half as much, may require that special attention be given to teaching both what these terms mean and how they are used in context in prose sentences. For example, in a classroom of fifth graders, Khisty (1995) reports how a teacher effectively begins a unit on fractions by having all her students copy in a notebook key terms that will be used throughout the unit, along with corresponding written explanations, examples of how they are used in writing, and numerical examples of what they mean.

It is important also to identify words that might cause possible confusion. For instance, words such as *sum* and *whole* can easily be mistaken for their homonyms, *some* and *hole,* just as *fourths* (if the "th" is not clearly enunciated) can be mistaken for *fours.* Likewise, second-language learners usually first learn the nonmathematical meanings of such words as *quarters* (as in three-quarters of a pie) and *left* (as in "How many are left?"). Again, without clarification, comprehension can be less than adequate.

Making lessons comprehensible, or providing students with "comprehensible input" (Krashen 1982), implies taking steps to make sure that what students hear is as unambiguous as possible. Teachers accomplish part of this by being very conscious of their speech and modifying it to incorporate clearer word boundaries, a slower speech rate, fewer idiomatic expressions, and a simpler syntax (Krashen 1982). The other part includes writing key words and ideas and providing such linguistic supports as visual aids, concrete objects, diagrams, or examples from students' experiences and background.

Much of this approach seems similar to what is discussed in general mathematics conversations about the importance of manipulatives or concrete objects in learning. How is it unique for the Latino student? Concrete aids are usually thought of only in terms of enhancing the development of a concept. For Latinos, the purpose of concrete aids extends to supporting what a student hears and subsequently understands. Making instruction context embedded and more comprehensible can never be a secondary consideration; it may require using *all* the aids mentioned above. Khisty and her colleagues (1990) found that teachers of Latinos who effectively created language-sensitive environments with comprehensible lessons in mathematics used such strategies as writing much of what is said as it is spoken, using voice tone and inflection as a tool to focus students' attention on a target word or phrase, and pointing to and pronouncing possibly troublesome words in texts to further draw students' attention to them.

MAKING GROUP WORK EFFECTIVE

Group work, or students' working collaboratively, has become an important instructional strategy in reformed mathematics teaching. Clearly, students can gain much cognitively through expressing themselves and through listening to others' thinking. Group work also benefits Latinos' second-language acquisition by giving them opportunities to use and hear the language of instruction in a more context-embedded situation (Faltis 1993). However, the intellectual progress and gains in second-language acquisition that could result from group work are based on certain assumptions. These assumptions imply instructional considerations that, if overlooked, can negate the intended benefits.

The first assumption is that effective learning through group work requires that all students in a group have the opportunity to participate on an equal basis or that there is what Cohen (1986) calls *status equalization*. This means that all students have an equal chance of contributing ideas, questioning for clarification, and understanding the task at hand. However, as in any other small-group situation, hierarchies develop in which some group members dominate and others are passive. These hierarchies frequently reflect the differential statuses that exist in classrooms, with those students with higher status tending to dominate and conversely, those with lower status tending to be passive—or worse, not even to participate.

Classrooms mirror social conditions outside the school. In a school environment, status differentials can develop based not only on a student's perceived expertise in a subject or general academic ability but also on membership in one or more of the social categories of gender, class, ethnicity, and language group (Cohen 1986). In light of this, group work may actually put Latinos at a disadvantage. They enter the situation already with a lower status because of minority-group membership, lower expectations that often accompany the minority status, and language affiliation.

Consequently, the instructional task for the teacher becomes twofold: (1) to design appropriate tasks that require collaborative work and (2) to develop and set norms that promote status equalization. In this task, norms differ from guidelines in that norms refer to deeper values and ways of relating. They develop through a process of internalization over time and through varied experiences. Guidelines, however, are often defined as a set of rules that, by their nature, require relatively little time to establish. The norms for status equalization should particularly emphasize that (1) everyone in the group *ought* to have a chance to talk, (2) everyone's contribution should receive a fair hearing, and (3) not everyone has the same abilities but all are worthwhile (Cohen 1986).

Much of the current discussion in mathematics education addresses the first task noted above; however, in spite of the fact that students do not inherently know how to work in groups, little attention has been given to the need for setting norms or procedures for doing so. Students need to be taught norms for group work with just as much thoughtfulness and specificity as are used to teach content. If group work is to be effective and not negatively affected by the existing differential statuses, the teacher has to pay specific attention to developing new social norms for students. Students need to understand not only what are the norms of "equal participation" but also *why* they are relevant. This implies that specific lessons are directed toward setting norms; that there is ongoing assessment of, and feedback for, students on how they are conforming to these norms; and as with any other internalization process, that a long time is devoted to developing these norms before students actually engage in the group work.

The second assumption for effective group work for Latinos is that the activity provide sufficient comprehensible input to foster gains. In other words, the environment must be such that students can listen to "talk" and have it add to their language skills and aid in their understanding of the concepts being learned (Khisty 1994). Language-sensitive learning environments take into consideration that second-language learners are operating with a weaker language, English, and that aural word recognition might not always be accurate or quick. In their eagerness to talk, native English-speaking children may clip word endings, run words together, or simply use incorrect grammar. If students' talking is too chaotic or unclear, then Latinos may not be able to comprehend fully what is being said, and gains will be minimized. Combine this situation with students' using mathematical words that may be special (e.g., *tens group, units digit,* or *equivalent*) or may have nonmathematical meanings (e.g., *right angle, quarters*), and Latinos will have a much more difficult time comprehending. To help minimize such difficulties, the teacher must pay close attention to how students speak with one another and note possible confusions that later should be checked and clarified.

The language acquisition also involves repeatedly hearing the language used in context. Unfortunately, if a student hears the language used incorrectly enough times, the error—be it in pronunciation or in grammar—can become fossilized in the student's repertoire. Wong Fillmore (1985) cautions that the teacher must recognize her or his role as a model for the appropriate use of the language. This advice implies that group work should be complemented with an activity, perhaps whole-class instruction, in which the teacher models or consciously uses her or his own talk to teach academic language, both English and mathematics.

Concluding Thoughts

This discussion's purpose has been to demonstrate that creating effective mathematics learning environments for Latinos—and other language-minority students—involves thoughtfully integrating the principles of bilingual education and second-language acquisition with content instruction. This discussion has suggested that the home language has an important role in the all-English classroom, especially if Latinos are to feel that they and their families and communities are valued and valid in school. I also have suggested that teaching the language we use to communicate mathematically is as important as the content and cannot be separated from it.

However, the true essence of effective instructional reform that is capable of reaching *all* students lies in changing the prevailing beliefs and thinking that guide decision making. We cannot assume that good teaching is simply good teaching and then carry on with the same set of assumptions about language, ethnicity, and class. As Secada and Carey (1990) question, do students hesitate or seem unwilling to communicate mathematically because of the mathematics or because of their lack of confidence or insufficient proficiency in a second language? Are students' written explanations unclear or not forthcoming perhaps because their writing proficiency in L_2 is still underdeveloped? Likewise, do students have difficulty understanding because of the mathematics or because information was aurally misunderstood or lacked meaning in light of knowledge and experiences from their home and community?

Much of improved learning for Latinos and other ethnic- and language-minority students rests with teachers' dispelling the myths of "disadvantages" among students, understanding how students' characteristics can be learning capital, and using abundant resources and strategies to accommodate students' unique needs instead of excluding them. It also rests with teachers' understanding the need to work collaboratively with specialists in bilingual and ESL programs. Finally, a truly viable agenda for equity in mathematics will draw into the conversation new approaches to teacher preparation and staff development that incorporate the research and strategies from this same area.

REFERENCES

Adams, Verna, and Lena Licón Khisty. "Teacher Talk: Its role in Orienting Student Thinking." Unpublished manuscript. Pullman, Wash.: Washington State University, 1995.

Cardenas, Jose, Maria Robledo, and Dorothy Waggoner. *The Under-Education of American Youth.* San Antonio, Tex.: Intercultural Development Research Association, 1988.

Cohen, Elizabeth. *Designing Groupwork: Strategies for the Heterogeneous Classroom.* New York: Teachers College Press, 1986.

Cummins, James. "Bilingualism and Second Language Learning." *Annual Review of Applied Linguistics* 13 (February 1992): 51–70.

———."The Role of Primary Language Development in Promoting Educational Success for Language Minority Students." In *Schooling and Language Minority Students: A Theoretical Framework,* edited by California State Department of Education, pp. 3–50. Los Angeles: Evaluation, Dissemination and Assessment Center, 1981.

Faltis, Christian. *Joinfostering: Adapting Teaching Strategies for the Multilingual Classroom.* New York: Macmillan Publishing Co., 1993.

Garcia, Eugene. *The Education of Linguistically and Culturally Diverse Students: Effective Instructional Practices.* Santa Cruz, Calif.: Center for Research on Cultural Diversity and Second Language Learning, 1991.

Khisty, Lena L. "Exemplary Practices in Bilingual Education: Implications for Mathematics Teachers' Professional Development." Paper presented at the annual meeting of the American Educational Research Association, New Orleans, April 1994.

————. "Making Inequality: Issues of Language and Meanings in Mathematics Teaching with Hispanic Students." In *New Agendas for Equity in Mathematics Education,* edited by Walter Secada, Elizabeth Fennema, and Lisa B. Adijian, pp. 279–97. New York: Cambridge University Press, 1995.

Khisty, Lena L., Douglas B. McLeod, and Kathryn Bertilson. "Speaking Mathematically in Bilingual Classrooms: An Exploratory Study of Teacher Discourse." In *Proceedings of the Fourteenth International Conference for the Psychology of Mathematics Education,* vol. 3, edited by George Booker, Paul Cobb, and Teresa Mendicutti, pp. 105–12. Mexico City: Program Committee of the 14th PME Conference, Mexico, 1990.

Krashen, Stephen. *Principles and Practice in Second Language Acquisition.* New York: Pergamon Press, 1982.

Milk, Robert, Carmen Mercado, and Alexander Sapiens. *Rethinking the Education of Teachers of Language Minority Children: Developing Reflective Teachers for Changing Schools.* Washington, D.C.: National Clearinghouse for Bilingual Education, 1992.

Moll, Luis, ed. *Vygotsky and Education: Instructional Implications and Applications of Sociohistorical Psychology.* New York: Cambridge University Press, 1990.

National Council of Teachers of Mathematics. *Curriculum and Evaluation Standards for School Mathematics.* Reston, Va.: National Council of Teachers of Mathematics, 1989.

Orum, Laurie. *The Education of Hispanics: Status and Implications.* Washington, D.C.: National Council La Raza, 1990.

Scarcella, Robin. *Teaching Language Minority Students in the Multicultural Classroom.* Englewood Cliffs, N.J.: Prentice Hall Regents, 1990.

Secada, Walter, and Deborah A. Carey. *Teaching Mathematics with Understanding to Limited English Proficient Students.* New York: Educational Resource Information Center Clearinghouse on Urban Education, 1990.

U.S. Bureau of the Census. *The Hispanic Population in the United States: March, 1990.* Washington, D.C.: U.S. Government Printing Office, 1991.

Wong Fillmore, Lily. "When Does Teacher Talk Work as Input?" In *Input in Second Language Acquisition,* edited by Susan Gass and Carolyn Madden, pp. 17–50. Rowley, Mass.: Newbury House, 1985.

10

Uncovering Bias in the Classroom—a Personal Journey

Maryann Wickett

We hear about it often. The evidence is out there—boys have greater opportunity in mathematics (American Association of University Women 1992); teachers call on boys more often than they do on girls (Kaplan and Aronson 1994; American Association of University Women 1992).

Not in my classroom—I hoped! Secretly I had wondered about this for years. Are my girls being cheated in mathematics because of whom I call on and when? If girls are being cheated, who else is? Are my second-language students being treated equitably? Why is it that in my multi-grade classroom, my first-year students (usually third graders) are much more reluctant to share their thinking than my fourth graders (usually my second-year students)? Is the difference really due to the ages of the students or the older children's greater comfort level with me, or do I have unconscious practices that are systematically silencing these newer, younger students during class discussions? Have my behaviors hindered some while giving greater access to others?

The story I am about to share is the result of an intimate look I took at myself and my practices as I searched for honest answers to the questions above. No one is born prejudiced. Prejudices, ranging from extreme bigotry to unconscious cultural biases, are acquired by—actually imposed on—the young person. All forms of bias are dysfunctional (Weissglass 1996). To become aware of equity and deal with it meaningfully, I had to look deep inside myself to understand how my life experiences have affected who I am and my biases. As a participant in the Equity in Mathematics Education Project sponsored by the California Mathematics Project, I had the opportunity to do just that. I listened as people shared their stories, and I shared mine. From this sharing, I began to discover how biases imposed on me were affecting my classroom practices. As I gained a deeper understanding of myself, I discovered that I had a voice and the power to make changes. My passivity was no longer useful. Using my voice by giving permission for some of my writings to be published in a newsletter was my first step. With greater self-understanding, I could change what needed to be changed. Change in educational practices must be grounded in personal and concrete understandings (Weissglass 1996). The focus of my self-reflection was to gain personal and concrete insights enabling me to become a more effective teacher. In this instance, becoming a more effective teacher meant giving support, respect, and opportunities to participate to all students during whole-group class discussion.

Gathering information about my classroom practices posed a problem. I had considered videotaping as a means to find out what I was doing. The problem was that I would know I was being taped and consequently I would be on my best behavior. I wanted information on what I was doing subconsciously from day to day. Audiotaping and peer scripting my lessons posed the same problems as videotaping. As I pursued my self-study, I found research that contradicted these beliefs. This research indicates that even when one knows the camera is on, videotaping will show many teachers unintentionally demonstrating their biases (Kaplan and Aronson 1994). Despite this research, I still had my doubts.

As part of class discussions, I routinely record students' responses in writing on chart paper as the discussion progresses. I record the student's contribution word for word and put the student's name after the contribution. (In the beginning, I ask students for their permission to record their thinking. The students understand that they always have the right to revise their ideas or ask that their thinking not be recorded.) I like to make a written record of students' contributions for several reasons: writing students' responses gives a context for modeling the correct use of punctuation, capitalization, and spelling; it helps students see the relationship between the spoken and the written word; it gives students both auditory and visual access; it gives me a written record of students' responses, which I can use for reflection after the lesson; it allows students to read and reflect about previous related experiences, which helps them to make connections from one activity to another; and *most important,* it shows students that I respect their thinking, that their ideas are important enough to be written down. This respect encourages their thinking—often at a deeper level.

My recording of class discussions gave me the insight I needed about my unconscious practices. Since I had charts that covered several weeks, I was able to use these charts to take an honest look at the dynamics of whole-group discussions in my classroom. With this information I was able to make sound, conscious changes in my behavior that improved my teaching by giving greater opportunity and respect to all students.

Here's what I found: In almost all instances, I had called on two boys first, then a girl. Overall, I had called on more girls (52 percent of the time in a class that was 50 percent girls), but the boys were given the first opportunity. I found that I had tended to call on fourth graders before third graders. Second-language students had often been included toward the end of discussions. I found unexpected patterns of bias. These practices were upsetting. I had thought that such lapses did not occur in my classroom, yet the evidence was clearly recorded by me on nine charts of student discussion covering several weeks.

Why was this happening? The boys I usually called on first were bright, enthusiastic, verbal, and wriggly. Their behavior caught my attention, and I think I may have called on them partly to control behavior. I knew the others—the girls, the first-year students, and the second-language children—would wait. I also believed these boys had a lot to contribute to the discussion. Sometimes their comments triggered the thinking of other students.

Soon after my personal discovery, I asked the students about their perceptions. I asked them who they thought I called on first. Their responses were very interesting. In language arts, they thought I called on girls first, but in mathematics, they said I called on boys first. Their perception matched the reality recorded on the class-discussion charts in mathematics. Although I was disappointed with myself, the discovery of this new information provided an ideal opportunity to make positive changes in the way I ran class discussions.

The charts captured an important part of the discourse in my classroom, but they didn't capture everything. I was recording only the students' responses—not who was volunteering but not being called on, not my questioning, not my responses, not my body language.

This account is not intended to be a scientific study but rather the sharing of the method I used to look at my own biases. I had enough information to make positive changes yet not so much information that I felt overwhelmed and defeated. The idea of using the class-discussion charts to look at my behaviors came to me after I had done the charts, so I knew they represented day-to-day practices for the few areas I was thinking about. Other possible sources of information I could have used are student work reflecting what went on in class, including journal entries, group projects, reflections, and responses to such questions as "How did you feel about your learning?" or "How do you feel about this discussion?"

By looking at my practices honestly and without condemning myself, I began the process of recovery and change. "No one is born prejudiced. It is possible to recover one's full humanness. The recovery process is uncomfortable because we have numbed out the pain we endured while acquiring the bias, but recovery is possible" (Weissglass 1996). I was able to remain open, freeing myself to try new ideas with my students' best interests in mind. The following are some changes I've made as a result.

I now make a conscious effort to give all children equal opportunities to respond first and equally in all class discussions. Whenever possible, I have visitors or my student-teachers script class discussions. I continue to monitor myself through the charted records of class discussions. Before calling on a child, I pause to carefully consider who has been heard and who still is waiting to be heard. This pause helps me make better decisions about whom to call on, and it allows students additional think time. This additional think time gives students who process information a bit slower a greater opportunity to formulate their thoughts, which allows them greater access to discussions.

Besides making a conscious effort to give students equal opportunity and access to class discussion, I also consider the types of questions I ask all students. Because I want them to think as deeply as possible about their ideas, I routinely ask questions that require an explanation or a justification of their thinking. Students are encouraged to question or state their agreement or disagreement with one another or me.

Drawing out second-language students remains a personal struggle. Because these students don't initially volunteer to share their thinking, their participation is limited to the later part of class discussions. I am honoring their hesitation for now for two reasons: first, they may need to listen longer in order to process in a second language, and second, I rarely call on students unless they volunteer. I rarely share in large-group discussions. The thought of doing so paralyzes me with fear. To be singled out when I haven't volunteered renders me speechless and embarrassed. Even though I am silent, I am listening and learning from my peers throughout the discussion. The problem for me as a teacher occurs when students don't volunteer. Because of who I am and my own anxieties, I don't usually force students to participate by calling on them. So, how do I encourage students? In an attempt to draw in these students, I now use dyads routinely. A dyad is a structure in which children are paired. Each receives equal time to share while the other listens without interrupting. This approach helps all children clarify their thinking and thus builds confidence before sharing with the whole group. Dyads allow everyone to listen carefully and to be heard by someone. Dyads occur before, after, or even during class discussions. In dyads, students can use their primary language if they wish, which not only gives all students a voice but helps all students clarify and deepen their thinking.

I have found another approach helpful for encouraging participation: When I observe mathematically powerful thinking during students' work time, I ask the students if they are willing to share their thinking later as part of processing the activity. Doing so tells the children their thinking is valued before they share it publicly with the class, and it builds confidence. If the children choose not to share, I ask permission to share their thinking, again valuing the children's thinking and building their confidence yet respecting their decision.

During the past school year as I have reflected on these matters, I have observed changes in the dynamics of discussions in my classroom that seem to validate my efforts. Girls are responding first about half the time and justifying their answers with confidence. They are willing to question. They will state their ideas and back up their thinking with sensible arguments.

I have just begun a new school year. I am pleased with my new group of first-year students. I have had them for just four weeks. During class discussions in the first week, about five to seven students volunteered. These volunteers were mostly second-year students. Now, after I have used the new methods intensively for four weeks, about twelve to eighteen students out of thirty actively volunteer throughout discussions. These volunteers include boys, girls, first-year students, second-year students, and a few second-language students. Scripting by observers and recordings of class discussions support these observations. When students were asked recently, their perceptions also supported mine.

Although my data are incomplete, they offer a glimpse of what is going on with my behaviors and my biases. Recording class discussions has given me a way to perceive behaviors I wasn't seeing before and to make better decisions. Race, class, and gender bias are serious issues facing American society and education that are usually not discussed. Talking about them is necessary, not to lay blame but to figure out better ways of educating our children (Weissglass 1996). By understanding myself and looking at my biases openly and honestly—without self-condemnation—I am trying to figure out better ways to educate children. I am giving more students respect and opportunities. I also know that this is just the beginning of my journey.

REFERENCES

American Association of University Women. *How Schools Shortchange Girls.* Washington, D.C.: American Association of University Women, 1992.

Kaplan, Joel, and David Aronson. "The Numbers Gap." *Teaching Tolerance* 3 (Spring 1994): 20–27.

Weissglass, Julian. "Transforming Schools into Caring Learning Communities: The Social and Psychological Dimensions of Educational Change." *Journal for a Just and Caring Education* 2 (2) (1996): 175–89.

11

Creating a Gender-Equitable Multicultural Classroom Using Feminist Pedagogy

Judith E. Jacobs

Joanne Rossi Becker

Feminist pedagogy can be an important part of building a gender-equitable multicultural classroom environment. Such a pedagogy builds on how students come to know mathematics. It also requires examining the discipline of mathematics from a feminist perspective.

A FEMINIST PERSPECTIVE ON KNOWING

As with many other theoretical frameworks, Perry's model (1970) of how students acquire knowledge was developed using an all-male sample, then generalized to include women. One of the major advances in our understanding of women's development of knowledge comes from Belenky, Clinchy, Goldberger, and Tarule's (1986) all-female sample. In their work, *Women's Ways of Knowing,* they describe the following five categories that describe how women come to know things:

- *Silent knowers* accept what they know without stating what it is they know.
- *Received knowers* focus on attaining knowledge from authority figures, usually through listening.
- *Subjective knowers* listen to their own internal voices.
- *Procedural knowers* fall into two categories: separate and connected.
  Separate knowers learn separately from others.
  Connected knowers gain knowledge through access to others' experience.
- *Constructed knowers* judge evidence within its context—an integration, the book's authors maintain, of both separate and connected approaches.

More detail on interpretations relating this theoretical model to mathematics can be found in Becker (1995) and Jacobs (1994).

The most important point to stress here is that in the *procedural knowing* category, Belenky, Clinchy, Goldberger, and Tarule (1986) found women predisposed to be *connected knowers,* whereas Perry's studies (1970) had found *separate knowing* more prevalent in male populations. Mathematics has traditionally been taught in a manner more consistent with *separate knowing:* stressing deductive proof, absolute truth, and certainty; using algorithms; and emphasizing abstraction, logic, and rigor. To build on the strengths and propensities of *connected knowers* as well, our teaching needs to include more intuition and experience; conjecture, generalization, and induction; creativity; and context.

FEMINIST PEDAGOGY IN THE MATHEMATICS CLASSROOM

This new knowledge gleaned from *Women's Ways of Knowing* provides directions for pedagogical strategies that facilitate using connected teaching to reach all students. Four principles of feminist pedagogy will be discussed here as an approach to building a gender-equitable, multicultural mathematics classroom. These four principles are using students' own experiences, writing, cooperative learning, and developing a community of learners.

Using Students' Own Experiences to Build Knowledge

As illustrated by our discussion of *Women's Ways of Knowing, connected knowing* is an important perspective, especially for women. In this stage, the student builds knowledge from personal experience. Instruction should include experiences designed to allow students to build on their intuitive understanding, to provide insight into the reasons for the area of study, and to encourage activity versus passivity. Such instruction might involve applications, drawing and constructing models, using visual representations of mathematical concepts, and using technological tools such as calculators and computers.

Everyday uses of mathematics can help promote the study of particular topics by connecting mathematics to experiences from everyday life. As Meiring, Rubenstein, Schultz, de Lange, and Chambers (1992) point out, giving applications more prominence can bring out the relevance of mathematical ideas and help motivate reluctant learners (p. 117).

Example 1

A real-life problem involving force relates to air bags in the front passenger seat of a car when an infant or child seat is being used. Why might one want *not* to use an air bag in that situation? Could the air bag be modified to help prevent possible injuries to the child, better complementing the protection the child seat provides?

Example 2

High school students might choose a problem of importance to them, their school, or their community to survey, analyze, and present results to an appropriate agency to seek change. Potential topics might be a survey and analysis of the food that is thrown away uneaten in the school cafeteria, with recommendations to cafeteria staff about menu changes; an analysis of crime statistics, comparing those of a shopping center having a liquor store to those of one without a liquor store, with a report and recommendations to the city council; or a survey and analysis of local traffic bottlenecks, with a report to appropriate officials.

Example 3

Another way to involve students' lives occurs in December and early January, when many ethnic and religious groups celebrate holidays. Multiculturalism is not just a means of affirming one's own identity; it also should promote knowledge and understanding of others. Looking at different groups' celebrations helps us know each other better. Western- and Eastern-rite Christian churches celebrate Christmas, Jews celebrate Chanukah, and African Americans celebrate Kwanzaa. Many different mathematical questions arise from studying these celebrations. Why is Kwanzaa celebrated between Christmas (25 December) and New Year's (1 January)? Why do the different Christian churches celebrate Christmas on different dates? How many different New Year's Days are celebrated around the world? Why are the dates different from year to year for many of these holidays?

Seven candles are used for Kwanzaa, symbolizing the seven days of celebration and the seven beliefs that are held by people in many parts of Africa. There is one black candle, three red candles, and three green candles. On the first night the black candle is lit in the middle position. The second night the black candle and a red candle are lit. The third night the black, the red, and a green candle are lit. This pattern continues with each night having an additional candle lit, alternating red and green as the additional candle. On the seventh night, all candles are lit, with three red, then a black candle, and then three green. If each night's candles are burned completely in a single night, what is the total number of candles used and how many of each color are used over the seven days?

Chanukah involves lighting candles on a menorah (a candlestick with holders for nine candles). The first night the *shamus,* or worker, candle is lit; it then lights one other candle commemorating the first night. On the second night the shamus candle lights two candles; on the third night, three candles; and so on. Chanukah lasts eight nights, and each night's candles are all burned completely in a single night. How many candles are needed for all eight nights?

Chanukah and Kwanzaa present opportunities for finding the sum of arithmetic progressions as students find the answers to the questions posed above. In addition to all the mathematics involved, students can learn about the cultures and religions and bring in their own customs for these celebrations. The possibilities are endless.

Writing in the Mathematics Classroom

A great deal of attention has been paid of late to using writing in mathematics. Writing is essential to connected teaching for a number of reasons.

First, writing out explanations helps students develop their own voices and move away from the authority of the teacher. It allows the learner to gain a sense of self and become more independent. Sharing writing with other students allows one to listen to others' reasons and ideas and learn from the variety of approaches that might be taken on any one problem situation. Writing emphasizes the process, not just a correct answer.

There are a number of ways to integrate writing into the mathematics classroom. Students can give feedback on the class, anonymously if need be. Students of most ages can inform the teacher about the pacing of the class, whether specific activities or topics were interesting or boring, or how they prefer to work and learn.

A journal might be used to gather both affective and cognitive information from the student. Prompts related to specific concepts can furnish the teacher with considerable information about students' understanding, both individually and for the class as a whole. In algebra, for example, students can explain what an algebraic expression and an algebraic equation are and compare the two concepts. A journal can also be used to gather important information about students' feelings about themselves as learners of mathematics. A mathematics autobiography early in the academic year and follow-ups throughout the year will give the teacher a wealth of knowledge about what past experiences affect students' current learning patterns.

Writing out a full explanation of how a problem was solved, including dead ends, encourages students to reflect on their own thinking and learning processes and to learn from their mistakes. At the same time, it gives the teacher insight into problem-solving abilities.

Cooperative Learning in the Mathematics Classroom

There is evidence that women (and students of color) not only prefer a more collaborative, less competitive atmosphere in the classroom but that they achieve more in that milieu as well (AAUW 1992). Traditional mathematics classrooms of the past might best be described as appealing most to Anglo-European male students in terms of both content and mode of instruction. Some men, however, do equally well in a collaborative environment.

For many girls and young women, successful learning takes place in an atmosphere that enables students to enter empathetically into mathematics through *connected knowing*. Although not the only methodology to achieve connected teaching, using collaborative, small groups is one of the best ways to accomplish several goals.

Developing the student's voice and ability to learn autonomously is hypothesized to be essential for eliminating gender differences in mathematics (Buerk 1985; Fennema and Leder 1990). In groups, students develop and support their own justifications, struggle for solutions to problems, and share problem solving. More-challenging problems can be chosen because a group has the benefit of several minds working toward a solution. With guidance from the teacher, students in one group can carry out investigations in further depth than other groups on a problem that interests them.

But one cannot view cooperative learning as the solution to all gender-equity problems. Although some advocates of cooperative learning stress the use of heterogeneous groups, cross-gender relationships may be more difficult to achieve than cross-race friendships or friendships among students with and without disabilities. Students may prefer working in single-gender groups. Also, gender differences in communication and interaction patterns may hinder effective cross-gender group dynamics. Research indicates that boys in small groups are more likely to receive help from girls when they ask, but that girls' requests are more likely to be ignored by boys (AAUW 1992). The teacher must therefore constantly monitor the groups' activities not only for mathematical content but also for the group dynamics to ensure that sex stereotyping is not reinforced and females' achievement is not impaired.

Developing a Community of Learners

One of the hallmarks of a feminist classroom is that it is a community of learners. Although teachers retain ultimate responsibility and authority, all in the class are there to learn together and from each other. Students need to validate their answers and generalizations so that their peers as well as their teacher understand and accept their work. In doing this, they often discover their own misunderstandings and correct them. Students need to be clear about how they arrive at their conclusions. When words fail, they often resort to graphic or pictorial displays or explanations that rely on counterexamples.

Students also need to determine what they will learn and how they will learn it. For example, if a school district decides to adopt a dress code, students usually will oppose this decision. After discussing the decision, students can explore its implications. Given the parts of the uniforms—skirts, long pants, short pants, blouses or shirts, blazers, vests, types of shoes and socks or stockings—students can determine how many different outfits they can wear (a counting problem). They can examine the cost factor involved, survey students' feelings about a dress code, and present their findings. An interesting twist to the problem would be to have them use the same data and present supportive or nonsupportive reports, addressing different audiences that are affected by, or involved in, the decision—such as students, parents, teachers, or the school board.

REEXAMINING MATHEMATICS AS A DISCIPLINE

Another way that feminist pedagogy changed the way we function in the classroom was by examining different academic disciplines to see how the disciplines themselves promote male involvement and discourage that of females. Mathematics needs to be examined from that perspective. We have already mentioned the emphasis in mathematics on deductive proof (the more male way of knowing) and a lack of emphasis on induction and experience (the more female way of knowing). In support of using different modes of knowing mathematics and understanding the fundamental basis of mathematics, we present the following two examples.

Abstract mathematical systems are the heart of most of mathematics. The author of a book retains control over definitions and determines the symbols used. Exploring different authors' definitions raises questions at many levels of sophistication about both the arbitrariness of mathematical definitions and how different definitions change mathematics in a system.

Most of us were taught that a trapezoid is defined as a quadrilateral with only one pair of parallel sides. A popular textbook for preparing elementary school teachers in mathematics (Billstein, Libeskind, and Lott 1993) defines a trapezoid as a quadrilateral with at least one pair of parallel sides. Discussions about the nature of mathematics can be pursued by examining such questions as these: Can we reconcile these two definitions? Does the second definition make any sense? Using the Geometer's Sketchpad (Jackiw 1994), people from upper-elementary-grade students to those holding Ph.D.'s in mathematics can come to appreciate the power and flexibility in an arbitrary system and chart the changes that a different definition can make.

By examining the sketch in figure 11.1, students can see that there is a good reason to think of a parallelogram as a special trapezoid. Of course, the dynamic experience of watching the transformation as you drag on one corner (D) of a nonparallelogram trapezoid, closing in on the one point (D') for which the transition from a trapezoid to a parallelogram occurs, and continuing to drag the corner (D'') so that the quadrilateral returns to being a nonparallelogram trapezoid is far more effective than just looking at the sketch.

In *Proof without Words* (Nelson 1993) there are many examples of how visual proofs can be even more powerful than deductive ones. Completing the square is one algebraic skill that students frequently are required to develop. Given $x^2 + ax$, how is the square completed? We know we want to get to $x^2 + ax = (x + a/2)^2 - (a/2)^2$. A visual proof of this identity (Nelson 1993, p. 19) is shown in figure 11.2.

SUMMARY

Feminist pedagogy can be a vehicle for promoting learning for all students. The four principles discussed in this article are promising strategies to reach

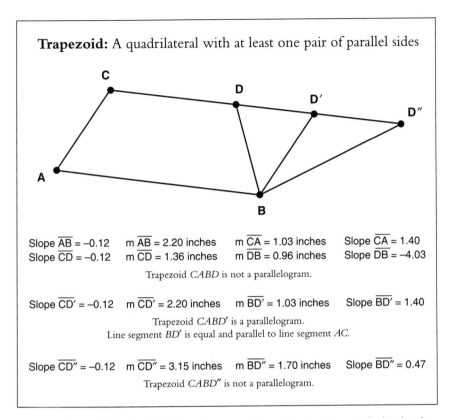

Trapezoid: A quadrilateral with at least one pair of parallel sides

Slope $\overline{AB}$ = –0.12   m $\overline{AB}$ = 2.20 inches   m $\overline{CA}$ = 1.03 inches   Slope $\overline{CA}$ = 1.40
Slope $\overline{CD}$ = –0.12   m $\overline{CD}$ = 1.36 inches   m $\overline{DB}$ = 0.96 inches   Slope $\overline{DB}$ = –4.03

Trapezoid $CABD$ is not a parallelogram.

Slope $\overline{CD'}$ = –0.12   m $\overline{CD'}$ = 2.20 inches   m $\overline{BD'}$ = 1.03 inches   Slope $\overline{BD'}$ = 1.40

Trapezoid $CABD'$ is a parallelogram.
Line segment BD' is equal and parallel to line segment AC.

Slope $\overline{CD''}$ = –0.12   m $\overline{CD''}$ = 3.15 inches   m $\overline{BD''}$ = 1.70 inches   Slope $\overline{BD''}$ = 0.47

Trapezoid $CABD''$ is not a parallelogram.

Fig. 11.1. Exploring the definition of a trapezoid by using the Geometer's Sketchpad

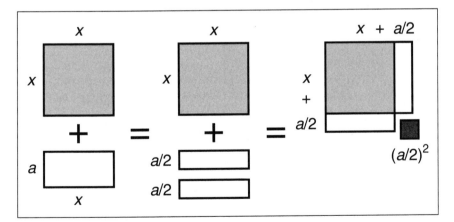

Fig. 11.2. Completing the square: a visual proof that

$$x^2 + ax = \left(x + \frac{a}{2}\right)^2 - \left(\frac{a}{2}\right)^2$$

students who previously have not been successful in mathematics. Using all four strategies of feminist pedagogy promotes connected teaching. Connected teaching promotes learning by allowing students to use their strengths and experiences to pursue knowledge, providing a supportive atmosphere in which students can direct their own learning, and allowing for a variety of approaches for doing mathematics. A broader view of mathematics as a discipline also makes it more inclusive. With increased emphasis on intuitive understanding and visual proofs, more students will become engaged in doing mathematics. By listening to women's voices and using feminist pedagogy, teachers can facilitate *all* students' mathematical growth.

REFEERNCES

American Association of University Women. *How Schools Shortchange Girls.* Washington, D.C.: AAUW Education Foundation, 1992.

Becker, Joanne Rossi. "Women's Ways of Knowing in Mathematics." In *Equity in Mathematics Education: Theoretical Issues and Cross-Cultural Perspectives,* edited by Pat Rogers and Gabriele Kaiser-Messmer. London: Falmer Press, 1995.

Belenky, Mary Field, Blythe McVicker Clinchy, Nancy Rule Goldberger, and Jill Mattuck Tarule. *Women's Ways of Knowing: The Development of Self, Voice, and Mind.* New York: Basic Books, 1986.

Billstein, Rick, Shlomo Libeskind, and Johnny W. Lott. *A Problem Solving Approach to Mathematics for Elementary School Teachers.* 5th ed. Reading, Mass.: Addison-Wesley, 1993.

Buerk, Dorothy. "The Voices of Women Making Meaning in Mathematics." *Journal of Education* 167, no. 3 (1985): 59–70.

Fennema, Elizabeth, and Gilah C. Leder. *Mathematics and Gender.* New York: Teachers College Press, 1990.

Jackiw, Nicholas. The Geometer's Sketchpad. Berkeley, Calif.: Key Curriculum Press, 1994.

Jacobs, Judith E. "Feminist Pedagogy and Mathematics." *Zentralblatt für Didaktik der Mathematik [International Reviews on Mathematical Education]* (1994): 12–17.

Meiring, Steven P., Rheta N. Rubenstein, James E. Schultz, Jan de Lange, and Donald L. Chambers. *A Core Curriculum: Making Mathematics Count for Everyone.* Reston, Va.: National Council of Teachers of Mathematics, 1992.

Nelson, Roger B. *Proof without Words: Exercises in Visual Thinking.* Washington, D.C.: Mathematical Association of America, 1993.

Perry, William. *Forms of Intellectual Development in the College Years.* New York: Holt, Rinehart, & Winston, 1970.

12

Using Ethnomathematics as a Classroom Tool

Joanna O. Masingila

K. Jamie King

Ethnomathematics refers to any form of cultural knowledge or social activity characteristic of a social and/or cultural group, that can be recognized by other groups such as "Western" anthropologists, but not necessarily by the group of origin, as mathematical knowledge or mathematical activity.

—Geraldo Pompeu, Jr., "Another Definition of Ethnomathematics?"

RESEARCHERS in ethnomathematics have tended to examine how people learn and use mathematics in two areas: (*a*) distinct cultures and (*b*) everyday situations within cultures. In the second area, research has focused on one situation or work context within a culture, whereas in the first area researchers have tended to look at the mathematics practice of a whole culture. Some examples of the first type of research are described below.

Saxe (1979, 1981, 1982, 1991) studied the Oksapmin in Papua New Guinea and found many differences between their indigenous mathematical practices and his own. He observed these differences in activities such as building houses, making arrowheads, weaving string bags, and counting. Gerdes (1985, 1986, 1988) examined mathematical ideas developed in the traditional culture of Mozambique. He started by examining the geometrical forms and patterns of everyday items such as baskets, mats, pots, houses, and fishtraps made by persons from that culture.

Other researchers have studied how people learn and use mathematics in everyday situations within cultures. For example, Lave collaborated with Murtaugh and de la Rocha to investigate arithmetic practice by grocery shoppers and cooks who were dieting in California (de la Rocha 1985, 1986; Lave 1988; Lave, Murtaugh, and de la Rocha 1984; Murtaugh 1985a, 1985b). Both of these investigations focused on the relationship between problem formation and problem solving. Masingila (1992, 1994a) examined the mathematics concepts and processes used by carpet layers in estimating and installing floor coverings.

If we think of ethnomathematics as knowledge or activities that someone can recognize as mathematical (paraphrasing Pompeu), then ethnomathematics becomes a tool usable in the mathematics classroom to help students make connections and develop deeper mathematical understanding. We shall discuss two ways in which we think ethnomathematics can be a classroom tool: (1) as the mathematics practice of others, and (2) as our own mathematics practice.

Ethnomathematics as Others' Mathematics Practice

A number of resources have been published under the description of multicultural mathematics. The goals of these resources are that teachers "can promote international understanding by exposing students to the mathematical practices of other peoples" (Zaslavsky 1993, p. vii) and that the resources' activities can "bring to the ... mathematics curriculum the vitality of ethnic and cultural diversity" (Krause 1983, p. iv).

These activities are examples of ethnomathematics as mathematics practice in distinct cultures. The activities cover a range of content and cultures—different numeration systems and their properties; geometry and measurement ideas in art, symbols, baskets, and the shapes of houses; and logic and probability in games.

We can find examples of ethnomathematics as mathematics practice in everyday situations within cultures in articles that discuss the types of problems that people encounter in these situations (Masingila 1995; Millroy 1992). Other examples can sometimes be found in resource books or in textbooks. For example, a lesson on perimeter, area, and volume in a middle school textbook has students explore laying carpet and installing baseboards while considering the activities' related constraints (Chapin et al. 1995).

Other ideas can come from outside the classroom. A local teacher, Chérie Winnicki, has her students write to people in the community. The students ask them to describe the mathematics they do in their jobs and relate some problems that they encounter in their work.

One student wrote to a pharmacy clerk, who explained that her job included unloading the shipments of drugs and pricing them. A typical problem for her would be the following:

A customer needs two pills a day for a heart condition. The drug costs the pharmacist $10 for 100 pills.

a. What will 60 pills cost?

b. The pharmacist wants a 25% profit on the prescription for this drug. What should be the pharmacist's selling price for the 60 pills?

c. If this patient's health insurance pays 80% of the cost of prescription drugs, how much will this prescription cost the customer?

The teacher uses problems like these to develop activities that introduce students to different mathematical concepts. As students solve constraint-filled problems in a context, the mathematics comes alive and students are more likely to understand the mathematical concepts and processes involved.

Teachers need to be careful, however, in using what are often called application problems; sometimes these tasks are little more than computational exercises set in an artificial context that is irrelevant to finding a solution. Most everyday problems have constraints that must be considered when solving the problem. In order to engage students in solving problems resembling everyday situations, the problems must have realistic constraints.

ETHNOMATHEMATICS AS OUR OWN MATHEMATICS PRACTICE

Although the mathematics practice of others can be a valuable tool to use in the classroom, there is another, often overlooked, resource readily available: the ethnomathematics of the students and the teacher. In order for teachers to use this resource, however, teachers and students need to perceive that they use mathematics in everyday situations and to be aware of how they use it.

One method we have used to promote this awareness is having students keep a log of how they think they used mathematics over a specific length of time, such as a day or a week (Masingila 1994b). In a 1993 study, we interviewed twenty sixth- and eighth-grade students, had them and some of their classmates keep a log for a week of their mathematical activity outside the classroom, and then interviewed the twenty students again. By analyzing the logs and specific situations the students listed, we gained insight into how these students perceived that they used mathematics in everyday situations.

Teachers who learn about students' mathematics practice can then use what they have learned as contexts for problem solving. One student in our study noted that her friend bought a bike at a garage sale but did not know how many speeds it had. The two girls saw that the bike had "three main gears and seven little gears" and figured out that it had a total of twenty-one speeds. This context is a rich one; teachers could use it to create an activity in which students explore concepts of combinations and permutations.

In a current study, we are examining the out-of-school activities of some middle school students. One twelve-year-old respondent participated in a day camp during the summer. During the camp's arts-and-crafts period, she created key chains, zipper pulls, and creative designs from thin, flat plastic strings of different colors known as braiding lace. Camp participants call the craft "boondoggle."

Rebecca, our respondent, described boondoggle as "weaving together" multiples of two strings to make various designs named for their shapes—square, circle, brick, snake, snake on a pole. She said that snake on a pole "uses at least four strings but two have to be longer because the long ones have to wrap around the square every time" and that "if you know where the strings will end up, you can use certain colors to create patterns." When asked how she created various sizes of the same shape, Rebecca noted that "it's a ratio."

Boondoggle provides a hands-on activity for investigating and creating visual patterns as well as exploring ideas of ratio and proportion. Writing a log of group and individual progress would allow students to expand their beliefs about what mathematics is, along with developing a deeper understanding of the use of patterns in braiding, weaving, and other art forms.

We want to note a difficulty associated with investigating ethnomathematics in any situation, whether it be a researcher examining the mathematics practice of a certain culture or a student examining his or her own mathematics practice. The difficulty, as Millroy (1992) has noted, is that it is "impossible to recognize and describe anything without using one's own frameworks" (p. 11). Thus, a researcher examining the ethnomathematics of a certain culture interprets everything he or she sees according to his or her ideas about what mathematics is.

Likewise, students will interpret their own mathematics practice in light of what they think mathematics is. We noticed that, for the most part, the students who participated in our study perceived mathematics as equivalent to school mathematics. Some students, however, appeared to understand that there is more to mathematics than school mathematics. One student mentioned during an interview that he used mathematics and mathematical thinking a lot, but he could not articulate any specific examples that were different from ones involving school mathematics: "It's different from what we do in school—I can't explain it—but I know it is mathematics."

BROADENING STUDENTS' VIEWS OF WHAT MATHEMATICS IS

Differences between mathematics practice in school and out of school appear to be explained by the following: (a) problems in everyday situations are embedded in real contexts meaningful to the problem solver, and this encourages and sustains problem-solving activity (Lester 1989); and (b) "the mathematics used outside school is a tool in the service of some broader goal, and not an aim in itself as it is in school" (Nunes 1993, p. 30). Engaging students in activities situated in meaningful contexts and where students use mathematics as a tool will challenge and broaden students' beliefs about what mathematics is.

In order to draw on students' ethnomathematics and help them recognize their mathematics practice, teachers can have students list their activities for one day. Students then select one activity from their list and describe what they did. These descriptions may allow students to decide that an activity is mathematical even if they cannot articulate how it is mathematical.

Students should also be encouraged to generate conventions that may help them as they solve problems. For example, as students work in a measurement context, they may invent notation to indicate when objects are the same size and shape before they have learned about congruence.

Teachers can also encourage students to use their own ethnomathematics by having them (*a*) create their own problems, (*b*) solve problems in more than one way and share their solution methods with one another (Lester 1989), and (*c*) focus on semantics rather than syntax.

Ethnomathematics can be a valuable tool in the mathematics classroom. By encouraging students to do mathematics that uses both others' mathematics practice and their own, teachers can help students make connections, develop deeper mathematical understandings, and expand their beliefs about what mathematics is.

REFERENCES

Chapin, Suzanne H., Mark Illingworth, Marsha S. Landau, Joanna O. Masingila, and Leah McCracken. *Middle Grades Mathematics: An Interactive Approach, Course 2.* Needham, Mass.: Prentice Hall, 1995.

de la Rocha, Olivia. "Problems of Sense and Problems of Scale: An Ethnographic Study of Arithmetic in Everyday Life." (Doctoral dissertation, University of California, Irvine, 1986.) *Dissertation Abstracts International* 47 (1986): 4198A.

———."The Reorganization of Arithmetic Practice in the Kitchen." *Anthropology and Education Quarterly* 16 (1985): 193–98.

Gerdes, Paulus. "Conditions and Strategies for Emancipatory Mathematics Education in Underdeveloped Countries." *For the Learning of Mathematics* 5 (February 1985): 15–20.

———."How to Recognize Hidden Geometrical Thinking: A Contribution to the Development of Anthropological Mathematics." *For the Learning of Mathematics* 6 (June 1986): 10–12, 17.

———."On Culture, Geometrical Thinking, and Mathematics Education." *Educational Studies in Mathematics* 19 (1988): 137–62.

Krause, Marina C. *Multicultural Mathematics Materials.* Reston, Va.: National Council of Teachers of Mathematics, 1983.

Lave, Jean. *Cognition in Practice: Mind, Mathematics, and Culture in Everyday Life.* Cambridge: Cambridge University Press, 1988.

Lave, Jean, Michael Murtaugh, and Olivia de la Rocha. "The Dialectic of Arithmetic in Grocery Shopping." In *Everyday Cognition: Its Development in Social Context,* edited by Barbara Rogoff and Jean Lave, pp. 67–94. Cambridge, Mass.: Harvard University Press, 1984.

Lester, Frank K., Jr. "Mathematical Problem Solving in and out of School." *Arithmetic Teacher* 37 (November 1989): 33–35.

Masingila, Joanna O. "Carpet Laying: An Illustration of Everyday Mathematics." In *Connecting Mathematics across the Curriculum,* 1995 Yearbook of the National Council of Teachers of Mathematics, edited by Peggy A. House, pp. 163–69. Reston, Va.: National Council of Teachers of Mathematics, 1995.

————."Mathematics Practice and Apprenticeship in Carpet Laying: Suggestions for Mathematics Education." (Doctoral dissertation, Indiana University—Bloomington, 1992.) *Dissertation Abstracts International* 53 (1992): 1833A.

————."Mathematics Practice in Carpet Laying." *Anthropology and Education Quarterly* 25 (1994a): 430–62.

————."Middle School Students' Perceptions of Their Everyday Mathematics Practice." In *Proceedings of the 16th Annual Meeting of the North American Chapter of the International Group for the Psychology of Mathematics Education,* edited by David Kirshner, vol. 2, pp. 77–83. Baton Rouge, La.: Louisiana State University, 1994b.

Millroy, Wendy Lesley. *An Ethnographic Study of the Mathematical Ideas of a Group of Carpenters. Journal for Research in Mathematics Education* Monograph No. 5. Reston, Va.: National Council of Teachers of Mathematics, 1992.

Murtaugh, Michael. "A Hierarchical Decision Process Model of American Grocery Shopping." (Doctoral dissertation, University of California, Irvine, 1985.) *Dissertation Abstracts International* 46 (1985a): 1675A.

————."The Practice of Arithmetic by American Grocery Shoppers." *Anthropology and Education Quarterly* 16 (1985b): 186–92.

Nunes, Terezinha. "The Socio-Cultural Context of Mathematical Thinking: Research Findings and Educational Implications." In *Significant Influences on Children's Learning of Mathematics,* edited by Alan J. Bishop, Kathleen Hart, Stephen Lerman, and Terezinha Nunes, pp. 27–42. Paris: UNESCO, 1993.

Saxe, Geoffrey B. "Body Parts as Numerals: A Developmental Analysis of Numeration among Remote Oksapmin Populations in Papua New Guinea." *Child Development* 52 (1981): 306–16.

————."A Comparative Analysis of the Acquisition of Enumeration: Studies from Papua New Guinea." *Quarterly Newsletter of the Laboratory of Comparative Human Cognition* 1 (January 1979): 37–43.

————.*Culture and Cognitive Development: Studies in Mathematical Understanding.* Hillsdale, N.J.: Lawrence Erlbaum Associates, 1991.

————."Developing Forms of Arithmetic Operations among the Oksapmin of Papua New Guinea." *Developmental Psychology* 18 (1982): 583–94.

Zaslavsky, Claudia. *Multicultural Mathematics: Interdisciplinary Cooperative-Learning Activities.* Portland, Maine: J. Weston Walch Publisher, 1993.

13

The History of Mathematics
A Journey of Diversity

Frank Swetz

Liu Hui, al-Khwarizmi, Niccolò Tartaglia, Sophie Germain, Benjamin Banneker, Sonya Kovalevski, and Srinivasa Ramanujan: a Chinese scholar, an Islamic astronomer, a temperamental Italian reckoning master, an aristocratic French lady who used a male pseudonym, an African American colonial mathematician, a Russian woman who won scientific acclaim in Sweden, and an unfulfilled Indian genius—certainly a diverse collection of people. They come from varied ethnic, racial, and socioeconomic backgrounds, and yet they share a common bond in their love and use of mathematics. These are some of the people from the history of mathematics, the contributors to, and participants in, its evolution.

PERSPECTIVES

Mathematics can be likened to an object in a painting that stands alone on an otherwise bare canvas. In itself, the object may be visually attractive, even interesting; without a background, however, it has limited meaning and no context. A sense of mystery and confusion prevails and may frustrate a viewer. If the viewer becomes frustrated, he or she will give up trying to understand what is being illustrated and walk away from the painting. A background would complete the picture, allowing the viewer's eye to travel and obtain a fuller understanding of the subject. The contextual background for mathematics is its legacy of human involvement, its history. A journey through the history of mathematics spans cultures, geographic regions, societal priorities, and gender. It offers a panoramic exposure to the persons and accomplishments that have contributed to the science. History testifies to the universal nature of mathematical concerns and solutions. Knowing this history can improve students' understanding in many ways. Viewed as a record of diversity, the history of mathematics can be a vehicle for developing appreciation for the accomplishments of various peoples as well as a source of personal ethnic or racial pride in the contributions of one's forebears. Students who have in the past felt culturally, racially, or sexually disenfranchised from mathematics can find its history empowering; they can realize that mathematics belongs to all people.

THE CULTURES OF MATHEMATICS

As the initial sample of historical figures demonstrates, just considering the life and work of individual contributors to mathematics makes one aware of the global nature of mathematical involvement, accomplishment, and interdependence. Modern scholarship is dispelling the myth that mathematics is a Western invention, discovered by the Greeks and transmitted, albeit with the assistance of Arab (Islamic) intermediaries, to Europe and the modern world. The old Eurocentric perspective of mathematics is giving way to one that more readily acknowledges the contributions of non-Western and non-Caucasian peoples (Joseph 1991).

One of the easiest ways to historically enrich classroom mathematics teaching and to reveal the subject's diversity is to consider the lives and work of selected mathematicians. Anecdotes, biographical videos or films, poster sets, and student reports all lend themselves to use in this effort (Swetz 1994). Incidents such as Archimedes' (287–212 B.C.) "Eureka episode" or young Carl Friedrich Gauss's (1777–1855) summation of the first 100 natural numbers impress students. Biographic sketches often reveal the drama—the Tartaglia-Cardano dispute over the solution of the cubic equation (1545); the suspense—Johannes Kepler's (1571–1630) quest for planetary orbits; and the intrigue of mathematics—François Viète's (1540–1603) use of secret codes. Such sketches also allow insights into personal aspects of the subjects' lives and work, opportunities available to them, and obstacles they overcame. For example, Kepler was disabled by smallpox, his eyesight impaired, and his hands crippled. He suffered religious persecution and lived most of his life in poverty. Despite these difficulties, he worked persistently for eighteen years to unravel the geometry of our solar system. In contrast, Sophie Germain (1776–1831) was a well-born French lady who lived her life in comfort and yet, as a woman, was denied the right to formally study higher mathematics. Through determined study on her own, she overcame this prejudice, eventually winning the accolades of the European mathematical community for her work in mathematics (Perl 1978). Both societal conventions and physical circumstances spawn diversity.

By necessity, biographical considerations span cultures. Although the Greek philosophical and scientific impact on the development of mathematics cannot be ignored, its primacy in the hierarchy of historical accomplishments has diminished. Pythagoras, Thales, Euclid, and Archimedes still stand as great mathematicians; recognition is also being given, however, to non-Mediterranean peoples and their influences. Early

China produced Liu Hui (ca. 250) and Zu Congzhi (429–500) (Li and Du 1987). Liu was a mathematical innovator and commentator on the *Nine Chapters of the Mathematical Art,* the most comprehensive mathematics text of the ancient world. He wrote the *Sea Island Mathematical Classic,* a manual for mathematical surveying. Zu derived the correct formula for the volume of a sphere and, employing a technique devised by Liu Hui, obtained $3.141592 < \pi < 3.1415927$, the most accurate estimate of π for the next 1000 years! A reassessment of medieval mathematics reveals that Islamic mathematicians were more than just middlemen for mathematical ideas—they were true innovators. Muhammad ibn-Musa al-Khwarizmi (ca. 800–847) compiled comprehensive texts on solving simple equations and on computation using the numerals we today call Hindu-Arabic. His principal work was the *Condensed Book on the Calculation of al-Jabr and al-Muqabala.* Our word *algebra* arose from the book's title. Al-Khwarizmi's name itself evolved into the modern term *algorithm.* There are many other Islamic and non-Western mathematicians whose accomplishments are noteworthy and who can readily serve as subjects for student research projects. See table 13.1.

Unfortunately, adversity and diversity sometimes go together. Culturally based preclusions have limited the number of women's names recorded in the history of mathematics. The roots of modern mathematics in Western tradition sprang from the activities of churchmen and merchants. In medieval Europe and throughout the Renaissance, mathematicians were men. Gender bias existed and has persisted in varied forms until modern times. When Sonya Kovalevski (1850–1891), a Russian noblewoman, wished to study higher mathematics in 1869, she was forced to travel to Germany. She eventually won acclaim for her mathematical ability in France and Sweden. The obstacles Kovalevski encountered in her own country have not been the same in other societies. It is known, for example, that the Mayas (300–900) of meso-America employed female scribe-mathematicians (Closs 1992). In any discussion on the development of mathematics, the existence of such historical prejudices should be fully acknowledged, the reasons for their existence examined, and misconceptions dispelled. Sadly, tradition changes slowly, but it is changing: women are winning fuller recognition for their contributions to mathematics (Grinstein and Campbell 1987). See table 13.2.

Mathematical achievement has been accomplished and human genius expressed despite physical limitations, racial discrimination, and lack of financial support. Niccolò Tartaglia (ca. 1499–1557) suffered a childhood injury that left his speech impaired. He stuttered and, as a result, suffered cruel taunts. Nevertheless, he emerged as one of the great innovators of algebra, solving the cubic equation. The African American Benjamin Banneker (1731–1806), son of a slave father and a free mother, went on to win recognition as a "mathematical practioner" in colonial America. Srinivasa Ramanujan

TABLE 13.1
Some Noteworthy Non-Western Mathematicians

Name	Dates	Region of Origin	Field of Activity
Aryabhata	b 476*	India	Devised sine tables
Brahmagupta	b 598	India	Indeterminant equations
Yi Xing	683–727	China	Spherical trigonometry
Thabit ibn Qurra	ca 830–890	Turkey	Solution of algebraic equations
Abu Kamil	ca 850–930	Egypt	Algebraic computation
ibn al-Haythan	965–1039	Iraq	Algebra
al-Biruni	973–1055	Uzbekistan	Refined use of trigonometric functions
al-Uqlidisi	ca 952	Syria	Used decimal fractions
al-Karaji	d 1019	Syria	Algebra of exponents
Omar Khayyam	1048–1131	Iran	Solution of cubic equation
Bhaskara	1114–1185	India	Algebra
Li Ye	1192–1279	China	Solution of algebraic equations
Qin Juishao	ca 1202–1261	China	Linear congruencies
al-Dini	d 1213	Iran	Algebra
Yang Hui	ca 1250	China	Solution of polynomial equations
Zhu Shijie	fl 1300	China	Four Element Method for solving systems of equations
Seki Kowa	1642–1708	Japan	Theory of determinants
Muhammad ibn Muhammad	fl 1741	Nigeria	Magic squares
Srinivasa Ramanujan	1887–1920	India	Number theory

*Where information on the dates is limited, the following abbreviations are used: b, *born;* ca, *circa;* d, *died;* and fl, *flourished.*

TABLE 13.2
Women Pioneers in Mathematics

Name	Dates	Region of Origin	Field of Activity
Hypatia	ca 370–415	Greek Alexandria	Astronomy and mechanics
Marquise du Châtelet	1706–1749	France	Analysis
Maria Agnesi	1718–1799	Italy	Analysis
Sophie Germain	1776–1831	France	Number theory
Mary Fairfax Somerville	1780–1872	Scotland	Celestial mechanics
Ada Lovelace	1815–1852	England	Computing
Sonya Kovalevski	1850–1891	Russia	Analysis
Charlotte Scott	1858–1931	England	Algebraic geometry
Grace Chisholm Young	1868–1944	England	Foundations
Emmy Noether	1882–1935	Germany	Noncommutative algebras
Grace Hopper	1906–1992	United States	Computer science

(1887–1920), an Indian customs clerk, loved mathematics and spent his spare time solving problems, but he could not afford higher education. His talent was recognized by the British mathematician G. H. Hardy, who sponsored Ramanujan to visit Cambridge University. In England the young Indian contracted tuberculosis, which cut short his mathematical career. Studying Ramanujan's notes today, mathematicians are uncovering amazing findings in number theory. A knowledge of the lives and mathematical work of such people can inspire students who may face similar problems.

A MULTITUDE OF ORIGINS AND CONCEPTIONS

Over the years, different peoples have viewed and used mathematics in different ways. These differences do not necessarily assume judgments of superior and inferior. They do demonstrate that mathematics can be done in different ways and that these different ways often produce the same results. For example, the desire to obtain a more accurate value of π was universal: the ancient Babylonians and Hebrews used 3, Archimedes arrived at an estimate of 3.140845, Zu obtained 3.1415927, the Hindu Bhaskara (1150) used 3.1416, and by the fifteenth century the Persian astronomer al-Kashi (d. 1429) had calculated π accurately to sixteen decimal places. It is interesting to note that although separated by time, distance, and cultures, many mathematicians used the same techniques. The Greek Archimedes and the Chinese scholar Liu Hui both derived π independently, using a limiting process and a dissection technique relying on polygonal approximation for the area of a unit circle. Liu's iterative method is easily adapted for calculator or computer use.

When discussing alternative numeration systems with our students, because of Western traditions, we most often mention the Roman numeral system. Historically, systems exist that are more efficient and more interesting. One such system, used by the Native American Mayas, is positional with vigesimal (base twenty) grouping and a zero placeholder. See figure 13.1. Mayan numerals consist of groupings of symbols written vertically; uppermost groupings indicate higher-position values. For example,

represents

$$17 \times (20)^2 + 6 \times (20)^1 + 7 \times (20)^0 = 6927$$

(Bidwell 1967).

An early base-ten system deserving pedagogical attention is the rod-numeral system of ancient China. Several scholars contend that our numeral system evolved from this rod system and that we should more appropriately call our system *Sino-Hindu-Arabic*. That's diversity! This system used colored rods, red and black, to designate positive and negative

1	•	5	——	9	••••	13	•••	17	••
2	••	6	•	10	==	14	••••	18	•••
3	•••	7	••	11	•	15	====	19	••••
4	••••	8	•••	12	••	16	===	0	🐚

Fig. 13.1. The Mayan numeral system

quantities, respectively. The same colors are employed today for similar designations, although reversed for bookkeeping (but not for electricity).

Another multicultural legacy of our mathematics is the representation of common fractions, that is, numerator/denominator. The Chinese were the first known people to designate a fraction by two numbers, one placed above the other; however, their upper number, termed "the mother," would be our denominator, and the lower number, the numerator, was "the son." Hindus used a similar format, but they reversed the order and placed the numerator over the denominator. The Arabs introduced a separating bar. Leonardo of Pisa (Fibonacci) imported this practice into Italy in 1202. Thus even the format of our modern fractions evolved from the practices of diverse cultures.

Similarly, the *gelosia* (lattice) algorithm of early multiplication (see fig. 13.2) originated in India, was adopted by Islamic traders, and found its way into thirteenth-century Italy. For many centuries, it was the most popular form of multiplication in Europe. Further, the gelosia scheme inspired Napier's bones, an early calculating device invented by the Scotsman John Napier (1550–1617). Students can easily make a set of Napier's bones and use it to do computations (Jones 1954).

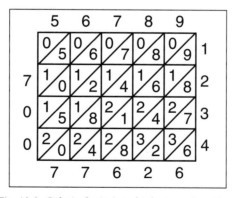

Fig. 13.2. Gelosia (lattice) multiplication algorithm

Comparing mathematical techniques or concepts between cultures, while noting possible different approaches, should also stress the similarities. To illustrate similar mathematical thinking, compare Heron of Alexandria's (ca. A.D. 75) formula for the area of a triangle with the Hindu Brahmagupta's (ca. 628) formula for the area of a cyclic quadrilateral (Eves 1990). A second-year-algebra class can explore the derivation of these formulas (fig. 13.3).

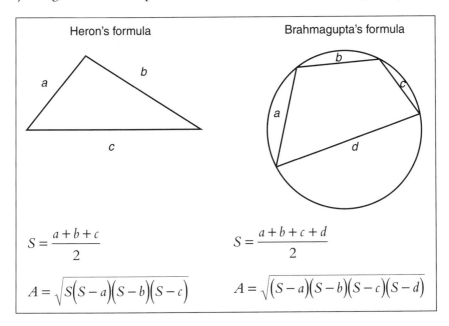

Heron's formula

Brahmagupta's formula

$$S = \frac{a+b+c}{2}$$

$$A = \sqrt{S(S-a)(S-b)(S-c)}$$

$$S = \frac{a+b+c+d}{2}$$

$$A = \sqrt{(S-a)(S-b)(S-c)(S-d)}$$

Fig. 13.3

All peoples have employed finger mathematics. The finger and body motions that medieval European merchants used to designate numerical quantities can be compared with the numerical finger gestures of contemporary people like the Kewa of Papua New Guinea. See figure 13.4. A "fun" classroom activity is to have students communicate a numerical quantity using such postures and gestures.

A modern topic of discrete mathematics can trace its Western origins to Leonhard Euler's (1707–1783) concern with the Bridges of Königsberg problem. His deliberations and methods of analysis gave rise to the study now known as *graph theory*. The Tshokwe people of southern Africa's Bantu culture, however, have used graph-theory principles in sand drawings, or *sona,* for centuries (Ascher 1991). See the examples in figure 13.5.

Even geometric considerations can be enlivened and made more thought-provoking by incorporating historical and intercultural insights. The circle with its perfect symmetry and continuous cyclic nature has fascinated peoples across time and cultures. The ancient Pythagoreans predicated cosmic harmony on "the music of the spheres"—synchronous vibrations of whirling planets in their circular orbits around the earth. Even when the later Greek astronomer Ptolemy (ca. A.D. 85–ca. 165) offered a more "scientific" theory of planetary motion, it depended on circles. Medieval European theologians and natural philosophers considered the circle divinely inspired. It would take the data-based computations of Johannes Kepler and Isaac Newton in the seventeenth century to remove the circle from celestial status. Traditional peoples also revere the circle. In Africa, circular houses are grouped in circular compounds; such an arrangement maximizes living space, affords protection, and minimizes required building materials (Zaslavsky 1973). For those who live in close contact with the cycles of life and nature, arcs and circles determine more natural spatial partitions and orderings than straight lines do. Certainly for the native peoples of North America, this was true. The Sioux chief Black Elk noted in his nineteenth-century comments on the prospects of reservation life (Neihart 1972, pp. 198–99):

> You have noticed that everything an Indian does is in a circle, and that is because the Power of the World always works in a circle, and everything tries to be round…. But the Waischus [white men] have put us in square boxes. Our power is gone and we are dying, for the power is not with us anymore.

Broader cultural and racial perspectives on the history of mathematics have altered perceptions of

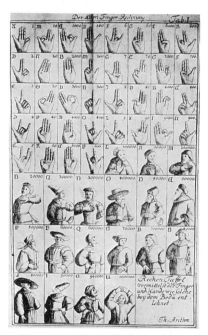

European Finger Mathematics

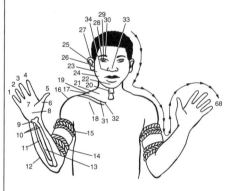

Kewa Hand Mathematics

Fig. 13.4. Two examples of the use of body parts and gestures to designate numerical quantities. European Finger Mathematics is adapted from Bede's finger counting as illustrated in *Theatrum arithmetica-geometricum*, by Jacob Leupold (1727); Kewa Hand Mathematics, from "The Kewa Calendar" (H. Pumuye, *Papua New Guinea Journal* 14 (1978): 47–56.) Used with permission.

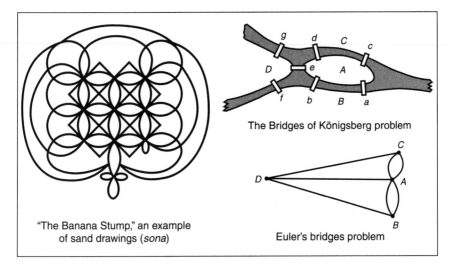

"The Banana Stump," an example
of sand drawings (*sona*)

The Bridges of Königsberg problem

Euler's bridges problem

Fig. 13.5. Examples of some uses of graph theory

historical priorities. It is widely recognized today that the Greek Pythagoreans were not the first people to recognize the mathematical relationship among the sides of a right triangle. Mathematicians in Babylonia, India, and China knew and used this relationship before the Pythagoreans existed (Katz 1993). In fact, the Chinese proof of this theorem is more intuitive and psychologically satisfying than that of the Pythagoreans (Swetz and Kao 1977). Similarly, the Chinese mathematician Jia Xian (ca. 1000) and the Persian astronomer al-Kashi (1427) used the Pascal's triangle technique of generating binomial coefficients well before the Frenchman Blaise Pascal (1623–1662), to whom it is credited, was born. Each instance of mathematical articulation was independent, resting only on its author's motivation and ability. Mathematical creativity and genius resides in, and has been demonstrated by, all peoples.

CONCLUSION

The history of mathematics provides a background for the subject. It offers a journey of diversity—a diversity of participation and a diversity of opportunity. Mathematics grows and develops through the efforts of a multitude of peoples—male, female, from all races and ethnic groups. A most recent illustration of this phenomenon is the announced solution of one of the most perplexing and persistent problems in the history of mathematics, Fermat's last theorem. The problem, which can be traced to Greek origins (Diophantus, ca. A.D. 250), builds on the Pythagorean relationship for a right triangle with legs of length x and y and hypotenuse of length z, that is, $x^2 + y^2 = z^2$. Can this solution be generalized for the situation $x^n + y^n = z^n$ for $n > 2$? It was conjectured that integral solutions could not be found, but the case remained to be proved. The French mathematician Pierre de Fermat (1601?–1665) indicated he had such a proof but inconveniently died before he could reveal it. Since that time, mathematicians have tried to resolve the issue and prove Fermat's last theorem. It became the most famous unsolved problem in recent history. On 23 June 1993, Andrew Wiles of Princeton University delivered a talk in England at Cambridge University in which he outlined a scheme for solving Fermat's last theorem. Wiles, like Sir Isaac Newton in his work on calculus, had to build on the work of many mathematical predecessors. Wiles relied on research findings from colleagues in France, Germany, Italy, Japan, Australia, Colombia, Brazil, Russia, and the United States. Fermat's last theorem was solved, as most problems are, by a truly diverse effort of peoples and ideas. Might we not all learn from this accomplishment?

REFERENCES

Ascher, Marcia. *Ethnomathematics: A Multicultural View of Mathematical Ideas.* Pacific Grove, Calif.: Brooks/Cole Publishing Co., 1991.

Bidwell, James K. "Mayan Arithmetic." *Mathematics Teacher* 74 (November 1967): 762–68.

Closs, Michael P. "I Am Kahal; My Parents Were Scribes." *Research Reports on Ancient Maya Writing,* May 1992, pp. 7–22.

Eves, Howard. *An Introduction to the History of Mathematics.* 6th ed. Philadelphia: Saunders College Publishing, 1990.

Grinstein, Louise, and Paul Campbell. *Women of Mathematics: A Biobibliographic Sourcebook.* Westport, Conn.: Greenwood Press, 1987.

Jones, Phillip S. "Tangible Arithmetic I: Napier's and Genaille's Rods." *Mathematics Teacher* 47 (November 1954): 482–87.

Joseph, George G. *The Crest of the Peacock: Non-European Roots of Mathematics.* New York: St. Martin's Press, 1991.

Katz, Victor. *A History of Mathematics: An Introduction.* New York: HarperCollins Publishers, 1993.

Li Yan and Du Shiran. *Chinese Mathematics: A Concise History.* New York: Oxford University Press, 1987.

Neihardt, John G. *Black Elk Speaks.* Lincoln: University of Nebraska Press, 1972.

Perl, Teri. *Math Equals: Biographies of Women Mathematicians and Related Activities.* Reading, Mass.: Addison-Wesley Publishing Co., 1978.

Swetz, Frank J. *Learning Activities from the History of Mathematics.* Portland, Maine: J. Weston Walch Publishers, 1994.

Swetz, Frank J., and T. I. Kao. *Was Pythagoras Chinese? An Examination of Right Triangle Theory in Ancient China.* University Park, Pa.: Pennsylvania State University Press, 1977.

Zaslavsky, Claudia. *Africa Counts: Number and Pattern in African Culture.* Boston: Prindle, Weber & Schmidt, 1973.

14

Integrating with Integrity
Curriculum, Instruction, and Culture in the Mathematics Classroom

Ellen Davidson
Leslie Kramer

CREATING equity in mathematics education is inherently complex. If we are to move to a true equity model, we must make concurrent and deep changes in several areas. A change in only one of these areas would not be substantial enough to bring about equity in our mathematics classrooms. When we cross the conceptual boundaries between curriculum, instruction, and the social structure of the classroom, we are empowered to see the complexity and interrelatedness of these areas. We can then change not only what we *do* but also how we *think*. We can change the lens we use to look at every aspect of our classrooms. We can change what we take for granted and what we see as "normal."

The gift of diversity is one of a classroom's most powerful assets no matter what the age level. The teaching dilemmas provoked by the call to equity—in curriculum, in instruction, and in classroom culture—have many commonalities across all developmental stages. If we embrace and build on diversity, elementary school students can become stronger both academically and socially.

We thank Jim Hammerman and Leigh Peake for their thoughtful contributions to this paper. The work of Mathematics for Tomorrow on which this paper is based, in part, has been supported by grant no. ESI-92-54479. Any opinions, findings, and conclusions or recommendations expressed in this paper are those of the authors and do not necessarily reflect the views of the National Science Foundation. In writing this chapter we have chosen to use the pronoun *we* when referring to an experience or belief we have in common and *I* when referring to an experience particular to just one of us.

CHANGES IN CURRICULUM

Changes in the curriculum are, in many ways, the most common and accessible of the changes we can make. Many multicultural curricula are available (Eicholz 1992; Grant and Croom 1992; Zaslavsky 1993) that offer an excellent entry point into a more multicultural mathematics class. But changing the curriculum alone doesn't necessarily result in changes in thinking about teaching and learning. To be most powerful, the changes in the curriculum must be integrated with changes in both instruction and classroom culture.

Even a change in the curriculum alone, however, can be made more powerful if it meets two essential criteria—integration in time and integration in ideas. Rather than do enrichment activities on Fridays or at the ends of chapters, a more meaningful approach fully integrates mathematical ideas, concepts, and systems from all over the world into the everyday life of the classroom. By regularly using this mathematics to learn developmentally appropriate content, students also learn that all peoples of the world use and have used important mathematics.

This approach contrasts with both the mathematics equivalent of Black History Month, in which multicultural mathematics is separate from "regular" mathematics, and with a "tourist curriculum," in which students see this type of mathematics as fun but not as a basis for essential mathematical learning (Derman-Sparks 1989, p. 7):

> Tourist curriculum is both patronizing, emphasizing the "exotic" differences between cultures, and trivializing, dealing not with the real-life daily problems and experiences of different peoples, but with surface aspects of their celebrations and modes of entertainment. Children "visit" non-White cultures and then "go home" to the daily classroom, which reflects only the dominant culture. The focus on holidays, although it provides drama and delight for both children and adults, gives the impression that that is all "other" people—usually people of color—do. What it fails to communicate is real understanding.

In the same way that we can teach the history of and for us all, we can teach the mathematics of and for all of us. We can take our standard mathematics curriculum—whole-number operations, fractions, geometry—and use mathematics from other cultures as a way to master necessary skills and understand important concepts.

An example of this kind of curriculum is one we have taught in elementary school classrooms, preservice courses, and in-service institutes. *Sona* are sand drawings used by the Tshokwe people of the region crossing portions of northern Angola, southern Zaire, and western Zambia. Sona (plural of *lusona*) are intricate patterns that are drawn to illustrate the story as it is told, and then wiped away soon after the telling is done. The drawings are considered integral to the craft of storytelling, which is handed down from one generation to the next. One important feature of these drawings is the grid of dots that underlies them. The grids are always sketched in ahead of time by using two fingers of one hand to obtain equal spacing between the dots, and serve as a reference grid for drawing the lusona proper (Ascher 1991; Gerdes 1991).

We have used an exploration of one type of lusona (two examples are shown in fig. 14.1) to investigate important ideas from number theory. When drawn correctly, each dot is enclosed in its own box, or cell. Sometimes you can draw the pattern without lifting the pencil from the paper; sometimes several separate passes of the pencil are needed.

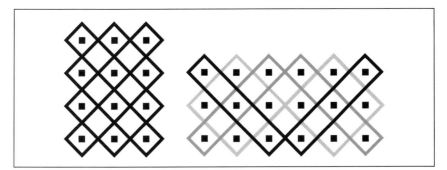

Fig. 14.1. Two examples of *sona*

The exploration involves changing the dimensions of the underlying grid and looking for patterns, making predictions, and creating general rules about how many passes of the pencil are required to complete any type of grid. The task of figuring out the patterns leads to a study of odd and even numbers, multiples, prime numbers, factoring, rules for divisibility, least common multiples, and greatest common factors. Sona provide a culturally relevant exploration in which these number ideas arise naturally.

Another curriculum example involves learning algorithms from many cultures as a way to better understand whole-number operations. When exploring and explaining a new algorithm, students often gain insights into both the new algorithm and the original one. As students develop the language to describe the systems being compared, they construct mathematical meaning for themselves.

Egyptian arithmetic gives students an opportunity to explore the rationale for alternative algorithms as well as the concepts of multiplication, division, powers of 2, and odd and even numbers (Hurd 1991). The example in figure 14.2 uses the problem 13×19 to illustrate the basic structure of Egyptian multiplication. Starting with 1 and 19 at the top of columns 1 and 2, respectively, we double the value of succeeding rows until the first column gets as close to 13 as possible without exceeding it. We choose the numbers in the first column that can be added to give the multiplier: $1 + 4 + 8 = 13$. We then add the corresponding numbers in the second column to get the product of 13×19: $19 + 76 + 152 = 247$.

Double the number in the previous row	Double the multiplicand
✔ 1	19
2	38
✔ 4	76
✔ 8	152

Fig. 14.2. Egyptian multiplication for 13 × 19

Figuring out why this algorithm works requires students to investigate the question "What is multiplication?" In designing their own division algorithm based on this multiplication algorithm and comparing theirs to that of the Egyptians, students must investigate the relationship between multiplication and division, a concept that is essential to really understanding these operations rather than seeing them as rote processes.

Sometimes, as with sona, mathematics from a culture serves as a powerful way for students to explore a developmentally appropriate mathematical concept. Other times, as in the following example, mathematics is presented when a culture is studied. In this instance, the teacher identifies a mathematics topic from the culture as being mathematically powerful and developmentally appropriate. The mathematics is thus contextualized within its culture.

During a yearlong study of Africa in my fifth-and-sixth-grade class, the students were challenged to build a model of a house from the culture each of them was studying individually. The assignment required the students to research and sketch a construction plan, describe the materials to be used, and calculate the square footage of the floor and walls. They needed to think about why a house is designed with particular features—a round or square shape, a flat or peaked roof, extravagant or economical materials, and vertical or horizontal strength. During the construction of the models, the students learned about the wall strength of round houses and the roominess of square and rectangular houses. The student studying the round houses of the Kikuyu people used less plasticene than the two students who built rectangular structures. The students developed a working vocabulary and an understanding of important ideas in solid and plane geometry, as well as spatial concepts (Denyer 1978; Education Development Center 1994b; Grifalconi 1986).

In Mathematics for Tomorrow (MFT), an in-service project for teachers who are in the process of changing their mathematics teaching, inquiry groups compared the counting systems of twenty ethnic groups from around the world. Given the transliterated names and numerical values of numbers up to and beyond 100, we spent two hours discussing the different base systems. We extended the inquiry and hypothesized about why a culture might have developed its particular number system.

After the MFT exploration, I brought into my class a chart of the number system (a base-twelve system) of the Mada people of central Nigeria. Working in pairs, some students shared quietly, but others needed additional input from the teacher. Some students created their own charts and wrote out word problems; other students wrote the English word for the equivalent in base ten for each base-twelve number and then created charts and wrote word problems. Through the Mada system, students created an understanding for themselves of "the first ten plus two digits" and regrouping, and they began developing the vocabulary necessary to communicate their computations. They then returned to the Hindu-Arabic base-ten system with a stronger understanding of what digits are and what the value of a place means. They also revisited the concept of zero and realized that zero is not just a place holder. In comparing different number systems, students develop both a richer knowledge of the ways different peoples of the world count and a deeper understanding of our own system (Education Development Center 1994a).

CHANGES IN INSTRUCTION

The second, more difficult type of change involves taking a hard look at *how* we teach. With each day of teaching we are faced with choices about using culturally relevant teaching, constructivism versus telling, and cooperative learning versus individual or competitive learning. All these choices require us to look at our underlying beliefs about how students learn—at where our beliefs fall on the continuum from knowledge transmitted from teachers to knowledge constructed by learners. We must also look at our students—at their backgrounds, styles, and needs.

We argue here for what Banks terms the *transformation approach* to multicultural education. In this approach, changes are required not only in the materials of the curriculum but also in the perspectives of teacher and students and in teaching methods. This transformation approach is defined by a number of important factors that influence instruction. One of these is *knowledge construction,* helping students understand multiple cultural perspectives and helping them become constructors of knowledge. Another is *prejudice reduction,* or active work on positive intergroup attitudes and beliefs. A third area is *equitable pedagogy,* or modifying teaching approaches to make them appropriate for children from a range of cultures. A final component, which we discuss in the next section of this paper, is *school culture and social structure* (Banks 1994).

Delpit (1986, 1988) raises several of these issues as she asks us to consider how students' different backgrounds affect what they need from the school environment. There is a culture of power in this country, the culture of those who control the country's institutions: government, education, health care, industry, and the military. Some students enter school better prepared than others to function productively in this culture of power of which education is a part. Their preparation depends on how well their home culture matches the culture of the school. Children who enter school with an understanding of the dominant culture do not need help from the school system in understanding that culture. Children who come from cultures with different rules need to be taught, in school, the rules of the middle- and upper-class white culture of power to have greater access to jobs, housing, education, power, and general success in our society (Delpit 1988).

Delpit specifically describes the need to focus on traditional skills with African American children rather than on the currently popular conceptual or developmental approaches. A careful reading of Delpit's work shows that she understands the tension between these approaches and clearly states that no single focus will serve the needs of these children (Delpit 1986, p. 384):

> I believe that skills are best taught through meaningful communication, best learned in meaningful contexts. I would further explain that skills are a necessary, but insufficient aspect of black and minority students' education. Students need technical skills to open doors, but they need to be able to think critically and creatively to participate in meaningful and potentially liberating work inside those doors. Let there be no doubt: a "skilled" minority person who is not also capable of critical analysis becomes the trainable, low-level functionary of dominant society, simply the grease that keeps the institutions which orchestrate his or her oppression running smoothly. On the other hand, a critical thinker who lacks the "skills" demanded by employers and institutions of higher learning can aspire to financial and social status only within the disenfranchised underworld. Yes, if minority people are to effect the change which will allow them to truly progress we must insist on "skills" *within the context* of critical and creative thinking.

Gloria Ladson-Billings, using the term *culturally relevant teaching,* supports many of the ideas in Banks's transformation approach. Culturally relevant teaching emphasizes the role of teacher as conductor or coach who validates and supports the cultures students bring to the classroom. This approach places less emphasis on skills and more emphasis on developmentally based practice. In a three-year, intensive study, she described and analyzed eight teachers (five African American and three white) who are highly successful with African American children. These teachers were defined as successful by parents, colleagues, and principals alike. The criteria for success included a willingness to involve parents as active partners, a demand for academic excellence, the ability to discipline and manage a class, an increase in students' attendance and enthusiasm, and an improvement in standardized-test scores. Ladson-Billings, in explaining why she focuses on teaching practice rather than on curriculum, says that *the way we teach* has the greatest impact on how students perceive *what we teach* (Ladson-Billings 1994).

We know from experience that the greatest success comes when teachers have paid attention to methodology as well as to content and classroom culture. Ladson-Billings argues emphatically that "teaching is not telling" and that all children, regardless of culture, must be involved in classrooms where they explore and collaborate to construct their own understanding. Although the classrooms she studied varied in the degree of "teacher centeredness," in all of them, the children were actively investigating the material and actively discussing their own findings (Ladson-Billings 1994).

Cooperative learning is consistently recommended in the current literature. Ladson-Billings found that all eight teachers in her study had a significant commitment to this approach as part of culturally relevant teaching (Ladson-Billings 1994). A major study that "reviewed research on every imaginable approach to increase student reading and mathematics achievement in the elementary grades" (Slavin and Madden 1989, p. 52) found that nearly all highly successful programs had two components in common: they were continuous progress models and they used some form of cooperative learning. In another study, Johnson and Johnson (1984) found that cooperative learning promoted higher achievement than competitive or individual learning for all age levels and in all subject areas for tasks involving concept attainment, problem solving, memory, judging, and predicting. Whereas the Ladson-Billings study focused primarily on African American students, Slavin and Johnson and Johnson considered the full range of American students. This style of teaching is geared for the success of *all* learners, not just students of color.

Despite these findings, the typical American classroom, at any level, is oriented toward competitive individualism. Students work mostly by themselves on individual tasks, and doing well implies doing better than others. We can contrast this model to classroom structures in which all students learn together and the primary task is to work collectively toward common goals, with all students invested in everyone's achievement (Schniedewind and Davidson 1987). Such a view supports the African attitude that "it takes a village to raise a child."

Extending the individual-as-group-member concept into the curriculum allows us to reinforce the importance of making school and other social units work. Students need real examples from both history and current events in order to develop more fully their understanding of interdependence within the community. It is incongruous and confusing to insist that students help each other during mathematics yet never to analyze with them how successful groups conduct themselves.

Another way to enhance learning at all levels is for students to develop metacognitive skills from a multicultural perspective. As they learn to reflect on *how* they learn, students can benefit from trying approaches developed in other cultural contexts. Uri Treisman encouraged black students to adopt a study method typical of Chinese American students. He found that the black students had developed a pattern of keeping their academic and social lives separate. In high school, this pattern had served them well and had enabled them to get to college. In college, this pattern precluded their working collaboratively to master the material. The academically successful Chinese American students, however, typically studied in groups they called *study gangs.* When the black students created study groups focused on academic excellence rather than remediation, they experienced a significant increase in course grades and a decrease in the drop-out rate (Watkins 1989).

Let us return to several of our curriculum examples to examine how each of these changes in instructional practice is woven with the culturally diverse curriculum content. In my preservice class on teaching mathematics, students begin work with sona as a whole class. The cultural context is introduced by drawing some sona on the overhead projector as a Tchokwe story is told. Students then work individually or collectively to learn how to draw the lusona. In order to make the lesson effective for a range of learners, the directions for the activity purposely give three different ways one might think of learning to draw the lusona—one using a billiards analogy and one using an optics analogy to explain how the angles are drawn and one that is strictly procedural. It quickly becomes apparent that "traditional" mathematics skills are not the most effective ones for this activity. Students who are visually adept often excel in learning how to draw the lusona and are thus able to help their more numerically oriented peers. By the end of class we check to be sure that *all* students are able to draw the lusona correctly. Success is the responsibility of the entire class, not just the instructor.

Students are then assigned to continue to work with sona between classes throughout the week. They may work individually or with others in the class or with friends outside of class. When the results are shared, we consistently find that a number of students have engaged their partners, children, parents, and roommates in this pursuit.

Students' understanding also stretches to many levels. Often students will find that the way another student looked at this problem is clearer than the way they had viewed it themselves. Students begin to experiment with strategies that were previously unfamiliar to them. Students' ideas build on one another; as they pool their information, they collaboratively create an overall theory.

CHANGES IN CLASSROOM CULTURE

I'm waiting for you to give up on me.

—Andrew, an African American fifth grader,
during a difficult transition

The third change, by necessity tightly woven with the other two, is in the culture of our classrooms. It entails building a community of learners by embracing a strength model rather than a deficit one; building on students' knowledge and interests; and respecting and appreciating cultural differences.

In such classrooms, teachers value themselves as professionals. Teachers value what their students bring with them from their homes and backgrounds. Classroom academic work *builds on* students' previous knowledge instead of ignoring or resisting this knowledge. Rather than expect students to give up their cultures for a central homogenized culture, teachers in these classrooms value and intermingle diverse cultures.

In addition to depriving us of the richness we can gain from appreciating and acknowledging cultural differences, disregarding these differences ignores the reality of the children in our classes (Derman-Sparks 1989). We need to see the children in our classrooms as whole children, bringing with them all their own experiences and backgrounds. We cannot understand the greater "norm" of our classrooms, and of this country, if we do not see the wholeness of each of our students. Ladson-Billings (1994, pp. 31–33) elaborates:

> My own experiences with white teachers, both preservice and veteran, indicate that many are uncomfortable acknowledging any student differences and particularly racial differences. Thus some teachers make statements such as "I don't really see color, I just see children" or "I don't care if they're red, green, or polka dot, I just treat them all like children." However these attempts at color blindness mask a "dysconscious racism," and "uncritical habit of mind that justifies inequity and exploitation by accepting the existing order of things as given"... by claiming not to notice, the teacher is saying that she is dismissing one of the most salient features of the child's identity and that she does not account for it in her curricular planning and instruction.

Often a change in the culture provides access for students who would otherwise not be full participants in our mathematics classrooms. When students experience the mathematics in a classroom as not relating to them or their culture, they may feel invisible and unconnected with the content. As quoted in a newsletter from my daughter's school, "when someone with the authority of a teacher, say, describes the world and you are not in it, there is a moment of psychic disequilibrium, as if you looked into a mirror and saw nothing."

In the fall of 1994 in my class in teaching mathematics, I had three Asian women—one from China, one from Japan, and one from the Philippines. All of them were uncomfortable with mathematics and with perceiving themselves as mathematicians. By the end of the semester, all three women were thoroughly involved in the course and participating eagerly. This change began when we were discussing games for our mathematics classrooms and games from many cultures. I gave the example of Mancala, which often is played in this country in a west African version. Victoria, the student from the Philippines, grew up playing the Filipino version called Sunka. She explained the game to the class, and we compared the strategies and mathematics of the two versions. I brought in my Filipino game board and my Ghanaian game board, and we looked at the different materials for the boards and for the playing pieces. By bringing her own experiences into the mathematics class, Victoria was able to see the mathematics as relevant and to see herself as someone who could do mathematics.

Another experience that reinforced the importance of making mathematics culturally relevant occurred during a one-time, after-school, in-service workshop for Boston teachers. One woman in the workshop,

Julie, appeared particularly uninterested. We were exploring a range of algorithms for addition and subtraction and what we might learn from each about the nature of these operations. I began sharing the following subtraction algorithm I had learned from Ralph, an elementary school teacher who had grown up in Barbados:

$$6\,{}^14$$
$$-\,{}^4\not{3}\,9$$
$$\overline{2\,5}$$

As we discussed why this algorithm worked, Julie became energized. She said she had learned this method in Barbados and it had always made much more sense to her than the "borrowing" she was expected to teach her current students. We explored how the alternative algorithm made sense mathematically, why it might be easier or harder for children to understand, and why it might be easier or harder for children to do. Julie was delighted with the interest and respect accorded to her from her Latina, Asian American, African American, and white colleagues.

In a discussion about different cultural styles in learning and discourse, the students in a preservice education course were talking about how underlying assumptions—often ones that are so normative for us that we're not conscious that they are assumptions—cause problems among people from different cultures. I commented that it often helps to be explicit about which culture is the context for a particular conversation. Ian, a student from England, suggested it might be easiest if we all adopted a "When in Rome, do as the Romans do" approach to this situation and when in someone's home, follow the norm in that setting. Becca then asked, "So whose home is the classroom?" Nieto (1994, p. 35) describes both the inherent complexity and possible benefits of grappling with these issues:

> Affirmation, solidarity and critique is based on the premise that the most powerful learning results when students work and struggle with one another, even if it is sometimes difficult and challenging. It begins with the assumption that the many differences that students and their families represent are embraced and accepted as legitimate vehicles for learning, and that these are then extended. What makes this level different from the others is that the conflict is not avoided, but rather accepted as an inevitable part of learning.

We *can* create classrooms that are homes to all of us. It is a daunting task, often overwhelming, always challenging, ever evolving—a task we can embrace with enthusiastic commitment, accurate knowledge, and careful thought as we enter the twenty-first century.

REFERENCES

Ascher, Marcia. *Ethnomathematics: A Multicultural View of Mathematical Ideas.* Pacific Grove, Calif.: Brooks/Cole Publishing Co., 1991.

Banks, James A. "Transforming the Mainstream Curriculum." *Educational Leadership* 51, no. 8 (1994): 4–8.

Delpit, Lisa. "The Silenced Dialogue: Power and Pedagogy in Educating Other People's Children." *Harvard Educational Review* 58, no. 3 (1988): 280–98.

———. "Skills and Other Dilemmas of a Progressive Black Educator." *Harvard Educational Review* 56, no. 4 (1986): 379–85.

Denyer, Susan. *African Traditional Architecture.* London: Heinemann, 1978.

Derman-Sparks, Louise. *Anti-Bias Curriculum Tools for Empowering Young Children.* Washington, D.C.: National Association for the Education of Young Children, 1989.

Education Development Center, ed. *From the Ground Up, Seeing and Thinking Mathematically.* Portsmouth, N.H.: Heinemann, 1994b.

———. *The Language of Numbers: Seeing and Thinking Mathematically in the Middle Grades.* Portsmouth, N.H.: Heinemann, 1994a.

Eicholz, Robert. *Building Bridges to Mathematics: Cultural Connections.* 9 vols. Reading, Mass.: Addison-Wesley Publishing Co., 1992.

Gerdes, Paulus. *Lusona: Geometrical Recreations of Africa.* Maputo, Mozambique: African Mathematical Union and Higher Pedagogical Institute's Faculty of Sciences, 1991.

Grant, Carl, and Lucille Croom. *Exploring Your Multicultural World Mathematics Projects.* 9 vols. Morristown, N.J.: Silver Burdett & Ginn, 1992.

Grifalconi, Ann. *The Village of Round and Square Houses.* Boston: Little, Brown & Co., 1986.

Hurd, Spencer S. "Egyptian Fractions: Ahmes to Fibonacci to Today." *Mathematics Teacher* 84 (October 1991): 561–68.

Johnson, David W., and Roger T. Johnson. *Circles of Learning: Cooperation in the Classroom.* Alexandria, Va.: Association for Supervision and Curriculum Development, 1984.

Ladson-Billings, Gloria. *The Dreamkeepers: Successful Teachers of African American Children.* San Francisco: Jossey-Bass Publishers, 1994.

Nieto, Sonia. "Moving beyond Tolerance in Multicultural Education." *Multicultural Education* 1 (Spring 1994): 9–12, 35–38.

Schniedewind, Nancy, and Ellen Davidson. *Cooperative Learning, Cooperative Lives.* Dubuque, Iowa: W. C. Brown, 1987.

Slavin, Robert E., and Nancy A. Madden. "What Works for Students at Risk: A Research Synthesis." *Educational Leadership* 46, no. 5 (1989): 4–13.

Watkins, Beverly. "Many Campuses Now Challenging Minority Students to Excel in Math and Science." *Chronicle of Higher Education,* 14 June 1989, pp. 13, 16–17.

Zaslavsky, Claudia. *Multicultural Mathematics: Interdisciplinary Cooperative Learning Activities.* Portland, Maine: J. Weston Walch Publisher, 1993.

15

Integrating Mathematics with Community Service

Gwendolyn Clinkscales

Claudia Zaslavsky

IMAGINE a place where sixth-grade students learn mathematics by teaching four- and five-year-olds and planning for their needs! This place, the brainchild of mathematics teacher Gwendolyn Clinkscales, is the Preschool Learning Center of the Community Service Academy of Intermediate School (IS) 218, situated in a low-income, working-class neighborhood of New York City. Although it is an inner-city school, IS 218 is as different as day and night from the stereotype so often depicted in the press of failing schools and disaffected students.

Innovation is the key word at IS 218, also known as the Salome Ureña Middle Academies (SUMA), named after a nineteenth-century educator in the Dominican Republic. The newly built school, the product of a partnership among the Children's Aid Society, the New York City Board of Education, local School District Six (one of thirty-two school districts in the city), and several community organizations, opened in March 1992. Designed as a full-service school, the institution offers social, dental, and medical services to students and their families; an after-school program; and evening classes for adults (Zaslavsky 1996).

Most of the students in SUMA are first- or second-generation immigrants from the Dominican Republic. They live in Washington Heights, a neighborhood that is an unofficial port of entry for newly arriving immigrants from the Dominican Republic. In 1987, 40 percent of the households in Washington Heights had incomes below $10 000, the highest percentage in that income bracket in the country. The school district ranked last in percentage of students reading at or above grade level, and second highest among New York City police precincts in the number of juvenile reports

We are grateful to Margaret DeLuca of the Center for Minority Achievement at the Bank Street College of Education for her expert advice.

filed for truancy, drug abuse, and child abuse (Children's Aid Society 1993). Yet, Dominican families are tightly knit and place a high value on education. SUMA is, indeed, an institution of which the community is proud.

The five academies in SUMA, of which the Community Service Academy (CSA) is one, function relatively independently of one another. CSA students are organized in heterogeneous groups, despite the general practice in the district and the city of tracking according to scores on standardized tests. Flexible scheduling and team planning among teachers are the rule. Each student is assigned to an advisory group of about fifteen students, which meets with an adult advisor for an hour each week, assuring each participant regular access to a sympathetic adult ear. This practice allows students to reflect on and assess their work with the preschoolers, their own school experiences, and their personal lives. Each student's voice is heard, thereby integrating all students into a meaningful community.

What is the purpose of community service? It is to empower students to be productive members of their community. Middle school students need to be actively engaged in order to build a knowledge base. They need to know how academic experiences affect the quality of daily life. Their mathematics teacher sees her role in the process as the coach who guides students to discovery, building on the strengths of early adolescents by combining service with active learning approaches and integrating them fully into the curriculum. For this teacher, with her prior experience in early childhood education, working with preschoolers was a natural choice for community service.

THE PRESCHOOL LEARNING CENTER IN ACTION

It is ten o'clock. Sixteen sixth graders are transforming their mathematics classroom into a preschool center. Theresa and Marlene are moving desks and chairs out of the block area. Theresa gives directives: "Put the cardboard blocks over there. They need room to fall. The little kids love building the blocks up high and knocking them over. I don't know why they keep doing this, but we better leave enough falling space." Marlene responds, "Yeah, but they need more space for the wooden blocks because they always make those long, long roadways with houses on top."

The sixth-grade class was exploring the topic of measurement. One activity was to estimate the space required for block-building. The two girls had cordoned off about a fifth of the classroom for that purpose.

In mathematics class the sixth graders were to determine which of several shapes had the largest area for a given fixed perimeter. Using the preschoolers' wooden unit blocks, string, and tape, they constructed a square "house" and a nonsquare, rectangular "house" having the same perimeter. Then they placed the same group of preschoolers into each structure in turn to determine which could contain more children. Having satisfied all participants that the square had a greater area, they continued the experiment by constructing a round "house" with the same perimeter (circumference).

The SUMA Preschool Learning Center project was started in the fall of 1993, with two classes of sixth graders and two preschool programs, in the regular mathematics classroom on the fourth floor. Each group came once a week at different times for an hour and a half. By the 1994–95 school year the entire CSA sixth-grade team was involved—six teachers, two teacher aides, and a social worker intern—working with three regular classes and one special education class, more than 100 sixth graders altogether.

The team plans the program jointly with the Center for Minority Achievement at the Bank Street College of Education during the invaluable twice weekly visits of its senior staff developer, Margaret Martinez-DeLuca. Together they have developed an innovative program of mathematical activities and relevant assessment strategies.

As an example of the activities, the sixth graders worked with preschoolers to build a town out of blocks on an eight-foot-square plastic floor mat with a grid. This led to algebraic thinking on the part of the older students, as reported by DeLuca in Jervis (1995, p. 28):

> Preschoolers select town center on the graph from which point they place their block buildings. As the preschoolers try to convey the direction from the point of origin to their chosen spot (left, right, up, down), the sixth graders discover the need to be clear in what they understand about movement on a graph. The sixth graders record the block placement in a notebook and on the graph paper. "Over there" is not enough information. Sixth graders must figure out that "over there" means "four to the right and three down," which leads to (4,-3). But as sixth graders begin to replicate on small graph paper what the preschoolers intend, they understand this exercise is about moving from and moving to. They begin to understand the necessity of axes and point of origin.... Students realize the need to simplify and use clear, precise language. Students say: "Remember how we explained to the preschoolers so it was clear enough for them to understand."

Incorporating the advisory group into the curriculum planning gives teachers the opportunity for establishing a close relationship with each student. This approach was carried further in the "reflection questionnaire" that each CSA student completed in the middle of the 1994–95 school year. The goal was for the adults to learn how students related to their work during the first half of the year—their projects and the role each one played, difficulties and how they overcame them, how they viewed their own leadership abilities, and whether they felt that they had improved academically. Some responses written to individual students are related here:

- "Pablo, you have improved greatly in being the leader for our advisory group. Which do you prefer, being the leader or a group member? Why? The preschoolers really seem to enjoy working with you. How can we incorporate area and perimeter in sand play? Let's talk about it in our advisory group. The object is to teach preschoolers what you are learning in mathematics class. Keep up the good work."
- "Shantel,... you do a wonderful job at circle time leading the preschoolers in games and songs. What other activity can we do at

Photo by Dick Corkery, courtesy of Impact II

circle time that will help the preschoolers to understand perimeter and area? I'm also glad to see you working harder in mathematics. Do you understand that the larger the scale, the less graph paper you will need to create the layout of the preschool? For example, if your scale is one graph-paper box equals one foot, then you will need more paper to make a classroom 450 square feet than if your scale is 1 box = 10 feet. Keep working hard, and you will succeed."

To a newcomer from Ethiopia, Clinkscales wrote the following comment:

- "Thank you for showing the preschoolers how to ride a bicycle. We are very happy that you are in our class. I see you have made lots of friends. I know it must be very confusing, but you are learning very quickly."

Active participation in a democracy is evident in the relationships among the ethnic and racial groups participating in SUMA Preschool, which include African American, Jewish, and Latino families. Children come from three centers: one sponsored by a Baptist church, another a Jewish community center, and a third that is independent. The preschool also includes siblings of SUMA students.

Planning for the Preschool Learning Center is democracy in action. During their advisory period and their daily hour-long mathematics class, the students discuss and map out the program for the upcoming visit on the basis of their experiences in their own mathematics class, observations of the preschoolers, and reflective discussions after each preschool class visit. The students are trusted to resolve any disagreements that may arise, and the teacher does her best not to intervene. Over time, students develop skills of effective action and citizenship: listening, problem solving, understanding power dynamics, and becoming accountable. The supportive learning environment enhances their self-confidence and social awareness, preparing them to participate as actively as adults do in the life of the community.

THE PRESCHOOL LEARNING CENTER AS A FOCUS FOR LEARNING MATHEMATICS

Mathematics projects are developed from the real-world needs of both the middle school students and the preschoolers. Assessment is integral to the curriculum.

As an example, the two-part midyear assessment given early in 1995 is summarized here. In the first part the students were to "sketch on scratch paper, then draw on graph paper, a dimensioned layout of [an imaginary] SUMA Preschool Learning Center using the following data." The list included entryways, two classrooms measuring at least 450 square feet each, offices, several types of bathrooms, parents' room, staff lounge, kitchen, laundry, and an outdoor play space measuring at least 1 200 square feet. The specific dimensions of each space were to be determined by each student.

In the second part the students were asked to answer five questions on a separate sheet of paper, showing and explaining all work. The first four questions dealt specifically with linear and area measurements of various parts of the center. The fifth question was, "The Health Department requires thirty

Photo by Dick Corkery, courtesy of Impact II

square feet of classroom space for each child. What is the maximum number of children your preschool can serve?" Students worked on this project for more than a week, both in school and at home.

One classroom project required the sixth graders to draw floor plans of their large, irregularly shaped classroom, which is almost twice the size of a typical classroom. They were to include the furniture for the sixth graders, occupying about two-thirds of the floor space, and the preschoolers' furniture in the remainder of the room. This was a cooperative group project, as are many of the mathematics assignments.

These floor plans show how middle school students are learning to look at existing space, to interpret and communicate that space's relationship to the surrounding environment, and the influence of the surrounding environment on a specific space. They are learning to create a site plan using concepts such as graphic scale, section drawings, and elevation.

Some students were unable to include all the furniture in the floor plan of their classroom, a difficulty that motivated them to look for better ways to plan their design. Their study of transformations helped them to solve the problem. To put across the concept of transformation, the students demonstrated with dances. As an illustration of translation, they did the electric slide, a popular dance in the African American community; to show rotation, they danced the Dominican merengue; and they mirrored each others' movements to illustrate reflection. When students went back to work on their designs, they were heard to make such comments as "Just slide it down a couple of boxes and it will fit" and "Rotate it clockwise and the garden might fit."

The architect's original floor plans for the school were shown to the students. They examined the linear dimensions on the plan and compared them with the actual dimensions of the classroom. That brought their attention to the architect's scale written on the floor plan. A discussion about scale led to the conclusion that "a scale drawing shows the same shape but not the same size."

The site plan became the floor plan from which each group created a three-dimensional model of the classroom, including the furniture, all done to scale. They had ingenious methods for judging the height of the room. Some measured the height of the tall cabinets and estimated the remaining distance; others stood on furniture or classmates' shoulders and used measuring devices for greater accuracy. They phoned relevant suppliers for catalogs, and used the data to calculate the cost of necessary building materials and furniture. Earlier in the year the students had carried out a homework assignment to draw floor plans of their own homes (see fig. 15.1). Subsequently their homework was to construct three-dimensional models of these homes.

The development of the outdoor play yard became the theme in the latter part of the 1994–95 school year. Two architects from the Salvadori Center on the Built Environment at the City College of New York joined the SUMA Preschool Learning Center team, devoting several

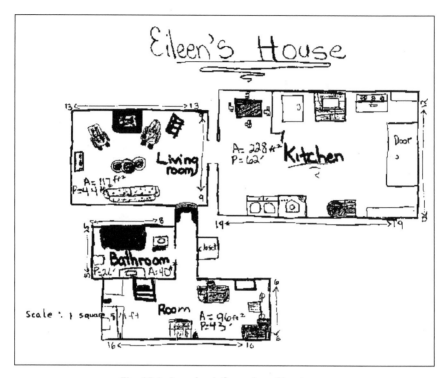

Fig. 15.1. A student's floor plan of her house

hours each week to the project. Before formulating their plans, the sixth graders visited local early childhood programs to observe the youngsters as they engaged in indoor and outdoor play. During the preschoolers' visits to the Preschool Learning Center, middle school students actively observed how the children used materials and equipment. In their journals and during their advisory sessions, they reflected on the ways that young children play and learn. Through visits to public parks and playgrounds they became aware of landscaping, the location and placement of structures, climate, and other construction factors. The culminating activity for this project was a display of site plans, three-dimensional models, and budget proposals for the outdoor play space for the SUMA Preschool Learning Center, to which the community and funding organizations were invited. In June all the paricipants in the project celebrated as their mathematics teacher, the school principal, and a preschooler dedicated the space for the new play yard.

Each week the middle school students receive their assignments for the entire week. Topics in the curriculum are not necessarily tied to preschool needs. Students might be asked to carry out exercises such as "Reflect the given triangle about the horizontal axis" or to define and give examples of various mathematical terms. References to the textbook are included, but assignments are never taken directly from the book. The textbook becomes a valuable resource.

Among the guiding principles of the mathematics program are these three: to relate the assignments to students' lives and interests, to integrate mathematics with other subject areas, and to give students choices. Descriptions of several assignments will exemplify how the guiding principles are carried out in practice.

One week the homework was based on a survey of the class on the movie they would like to see. The students used the data to calculate percents and draw graphs, but they also carried the assignment further by discussing ways to finance those classmates who could not afford to attend. The topic for another week's homework was the estimated Taino (indigenous) population of Hispaniola, the island that the Dominican Republic shares with Haiti. The students were given data for the years 1490 to 1510 in two-year intervals, based on two sets of old Spanish census figures. Besides graphing and interpreting the data, students were asked to write the reasons, in their opinion, for the disappearance of the Taino people by the year 1508.

PERFORMANCE-BASED ASSESSMENT VS. STANDARDIZED TESTS

SUMA teachers must cope with the results of students having been tracked through the fifth grade in the feeder elementary schools. The sixth-grade heterogeneous mathematics classes include students who had been tracked into advanced, average, and below-average elementary school classes. Nevertheless, their teacher finds that all the students are engaged in the sixth-grade mathematics activities. She firmly believes that some students had remained in the low track because little was expected of them and they were not motivated to achieve. Most of the mathematics activities are open-ended; some students will do more, others will do less, but no student who works at the assignment is given a failing grade.

As much as possible, the students are involved in decision making at all levels. This involvement requires a major adjustment on the part of the students, since they came from elementary schools where most of the day was spent in teacher-directed activities. Fortunately, there is a close relationship between the SUMA teachers and the elementary school teachers, many of whom are learning to model their methodology on that of SUMA.

To determine how to assign grades for the periodic report card, students discussed the weight to be assigned to each criterion and the kind of narrative comments that are appropriate. For the first marking period, they agreed that exams would count 50 percent; participation, 20 percent; and group projects, notebooks (or journals), and homework, 10 percent each. By the second marking period they felt that projects should receive the greatest weight. As one student commented, "We spend most of our time in mathematics class working on and talking about projects, so it should be the biggest part of our grade."

Group projects are presented to the entire class for evaluation. Each group must arrive at a consensus on the ratings for the items on an assessment sheet. For example, in evaluating the three-dimensional model of the basement classroom, groups were to rate each item on a scale of 1 to 4. The first ten items dealt with conformance to scale of the various parts of the model, and five items referred to the manner of presentation, one of which asked, "Is there evidence of cooperative group work?" Finally, each group was to "add some general words of encouragement and constructive criticism."

Students in the Preschool Learning Project have developed confidence in presenting their ideas to the public. They use mathematical terms with increasing ease, and they understand the connections among mathematics, the humanities, and the real world. However, SUMA does not devote an inordinate amount of class time to "drill and kill" exercises. Consequently, sixth-grade mathematics scores in spring 1994 on a standardized multiple-choice test were below the scores that the same children had attained in fifth grade the previous year. To a district that considers scores on traditional multiple-choice tests to be a most important measure of achievement, this decline in scores was a matter of great concern. Fortunately, the scores in spring 1995 were somewhat higher than those for sixth graders of the previous year.

It is generally acknowledged that the inquiry methods practiced in these SUMA classrooms are helping students to become better problem solvers. Children are encouraged to reflect on their own work and to evaluate the work of their peers. Their input into all phases of the learning experience—projects, types of assessment, evaluations, and grading—inspires them with the confidence to take control of their own learning, a form of empowerment that may remain with them throughout their lives. They are poised in public presentation, accustomed as they are to present their views to audiences of classmates and adults, to newspaper reporters, and in front of television cameras. Through their interaction with the preschoolers and their families, they are gaining experience in working with different age groups and with people in the community of diverse ethnic and racial backgrounds.

Perhaps most important of all, children who, in another setting, might have had little opportunity to realize their own worth can grow and blossom to their full potential in SUMA.

REFERENCES

Children's Aid Society. *Building a Community School: A Revolutionary Design in Public Education.* New York: Children's Aid Society, 1993.

Jervis, Kathe. "Collaboration in a Middle School—'You Can't Do It Alone.'" In *How We Are Changing Schools Collaboratively,* edited by Ellen Meyers, pp. 26–31. New York: Impact II—the Teacher Network, 1995.

Zaslavsky, Claudia. *The Multicultural Math Classroom: Bringing in the World.* Portsmouth, N.H.: Heinemann, 1996.

16

The Gift of Diversity in Learning through Mathematical Exploration

John C. Moyer

Jinfa Cai

Joan Grampp

MANY mathematics teachers who have modified their teaching practices to conform with the spirit of the NCTM *Standards* documents (National Council of Teachers of Mathematics [NCTM] 1989, 1991, 1995) have experienced the tension between two seemingly opposing perspectives. These are the need to allow students to construct their own mathematical knowledge (the constructivist perspective) and the need to have students learn standard mathematical ideas (the sociocultural perspective). At the same time, teachers are struggling with the demands presented by diversity. Every classroom is diverse in some form. Even students of the same race, gender, ethnicity, and culture may have very diverse levels of experience and knowledge. Many teachers seeking instructional approaches that achieve equity in learning mathematics often settle for small instructional changes that fall short of their goal. For example, it is quite common for teachers to use nonracist and nonsexist language in their classrooms or to reframe problems to reflect culturally diverse situations.

This chapter describes a high school mathematics teacher as she strives to teach meaningful mathematics to inner-city students in her bilingual (Spanish and English) classes. In the process she actually uses the diversity of her classroom to resolve the tension between the constructivist and sociocultural perspectives of learning mathematics. Although unconcerned

The authors gratefully acknowledge the helpful insights provided by William Rawles.

with the theoretical aspects of these two perspectives, she intuitively reconciles these two perspectives in complementary ways. In particular, she uses the diversity of her classroom to propel exploration in mathematics and achieve a balance between constructivist and sociocultural learning.

THE GIFT OF DIVERSITY IN MATHEMATICAL EXPLORATION: THEORETICAL PERSPECTIVES

Mathematics is considered to be fundamental for literacy in the twenty-first century. With respect to diversity, mathematics educators recently have focused on the need to provide all students with equal opportunities to learn mathematics (NCTM 1989; Secada 1990). Not enough emphasis has been placed on the benefits of using diversity as an asset in the learning process. Recently, the mathematics education community (e.g., Dossey [1992]; NCTM [1989, 1991]) has advocated that observation, experimentation, and discovery should be as much a part of mathematics as they are of natural science. Teaching mathematics should involve

> the notion that the very essence of studying mathematics is itself an exercise in exploring, conjecturing, examining, and testing—all aspects of problem solving. … Students should be given opportunities to formulate problems from given situations and create new problems by modifying the conditions of a given problem. (NCTM 1991, p. 95)

Learning through mathematical exploration in a diverse classroom is consistent with the NCTM's new vision of learning mathematics. Each student in a diverse classroom can bring unique views and perspectives to mathematical exploration in group settings. Each can learn by making unique contributions to the group exploration, and each can learn through the group's resolution of diverse points of view. Moreover, if group activities are specifically designed to take advantage of student diversity, then learning will be deep and powerful.

Learning through mathematical exploration in a diverse classroom is consistent not only with NCTM's vision but also with both the constructivist and the sociocultural perspectives of learning mathematics (Cobb 1994). According to the constructivist perspective of learning mathematics, all learners must actively construct their own knowledge through a complex process of accommodation and mutual adaptation. Learning is an individual process, and each individual responds to learning situations according to the meaning they have for him or her (Cobb 1994). From the constructivist perspective, the teacher's role is to provide appropriate environments and activities that induce students to construct their own knowledge. According to the sociocultural perspective, however, learners become acculturated by participating in cultural practices and by appropriating the contributions of experts. In this view, learning is a social process in which each individual learns mathematics through social interaction, meaning negotiation, and shared understanding. For socioculturalists,

> the teacher's role is characterized as that of mediating between students' personal meanings and the culturally established mathematical meanings of wider society. From this point of view, one of the teacher's primary responsibilities when negotiating mathematical meaning with students is to appropriate their actions into this wider system of mathematical practices. (Cobb 1994, p. 15)

Although the constructivist and sociocultural perspectives of learning mathematics appear to be different, even conflicting, Cobb (1994) argues that these two perspectives are complementary.

The learning that occurs through mathematical exploration in a diverse classroom can be understood by considering Cobb's complementary view of constructivism and socioculturalism. Students engage in group activities designed to take advantage of the diversity of the individuals. Students make individual contributions to the group activities, responding differently to the activities according to their backgrounds. By actively contributing to group exploration, individuals are constructing knowledge. Initially, the newly constructed knowledge of the individuals is often diverse, nonstandard, and incomplete. Further interaction with the group, however, modifies each individual's knowledge structure. Diverse knowledge is homogenized through the group process, especially when group discovery occurs. In other words, differences among individuals' understandings are exposed through group interaction, and through negotiation, individual knowledge becomes incorporated into shared knowledge. By engaging in group activities designed to benefit from diversity, individual students initially may construct nonstandard mathematical knowledge (constructivism), but as a group, they modify their individual constructions to conform more closely with the mathematical structures of the scientific community (socioculturalism).

THE GIFT OF DIVERSITY IN MATHEMATICAL EXPLORATION: PRACTICAL PERSPECTIVES

Our fundamental assertion is that the complementarity of constructivism and socioculturalism, as described by Cobb, is more than just theoretical. In the real world of the inner-city classroom, there are successful teachers guided by beliefs that are consistent with Cobb's views about the nature of learning. This section illustrates how Peg Miller, a high school mathematics teacher, strives to resolve the tension between constructivist and sociocultural perspectives as she guides her students through various activities designed to explore the concept of slope.

Description of the Classes

Ms. Miller is a bilingual teacher at Lake High School in a midwestern metropolitan area. Lake is a large (1800 students) high school in an area of the city with a predominately Hispanic population. The school qualifies for schoolwide Chapter 1 funding from the federal government. Students entering the school are performing well below national norms and are considered to be at risk academically. Over the years, Peg Miller and the other teachers at Lake High School have become increasingly concerned about the low percentage of students who pass algebra and who are ready for geometry. Before graduation, every student in the system is required to pass both algebra and geometry. Yet in 1993–94, only 41 percent of the ninth-grade students enrolled in algebra at Lake High School received a passing grade.

A passing grade in algebra is a prerequisite for enrolling in geometry at Lake High School. Large numbers of students barely pass with a D before moving on to a geometry class. In general, students struggle in geometry. They have trouble with measurement ideas: a majority are unable to use a ruler to measure sixteenths. They do not understand perimeter and area of rectangles, triangles, and circles and volume of rectangular solids. For them, a traditional geometry class, which places primary emphasis on proving theorems, is clearly inappropriate. In response, Peg Miller developed the Build-a-City geometry materials to improve students' achievement in bilingual (Spanish and English) classes. The ethnic groupings are Mexican, 50 percent; Puerto Rican, 45 percent; and Costa Rican, Salvadoran, and Venezuelan, 5 percent.

Description of Instruction and Materials

Over the past eight years, Peg Miller has collaborated with a few like-minded teachers at Lake High School to change the way the geometry course is organized and taught. Through these collaborations, her Build-a-City geometry project has evolved into a yearlong geometry course that incorporates all the important topics (except proof) of a standard course in tenth-grade geometry.

The students are told they will spend the year planning, designing, and constructing a model city. As the scope of the task becomes clearer, the teacher and students identify and organize the subtasks that are to be a part of this yearlong project. Figure 16.1 shows the components of the project. The experiences provided in this project lead the students to make connections between city living and formal geometric ideas that have evolved over centuries of mathematical exploration and discovery. The teacher is able to satisfy the dual demands of individual construction and standardized knowledge by furnishing good activities and skillful guidance based, in part, on comprehensive assessment.

In the spirit of the *Assessment Standards* (NCTM 1995), Ms. Miller's assessment is embedded in instruction, is multifaceted, and is used to make inferences about students' learning. She uses cognitive and affective, long- and short-term assessment to develop her instruction. Daily, she probes students' understandings as they work in groups. She also evaluates class

Subtask Categories		
Groundwork	**Construction**	**Details and Finishing**
Geometric Topics	**Geometric Topics**	**Geometric Topics**
• Measurement of lines and angles • Inductive and deductive reasoning • Coordinate graphing • Similarity • Parallel and perpendicular lines • Right triangles • Pythagorean theorem • Slope, rate, and scale	• Application of triangles • Application of properties of polygons and circles • Symmetry • Similarity • Congruence • Parallel and perpendicular lines • Pythagorean theorem • Simple trigonometry • Geometric solids • Slope, rate, and scale	• Area • Surface area • Volume • Tessellation • Networks • Locus • Slope, rate, and scale
Tasks	**Tasks**	**Tasks**

Preliminary planning, including the following:
 	
• The choice of a "global" location based on geographic, economic, cultural, and political concerns
• A more specific site selection based on the availability of sites and local geography
• Surveying and platting the city
• City planning, including water and sewer facilities, electrical and gas networks, and zoning
	Detailed drawings and construction of the following:
	
	• Infrastructure:
	  Roads and bridges
	  Parking
	  Sewers
	  Electrical networks
	  Gas networks
	  Water towers
	  Other utilities
	• Buildings
	  Municipal
	  Public
	  Business
	  Industrial
	  Apartment
	• Private homes
		All finishing work, including the following:
		
		• Landscaping
		• Tiling
		• Laying concrete (on driveways, patios, etc.)
		• Painting
		• Connecting utilities
		• Determining other details like expenses for heating, cooling, water, and sewer

Fig. 16.1. Components of the Build-a-City project

work and homework. Weekly, she evaluates students' journal writing as well as their work on multiday activities. Every six weeks, she administers individual performance tasks, and she requires completed projects, group reports, and self-assessments. Portfolios are obligatory each semester, and at the end of the year the students must write essays describing their perceived cognitive and affective growth.

In part, she uses inferences from her assessments to shape the amount and type of guidance she gives students. The following three examples of teaching slope illustrate how Ms. Miller's guidance is more or less directive according to her perception of the mix of three different factors: student, topic, and objective.

Teaching Slope

One of the important ideas in high school mathematics is that of slope and its connections to other mathematical and real-world topics. Unfortunately, most beginning algebra classes study slope almost exclusively in relation to graphs of linear equations, which are presented as abstract lines on coordinate axes. This standard approach is of limited effectiveness; the majority of Ms. Miller's students do not understand the concept, even though they have all passed beginning algebra. The standard approach to slope has at least four shortcomings, according to Ms. Miller: the approach does not build on students' informal knowledge; it does not illustrate the usefulness of slope in any realistic way; it does not connect slope to other mathematical concepts such as rate, ratio, and proportion; and most students find the formal definition of slope difficult and uninteresting.

In Peg Miller's Build-a-City geometry curriculum, the theme of slope permeates all three categories of subtasks (fig. 16.1) and serves as a thread that ties together many different algebraic and geometric ideas. The activities are designed to build on the students' existing knowledge, experience, and interests. Some of the activities with slope as a central theme are map reading (e.g., scale, examining the obliqueness of diagonal streets), global city planning (e.g., grades of roads, glide ratios of airplanes, sewer-system design), building design (e.g., ramps for the disabled, roof pitch, stair design, scale drawings), and budget estimation (e.g., unit price and other rates).

Peg Miller's approach is to plan activities designed to use students' existing knowledge, engage students in mathematically productive group activity, and gradually lead them to standardize their ideas through group negotiation. When students are given the responsibility to plan, design, and build their own city, the usefulness of the mathematical notion of slope in many of its manifestations becomes evident over time. Through these activities students can establish connections among mathematical topics they had considered to be unrelated.

Slope in roofs: Constructivist emphasis

The following example describes one of the many lessons that Peg Miller uses to teach the concept of slope. The example is structured to show how Ms. Miller's beliefs influence her pedagogical decision making. In particular, it shows how her belief in the complementarity of constructivism and socioculturalism drives her choices of activities and methods.

Although the classroom is diverse in terms of culture, nationality, family, and educational background, Peg Miller has identified some commonalities among the students, which she uses in planning the curriculum. Most of her students have experienced a very concrete approach to life and learning. They generally do not have role models who think and reason conditionally, so they are not used to hypothetical reasoning. As a result, the majority of the students have a difficult time reasoning abstractly—especially about unfamiliar ideas. These commonalities have led Ms. Miller to make two basic assumptions about planning lessons on slope: First, her lessons must build on her students' existing knowledge. Second, her students need concrete situations to help them learn new ideas. These two assumptions are of central importance in her lesson for teaching slope by using the pitch of roofs of different styles.

Ms. Miller realizes that she can use her students' daily experience to contribute to the exploration of slope. She knows her students have existing knowledge about steepness, which they have learned through their daily use of stairs, hills, roads, and so on. Her students also know that the roofs of buildings have different pitches. After a class discussion of various architectural styles of roofs, she prompts her students to examine the steepness of two different styles of roof: the A-frame and the ranch. She draws the outline of the roofs on a grid, hoping that some students will use the grid to quantify their comparisons (see fig. 16.2a). Some students do just that. For example, one student says the roof of the A-frame is steeper than that of the ranch because the height (CE) of the A-frame is greater than the height (DE) of the ranch. However, a few students disagree. They say the roof of the ranch is steeper than that of the A-frame because the span (AB) of the ranch roof is greater than the span (FG) of the A-frame roof.

Neither of the two views expressed by these students is mathematically correct, since they focus only on a single dimension. Ms. Miller realizes that she cannot simply explain the correct answer and move on. So she encourages her students to resolve the disparities through group discussion. She starts the discussion by asking the students who believed the A-frame roof is steeper to explain their reasoning more fully. One student says, "If you pretend that these two roofs are hills, the first hill will be harder to climb than the second." Other students nod their head, agreeing that the explanation is reasonable.

Ms. Miller decides that her students are relying on experientially based knowledge. So Ms. Miller draws the roof of a Tudor house (see fig. 16.2b) that has the same base as the A-frame roof and the same height as the ranch roof. She then asks students to compare the steepness of the roof of the Tudor to that of the A-frame and the ranch, respectively. One student raises her hand and says that the A-frame roof is steeper than the Tudor roof because they start from the same point but the A-frame rises more quickly than the Tudor. Peg Miller then asks the student who thought the ranch roof was steeper than the A-frame roof to compare the ranch and the Tudor roofs. According to his previous reasoning, the

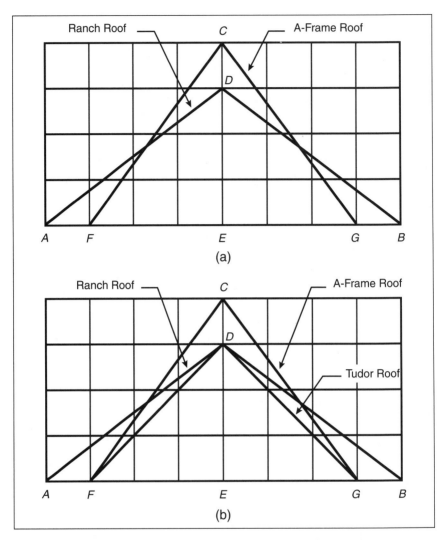

Fig. 16.2. Comparisons of the pitches of roofs of different styles

ranch roof would be steeper than the Tudor roof, but the previous student's explanation has convinced him that the Tudor roof is steeper than the ranch roof. He says, "The ranch starts farther left than the Tudor, but they both come to the same point. So it will be easier to climb the ranch than the Tudor." Peg Miller now directs the students' attention back to the comparison of the A-frame and ranch roofs. "So, who can tell us why the A-frame is steeper than the ranch?" Yolanda raises her hand and says, "Since the Tudor is steeper than the ranch and the A-frame is steeper than the Tudor, then the A-frame is steeper than the ranch."

It is still early in the year, and Peg Miller realizes that these constructivist conversations will later form the basis for an activity on the use of ratios to compare the steepness of roofs. For now, however, she does not pursue the issue.

Slope in ramps for persons with disabilities: Sociocultural emphasis

Another assumption that Ms. Miller has made about her students is that they are willing to work hard if they think they will experience success. Consequently, she organizes her activities so that the students experience some success quickly. For this reason, she begins most topics with some sort of hands-on activity with objects.

The following activity has a sociocultural emphasis. Ms. Miller thinks a sociocultural slant gives the students a greater likelihood of experiencing the success needed to encourage hard work. Continuing the theme of slope, Ms. Miller introduces her students to the federal requirements associated with the design and construction of ramps for persons with disabilities (see fig. 16.3). By this time the students have been in the class for more than a semester. Most of the students have established an informal concept of slope, which needs to become more formal, stable, and connected to other mathematical ideas. Ms. Miller decides her students' concept of slope is not yet stable enough for them to design their own ramps. Hence, she decides that she will design the ramp for her students and ask them to determine if the design falls within the federal requirements. Figure 16.3 presents the student worksheet. Ms. Miller realizes that the numbers on the design will make little sense to most of her students until they actually fold the ramp into a three-dimensional object. In other words, her students will not be able to determine if the design falls within the federal requirements solely by analyzing the labeled two-dimensional figure. So she provides students with step-by-step instructions for the hands-on construction of the ramps.

The students are expected to cut out and assemble the design shown in figure 16.3 into a three-dimensional object and determine if it complies with federal regulations. Because the students do not have to design the ramp, the success rate is quite high. They are freed to concentrate on the mechanics of building the ramps and on the relationships between the plane figures in the resulting three-dimensional object. As a result, instead of having a classroom of frustrated students, Ms. Miller has a roomful of hard-working, inquisitive teenaged students who are willing to discuss the important relationships between the steepness of the ramps and the sides of the triangles. Note the change of emphasis from the previous example, in which the learning was based mainly on the students' prior knowledge and experience (constructivism). In this second example, the students were given an incorrectly designed two-dimensional net as well as very strict guidance about the way to properly assemble it and judge its compliance (socioculturalism). In the end, the students were able to discuss

The following federal requirements apply to ramps for persons with disabilities:
1. The maximum slope of any ramp is 1/12.
2. A ramp that is longer than 30 feet must have a landing.
3. The landing must be as long as the ramp is wide.

Examine the following design of a ramp and determine if it falls within the federal requirements. If it does, explain why. If it does not, correct the design so that it will fall within federal requirements.

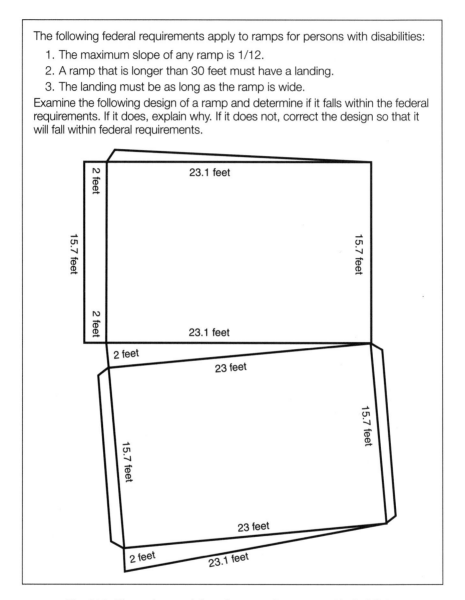

Fig. 16.3. The student worksheet for ramps for persons with disabilities

the noncompliance of their ramps with the federal guidelines and gain insight into the culturally accepted notion of slope as it applies to ramps for disabled persons. In subsequent classes, Peg Miller asks her students to correct the design so that it falls within the federal requirements for ramps for people with disabilities.

Slope in scale drawing: Complementary treatment

The fourth assumption that Peg Miller has made about her students relates to the importance of group processes in their learning. For the majority of these students, the most important people in their lives are their peers. Some of the students come from broken homes where they have been abused or neglected. These students find more acceptance, support, and motivation through their interaction with other students than they do from adult figures. Furthermore, by designing activities that require collaboration, negotiation, the resolution of differences, and shared responsibilities, Ms. Miller is taking advantage of the diversity that exists within her classroom.

As the year comes to a close, the students are fully engaged in the actual construction of the buildings in their city using Tyco blocks. To encourage hard work, Peg Miller maximizes her students' chance for success by allowing pairs of students to choose the city buildings they would like to build and by allowing students to build the buildings of their choice *before* they draw the plans. Finally, the students are shown the technique of using proportions to determine the relationship between the lengths on their drawing and the associated lengths of the full-scale building.

Each student brings unique views and perspectives into the group mathematical activity of maintaining the correct scale while planning, building, and drawing the models. During the process of building the models, some clear examples of learning through diversity invariably occur. For example, students often choose architectural styles based on their cultural backgrounds. Furthermore, the buildings the students choose for the city reflect their backgrounds and cultures. Some girls choose to build day-care centers because of their life experiences with children of their own. Other students choose sports arenas, shelters for the homeless, cultural centers, and so forth. Different buildings require different designs; they also exhibit roofs with different slopes, proportional relationships, and so on. Such differences are the subject of student discussion and learning.

Diversity also contributes to the quality of the group learning when the students make architectural drawings of their model buildings. For example, students in the art program are much more prepared to do the drawing that is required in the Build-a-City project. These students know how to use the T square and triangle to make parallel and perpendicular lines. They are able to help those that do not. Also, some students are very concerned with detail and precision. Because they are working as a group, these students encourage the others to pay attention to detail.

Once students make their architectural drawings, Ms. Miller asks them to use the scale to determine the dimensions of the actual building. From previous activities during the year, the students have learned the relationship between slope and ratio. Here the students learn to use the formal technique of solving proportions to find the dimensions of the actual building.

RESOLUTION: CONGRUENCE BETWEEN THEORY AND PRACTICE

Peg Miller's approach to teaching echoes the concerns of Ball (1993, p. 375):

> How do I create experiences for my students that connect with what they now know and care about but that also transcend the present? How do I value their interests and also connect them to ideas and traditions growing out of centuries of mathematical exploration and invention?

Peg Miller does not formally theorize about the tension between constructivism and socioculturalism, but her pragmatic approach to teaching meaningful mathematics reconciles these viewpoints. Having successfully combined the two approaches in her curriculum, she can move back and forth between the two complementary perspectives.

Of crucial importance is that Peg Miller's beliefs are very personal, experience-based theories about successful mathematics teaching. They have evolved over time, on the basis of her curriculum trials and revisions, successes and failures. They are mostly intuitive and informal, yet they are the source of tremendous drive and energy. It is interesting that they are also the source of a lingering sense of guilt. Just as a large portion of the mathematics education community views constructivism and socioculturalism as competing, so, too, does Peg Miller feel some conflict between her closely held dual beliefs about the nature of learning. She has struggled these past eight years to reconcile these opposing points of view and to apply them in her classroom. Yet from time to time, the reconciliation she has established in her mind is threatened by others around her. At these times she is bothered by feelings of self-doubt and guilt about the "impurity" of her constructivist teaching. Although she firmly believes that students must construct their knowledge, she knows that her teaching is not "purely" constructivist. Through twenty years of experience, she has decided that learning through a "pure" constructivist approach is neither possible nor desirable in a normal high school geometry class.

Hence, she takes a pragmatic approach that adopting the constructivist perspective "must be justified in terms of its potential to ... contribute to the improvement of students' education" (Cobb 1994, p. 18). She recognizes that this adoption must be done in context; that is, it must be done while addressing specific problems and issues. The approach she takes depends on what "makes sense" when she addresses the situated problems of her classroom.

Sometimes her approach is more clearly that of the socioculturalist. At these times she gives preeminence to the view that learning is acculturation through careful guidance and discourse. She expects that the negotiation process between student and teacher will lean heavily toward the students' appropriation of the socially and culturally accepted ideas. However, this type of teaching is done with the implicit assumption that the students will construct their own knowledge by actively participating in classroom discourse.

At other times her approach is more that of the constructivist. In these instances, Peg Miller believes her students must create mathematics in a highly personalized, individual fashion on the basis of their existing intellectual structures. Here she expects that the negotiation process between the student and others is a process of mutual adaptation. Of course, it is implicitly assumed that the student is being guided to learn the standard mathematics of our culture.

In spite of the cognitive conflict between constructivism and sociocuturalism that Peg Miller experiences from time to time, it is clear from her teaching that these two approaches are not operationally in conflict. Instead, they are complementary approaches, each of which assumes the other as a background. But even more important, they are the pragmatic ticket out of the dilemma articulated by Ball.

CONCLUSION

This article has provided specific examples of a high school teacher's approach to using diversity as a means to reconcile issues related to constructivist and sociocultural perspectives as she guides students to explore the concept of slope. In today's era of mathematics education reform, all teachers are confronted with the challenge of reconciling these two perspectives as they teach their mathematics classes each day. The examples used in this paper convey techniques that teachers might use to reconcile these two perspectives.

REFERENCES

Ball, Deborah L. "With an Eye on the Mathematical Horizon: Dilemmas of Teaching Elementary School Mathematics." *Elementary School Journal* 93 (March 1993): 373–97.

Cobb, Paul. "Where Is the Mind? Constructivist and Sociocultural Perspectives on Mathematical Development." *Educational Researcher* 23 (October 1994): 13–20.

Dossey, John A. "The Nature of Mathematics: Its Role and Its Influence." In *Handbook of Research on Mathematics Teaching and Learning,* edited by Douglas A. Grouws, pp. 39–48. New York: Macmillan Publishing Co., 1992.

National Council of Teachers of Mathematics. *Curriculum and Evaluation Standards for School Mathematics.* Reston, Va.: National Council of Teachers of Mathematics, 1989.

———. *Professional Standards for Teaching Mathematics.* Reston, Va.: National Council of Teachers of Mathematics, 1991.

———. *Assessment Standards for School Mathematics.* Reston, Va.: National Council of Teachers of Mathematics, 1995.

Secada, Walter G. "Student Diversity and Mathematics Education Reform." In *Dimensions of Cognitive Instruction,* edited by L. Idol and B. F. Jones, pp. 295–330. Hillsdale, N.J.: Lawrence Erlbaum Associates, 1990.

17

Dialectal Variations in the Language of Mathematics
A Source for Multicultural Experiences

Héctor Hirigoyen

Mathematicians are a species of Frenchmen: if you say something to them, they translate it into their own language and presto! it is something entirely different.

—Goethe, *Maxims*

DAVID Pimm (1987) devoted an entire book to the idea that mathematics is a language. One of the consequences of this idea is the use of foreign-language teaching techniques for mathematics. Mathematics education literature has spent some time on this idea. The Cockcroft report of 1982 states, "Mathematics provides a means of communication which is powerful and concise—this is the principal reason for teaching mathematics to all children."

One of the most interesting aspects of language—the idea of dialectal variations—is almost always ignored. The belief that the language of mathematics is universal is widespread. Unfortunately, *universal* in most American classrooms has a rather provincial tinge. We talk about multiculturalism yet ignore it in the language of mathematics. It is this richness of variations that allows students to affirm their culture and become active participants in the classroom discourse. Diversity becomes a challenge and a gift.

What do we mean by dialectal variations? Any teacher of mathematics in a large urban setting is aware, for example, that children from other parts of the world divide differently. I remember being chastised as a youth for crossing my sevens; crossing sevens, however, is popular now. This article provides a brief sample of these dialectal expressions to open the discourse in mathematics classes with students from all cultures. Exploring different modes of expression can be a source of inspiration and discussion in the classroom.

NUMBER REPRESENTATION

Besides the obvious number names and their relationships, arithmetical notation offers a wealth of dialectal variations. Rather than the decimal point, many countries use the comma as a separator. In Great Britain, however, a raised dot is used.

The writing of numerals is also interesting. Our 7 looks very much like what many cultures write as a 1. Are there advantages to their method over what we use? A German professor of mine pointed out that it is very difficult to differentiate the numeral for 111 from the absolute value of 1 if one does not use the "hat" on the 1. In other words, $|1|$ should not look like 111. For this reason many cultures cross the symbol for seven, distinguishing it from the way they write the symbol for one.

"Billion" is a curious linguistic affair. It would be interesting to investigate why the number we refer to as a *billion* in the United States is quite different from a billion in most other cultures. In the United States a billion is 10^9. In many countries, including Great Britain, France, Spain, and French- and Spanish-speaking countries, a billion refers to 10^{12}. This definition has dramatic implications for all other number names beyond a million. Table 17.1 illustrates the system.

TABLE 17.1
American and British Number Names for 10^6 and Beyond

	United States	Great Britain
10^6	million	million
10^9	billion	milliard
10^{12}	trillion	billion
10^{15}	quadrillion	thousand billion
10^{18}	quintillion	trillion

Number names are also a source of dialectal variations. Languages influenced by ancient Chinese, such as Japanese, Mandarin, and Vietnamese, tend to read numbers following the order of the digits, thus fifteen is read as "ten, five." In the Romance languages (those derived from Latin), the number names between eleven and fifteen do not have any reference to a grouping by ten, as four*teen*, fif*teen*, and so on. In Arabic one says, "Four, ten" for fourteen. In French, the number following sixty–nine (*soixante-neuf*) is "sixty-ten" (*soixante-dix*), eighty is "four-twenties"(*quatre-vingts*), and ninety is "four-twenties-ten" (*quatre-vingt-dix*).

Using fingers to represent numbers is also dialectal. In most of Europe a person raises the thumb, not the index finger, to indicate one. Two is usually represented by raising the thumb and the index finger. Thus, an American entering a European restaurant and requesting a table for two by raising the index and the middle finger is going to be misunderstood as wanting a table for three, since that is the visual image of the number three in most of Europe.

COMPUTATIONAL ALGORITHMS IN ARITHMETIC

The algorithms and notations usually taught in the United States are by no means universal. In many countries, division is presented in dramatically different ways. For instance, the long–division problem

$$
\begin{array}{r}
45 \\
8\overline{)360} \\
\underline{32} \\
40 \\
\underline{40} \\
0
\end{array}
$$

looks like this in most countries:

$$
\begin{array}{l}
360\ \underline{|8} \\
40\ \ 45 \\
\ \ 0
\end{array}
$$

In Miami, the method is commonly referred to as *Cuban division,* since it was first noted with the Cuban influx in the 1960s. The first printed example of the method, however, is in Calandri's *Arithmetic,* printed in Florence, Italy, in 1491. The method is used in many cultures, for example, Arabic, Lao, and Vietnamese. The method used in the United States seems to come to us from the Arabs through the Italians and was introduced by Greenwood in 1729. (Greenwood's *Arithmetic,* published anonymously, gave the United States not only this algorithm but also the use of the comma as a decimal separator and of *billion* for 10^9.) A similar algorithm is employed in the Netherlands and Poland.

In Japan, subtraction is performed by adding the "nines complement":

$$
\begin{array}{ccc}
531 & & 531 \\
-398 & \rightarrow & +601 \\
& & \overline{1\,132} \rightarrow 133
\end{array}
$$

The nines complement is formed by subtracting each digit in the subtrahend from 9. The nines complement of the subtrahend is then added to the original minuend. The "extra" digit is added to the ones place. Understanding this algorithm requires quite a bit of number sense.

Many other algorithms are found throughout the world. Acquainting students with several is an alternative to the usual process of presenting only one prescribed form, and it provides many students with cultural validation.

GEOMETRY

Teachers have many opportunities to discuss dialectal variations in geometry. The first of these is in the symbols themselves. In many countries the symbols for angle and triangle are placed above the name of the figure, not before it. Thus, $\triangle ABC$ becomes

$$\overset{\triangle}{ABC},$$

and $\angle ABC$ becomes

$$\overset{\wedge}{ABC}.$$

Using a bar above letters to indicate a segment is not universal. In many European countries, segments are designated by using brackets, for example, $[AB]$, whereas (AB) indicates the line and $\overline{AB}$ is often used for the length of the segment.

Another variation involves abbreviations. In Russian, the abbreviations for trigonometric functions are written in the Roman alphabet rather than the Cyrillic alphabet. In Spain and many Spanish-speaking countries the abbreviation for tangent is *tg* rather than *tan*. There are also variations in vocabulary. In Spanish, for example, the word for circle, *círculo*, refers to a circular region (disk); for the formal geometric meaning of *circle*, one uses the word *circunferencia*. The equivalent of *circumference* in Spanish is *longitud de la circunferencia* (length of the circle). The Spanish is closer to the usage in Euclid's *Elements*. The French use *cercle* and *disque*, and one must say *la longueur du cercle* for *circumference*.

In most Romance languages, a single word, *mediatrix*, conveys the meaning of perpendicular bisector. The word *trapezoid* is reserved for the quadrilateral without any parallel sides, whereas *trapezium* is used when there is one pair of parallel sides. (This is opposite to American-English usage.)

ALGEBRA

Algebraic vocabulary and syntax seem to be a bit more uniform. Here, too, however, there are variations. Linear functions are known as affine functions in many parts of the world. In referring to functions, the terms *injective* and *surjective* are used in place of *one-one* and *onto*, respectively. In the former Soviet Union, a period, rather than a comma, is used to separate the coordinates of a point.

CONCLUSIONS

The language of mathematics creates wonderful opportunities to explore a variety of topics and at the same time validate children's cultures. Mathematics teachers need to be aware of this variety so as not to make incorrect inferences about students' mathematical power. What may be perceived as a lack of understanding of mathematics may very well be a lack of understanding of the mathematical dialect. We must make a conscious effort to teach the language component of our subject.

Children from other cultures must be allowed to use their own processes. Forcing them into any particular algorithm not only is confusing but also may be demeaning. Encouraging them to present their methods validates their culture as well as their mathematical understanding. Classroom investigations of mathematical usage in other cultures are useful and exciting activities and an excellent opportunity to produce interdisciplinary units.

References

Cockcroft, W. H., ed. *Mathematics Counts.* London: Her Majesty's Stationery Office, 1982.

Pimm, David. *Speaking Mathematically: Communication in the Mathematics Classroom.* London: Routledge,& Kegan Paul, 1987.

Suggestions for Further Reading

Note: Some of these publications are series of textbooks for use by schoolchildren in various countries. The list is not exhaustive by any means but gives an indication of mathematical usage in different cultures.

Antibi, André, et al. *Math—nouveau transmath.* Paris: Editions Nathan, 1993.

Artigue, Christian, et al. *Mathématiques—collection Terracher.* Paris: Hachette, 1988.

Baruk, Stella. *Dictionnaire de mathématiques élémentaires.* Paris: Editions du Seuil, 1992.

Bonnefond, Gérard, et al. *Mathématiques—collection Pythagore.* Paris: Editions Hatier, 1987.

Bourbaki, Nicolas. *Eléments de mathématiques.* Paris: Masson, 1940–94.

de Guzmán, Miguel, et al. *Matemáticas—colección Anaya.* Madrid: Anaya Publishing Co., 1989.

James and James Mathematics Dictionary, 4th ed. New York: Van Nostrand Reinhold Co., 1976. (The author of this article warns that this dictionary has some serious mistranslations.)

Menninger, Karl. *Number Words and Number Symbols.* New York: Dover Publications, 1969.

Peck, Sharon, Pauline Simmons, and William Stark. *Math in a Limited English World.* Lansing, Mich.: Lansing School District, 1986.

Ramos, Antonio, et al. *Matemáticas—Santillana.* Madrid: Santillana Publishing Co., 1984.

Repiso, Consuelo S. *Diccionario de mathemáticas de E.G.B. a C.O.U.* Madrid: Editoral Escuela Española, 1986.

Smith, David E. *History of Mathematics.* New York: Dover Publications, 1958.

Such, Simone, et al. *Mathématiques—nouvelle collection Durrande.* Paris: Bordas, 1987.

Warufsel, André. *Diccionario razonado de matemáticas.* Madrid: Tecnos, 1972.

18

Integrating Mathematics and American Indian Cultures

Lyn Taylor

Rich opportunities for integrating mathematics with American Indian cultures are available to teachers. Teachers can create opportunities for students to make meaningful connections among mathematics, social studies, art, language arts, science, and physical education. At the core of integrated instruction lies the belief that knowing is multidimensional and requires information from a variety of sources. The real world is integrated, not fragmented; problems, whether childhood or adult, are connected and usually not isolated; and problem solving requires the skills and knowledge of several subjects.

Because content and procedures transcend individual disciplines, connected teaching is a natural way to teach and learn (Taylor and Quattromani in press). Lauritzen and Jaeger (1994) "use the word transdisciplinary to emphasize a transcendence beyond the boundaries of traditional. The interconnections are so vast they seem limitless; the theme, strategies, and skills seem to merge when set in a real-life context" (p. 581). Furthermore, it is likely that connected teaching provides a more equitable and meaningful environment for reaching the needs of all students, particularly females (Belenky et al. 1986) and persons of color (Secada 1992). Such a meaningful environment was created in the author's class at the 1995 Mount Holyoke SummerMath Program as well as in the 1989 Colorado School of Mines American Indian Program that the author evaluated. The culturally relevant mathematical experiences of middle school American Indian students in the summer program appeared to facilitate their developing positive attitudes toward mathematics (Taylor, Stevens, and Tonso 1989).

This chapter describes several problem–centered classroom activities that I have developed and used successfully with students of different ages. The Pueblo activities incorporate many standards from the *Curriculum and Evaluation Standards for School Mathematics* (NCTM 1989) as well as integrate Pueblo Indian culture with mathematics. Other educators with whom I have shared the following model-building activities have used them with students as young as third graders and as old as high school seniors. Graduate students in education and middle-grades teachers can become actively engaged in these activities as well. The estimation and literature activities have been used successfully with students from first through seventh grades.

MODEL BUILDING

Students become actively engaged in reasoning, estimating, measuring, and communicating as they create a three-dimensional scale model. As a preliminary activity a teacher can use her or his classroom, school, or other buildings the students are familiar with to build a scaled-down model. Taking actual measurements of the classroom gives students a hands-on experience with measuring. Scaling down the actual measurements to create a model involves students in making meaningful calculations.

An excellent resource book I have used is *The Complete Guide to Building Taos Pueblo* (Jordan 1989). This paperback-book kit, published by the Museum of New Mexico Press, includes materials to build an authentic scale model of the Taos Pueblo in New Mexico, as well as an accompanying story about the pueblo. Since "Taos Pueblo is the most famous Indian community in the United States" (Jordan 1989, p. 1), I have found that an activity such as this interests many people. Figure 18.1 is a photograph of a pueblo built by SummerMath students. The kit includes fifty-two buildings. One kit can be used for an entire class or a large team of students.

Fig. 18.1. An almost complete pueblo built by the author's 1995 SummerMath class of high school young women

Materials for a Construction Activity

Each group will need one Building Taos Pueblo kit, heavy paper for creating the second pueblo or scale model of your classroom (I have found recycled manila file folders work very well), scissors, glue, tape, measuring tapes or rulers, flat wooden toothpicks, calculators, and pencils. The sheets of roofing materials included in *Hands-on Design Math* (Reif 1994) resemble adobe bricks and can be used for building scale models of pueblos. Figure 18.2 depicts several student-created and -decorated buildings. One photo in figure 18.3 shows SummerMath students using these materials.

Fig. 18.2. Student-created buildings

Fig. 18.3. Students use the grid markings to assist them in measuring and creating scaled-up models in which the dimensions are doubled.

The grid markings on the materials make them especially useful for the scaling activities. The roofing materials have grid markings on the back, and other sheets have grid markings on both sides to use for practice buildings. Figure 18.3 depicts students using these markings to help them measure and scale up their second models.

We have used metric measurement tools for this activity, which serves as a meaningful context for students to become comfortable with using the metric system, especially centimeters and meters.

Building Procedure

Distribute one pueblo kit to each large group or class. The group selects the scaling factor they would like to use to create a second pueblo model (2 and 3 are popular scaling factors; more challenging ones might be 1/2 or 3/2). Then the building begins. Each person constructs at least one original printed building from the cut-out pieces included with the book. Then each student creates a second building that is proportionally scaled by the chosen factor.

Imagine all the problem solving, measuring, and other mathematics skills that the students use during this problem-centered activity. When all fifty-two buildings are completed, they are assembled into a scaled pueblo. (The inside cover of the book contains a map to use as a base for the village; see fig. 18.1.) The second scaled pueblo can be assembled on posterboard or wood of an appropriate size. Students can make trees, ladders, kiva fireplaces, and other additions to their pueblo.

Mathematical Communication Follow-Up

After completing the pueblo, it is good to have the students write about their experience and the mathematics they used. Journal comments can be shared in small-group discussions. One student was heard to say, "I am surprised how large the scaled-up pueblo is!" Shared journal comments can lead to a discussion of volume and surface area. Small blocks or centimeter cubes can be used to calculate the volume of various buildings (before they are attached to the base); students can be challenged to estimate the number of cubes that will fit in a given building. After placing a few blocks into the building, students can be given the opportunity to change their estimate.

The dimensions were doubled in the second pueblo created by the SummerMath students, which quadrupled the surface area of the kit buildings. The volume of the second model's buildings is eight times that of the original. Many students were surprised to see how much the surface area and volume were enlarged by just doubling the dimensions of the building.

The following are some other journal comments: "I now really understand measuring with fractions better. I used to just call anything between two whole numbers a half. When I tried to do this with my building dimensions it messed up the building." "Next, I'm going to challenge myself by building a more complicated structure." Most of the buildings in the pueblo kit are rectangular solids. The decorated building depicted in figure 18.2 is one of the few that are more-complicated solids.

After building a pueblo during a workshop, two in-service elementary school teachers brought me a gift of another kit; it includes several Victorian homes (Gillon 1979) with some interesting angles and octagonal rooms. It came with a wonderful note about their mathematical learning experiences with building the pueblo and about their attitudes toward learning and teaching mathematics having become much more positive!

Pueblo Activities That Integrate Other Subjects

The Building Taos Pueblo kit comes with twenty-four minipages of text, pictures, and a recipe for Pueblo bread. Each minipage is one-fourth of a book page. It is made to be cut apart and assembled into a small booklet to accompany the pueblo. This minibook can be used before the pueblo activity as an introductory social studies lesson. Students can learn that adobe bricks are created of sun-dried earth mixed with straw, canals are wooden drain spouts in pueblo buildings, hornos are "round adobe ovens used for baking bread," and *pueblo* is a Spanish word for *village* that was "given by the Spaniards to the modern Indians of New Spain (New Mexico) because of the large, complex adobe villages they built" (Jordan 1989, p. 4), and so on. Taos Pueblo has been continuously occupied since 1400. Except for the increase in size, the pueblo has not changed appreciably since the 1700s.

After building the pueblo, students can be asked to create their own books about the pueblo. They can include drawings as well as text. Students preferring to create a story can use creative writing. Storytelling is very important to Pueblo people and is a natural extension activity. (See Livo [1985] for further discussion of storytelling.)

Booklets can be made by individual students or teams of students. A whole class can even make a "big" book. Although some may think that only elementary school students enjoy creating "big" books, I know of several classes of middle school students—including eighth graders—that found the activity very meaningful.

Making the Pueblo bread recipe included in the kit can lead to a hands-on measurement experience that integrates mathematics with family studies. Students can be challenged to double or halve the recipe. Experiencing mathematics can enhance students' understanding. Doing so requires recognizing relationships among different mathematical topics and being able to use mathematics in other curriculum areas as well as in daily in life. The connections that we want students to explore should reflect authentic learning experiences rather than contrived ones.

INTEGRATING MATHEMATICS AND LITERATURE

The Popcorn Book (de Paola 1978) tells a story about the history of popcorn and its use among American Indians. De Paola tells us that "popcorn was discovered by the Indian people in the Americas many thousands of years ago" (p. 10). He also writes that "archeologists found some popped corn that was 5600 years old" in a "bat cave in New Mexico" (p. 11). This book creates the context for a popcorn-estimation activity that incorporates various Standards. The estimation jar can be filled with popcorn kernels or popped popcorn. Since popcorn kernels are fairly small, students find estimating kernels more challenging than estimating the number of pieces of popped popcorn. Estimating the weight of the kernels and popped corn are other challenging activities.

The Popcorn Book can introduce a study of author Tomie de Paola. *The Legend of the Indian Paintbrush* (de Paola 1988) is an Indian story that was retold to de Paola and published by Putnam. Other literature books that can be used to create integrated lessons include *Turquoise Boy, A Navajo Legend* (Cohlene 1990), *Iktomi and the Boulder, a Plains Indian Story* (Goble 1988), and *Children of the Earth and Sky* (Krensky 1991).

AMERICAN INDIAN MATHEMATICS ACTIVITIES

Another culturally appropriate activity can use designs from American Indian artwork. These designs can be reproduced on the computer by using Logo. Bradley (1992) discusses this idea further by using a Sioux "four directions" sign; Bradley (1993) uses a Navajo blanket pattern. Bahti (1983) is a good resource for southwestern Indian designs and information. Bradley (1975) discusses ways that Indian beadwork can be used to teach mathematics. An *Arithmetic Teacher* article by Taylor, Stevens, Peregoy, and Bath (1991) discusses several activities involving American Indian mathematics and designs.

Pattern blocks are very useful in creating additional design patterns. Elementary and middle school students can be challenged to extend a design created by their peers. This extension can be done with manipulative materials or on the iconic level by using drawings. Geoboards can be used effectively to have students create designs that are representative of a particular culture. The mathematics of the student-created designs can then be explored and discussed. The teacher may direct students to create a design that has line symmetry. I have also used the geoboard to have students create a design that has rotational symmetry or translational symmetry. During my SummerMath class I was surprised to find out how few of the high school students knew about symmetry. Three knew about line symmetry, but none knew about rotational or translational symmetry. Figure 18.4 shows a student-taken photograph depicting line, translational, and rotational symmetry. Symmetry and geometric patterns can be explored by using a Mira with designs from books or student-created designs. A Mira can also be used to create the other half of a student-created totem pole. See figure 18.5. Totem poles are typically carved by North American Indians from western Canada and the northwestern sections of

Fig. 18.4. This photograph taken by a student for posing a problem on symmetry demonstrates line, translational, and rotational symmetry.

Can you draw the other half of this totem pole?

Fig. 18.5. A student-created totem pole worksheet

the United States. Some people falsely believe that all American Indian people carve totem poles.

CONCLUDING THOUGHTS

This chapter has presented information about planning integrated lessons as well as several culturally connected activities that can make mathematics more appealing to students. These activities are designed to be noncompetitive and cooperative, which has likely contributed to their successful implementation with American Indian students. They are also beneficial for non-Indian students.

REFERENCES

Bahti, Mark. *Southwestern Indian Arts and Crafts.* Las Vegas: The Story Behind the Scenery Publications, 1983.

Belenky, Mary Field, Blythe McVicker Clinchy, Nancy Rule Goldberger, and Jill Mattuck Tarule. *Women's Ways of Knowing.* New York: Basic Books, 1986.

Bradley, Claudette. "Native American Beadwork Can Teach Mathematics." Unpublished manuscript available from Harvard University Library, 1975.

———."Teaching Mathematics with Technology: Making a Navajo Blanket Design with Logo." *Arithmetic Teacher* 40 (May 1993): 520–23.

———."Teaching Mathematics with Technology: The Four Directions Indian Beadwork Design with Logo." *Arithmetic Teacher* 39 (May 1992): 46–49.

Cohlene, Terri. *Turquoise Boy, a Navajo Legend*. Mahwah, N.J.: Watermill Press, 1990.

de Paola, Tomie. *The Legend of the Indian Paintbrush*. New York: G. P. Putnam's Sons, 1988.

———. *The Popcorn Book*. New York: Scholastic Book Services, 1978.

Gillon, Edmund V., Jr. *Cut and Assemble Victorian Houses*. New York: Dover Publications, 1979.

Goble, Paul. *Iktomi and the Boulder, a Plains Indian Story*. New York: Orchard Books, 1988.

Jordan, Louann C. *The Complete Guide to Building Taos Pueblo*. Santa Fe, N.M.: Museum of New Mexico Press, 1989.

Krensky, Stephen. *Children of the Earth and Sky*. New York: Scholastic, 1991.

Lauritzen, Carol, and Michael Jaeger. "Language Arts Teacher Education within a Transdisciplinary Curriculum." *Language Arts* 71 (December 1994): 581–87.

Livo, Norma. *Storytelling*. Denver, Colo.: Libraries Unlimited, 1985.

National Council of Teachers of Mathematics. *Curriculum and Evaluation Standards for School Mathematics*. Reston, Va.: National Council of Teachers of Mathematics, 1989.

Reif, Daniel K. *Hands-On Design Math*. Palo Alto, Calif.: Dale Seymour Publications, 1994.

Secada, Walter. "Race, Ethnicity, Social Class, Language, and Achievement in Mathematics." In *Handbook of Research on Mathematics Teaching and Learning*, edited by Douglas A. Grouws, pp. 623–60. New York: Macmillan Publishing Co., 1992.

Taylor, Lyn, and Libby Quattromani. "Integrating Elementary School Mathematics with Other Subjects." In *Mathematics Education: An Encyclopedia*, edited by Louise Grinstein and Sally I. Lipsey. New York: Garland Publishing, in press.

Taylor, Lyn, Ellen Stevens, John J. Peregoy, and Barbara Bath. "American Indians, Mathematical Attitudes, and the *Standards*." *Arithmetic Teacher* 38 (February 1991): 14–21.

Taylor, Lyn, Ellen Stevens, and Karen Tonso. *American Indian Student Summer Math Camp*. Final Report to the National Science Foundation, 1989.

19

Grounded Practice
Lessons in Anasazi Mathematics Emerging from the Multicultural Classroom

Clo Mingo

PRACTICE 1

The lights dim in the noisy, crowded classroom. Zuni Pueblo flute music quickly grabs the attention of the four or five seated students clustered around each of six slightly mismatched tables that furnish the cluttered mathematics classroom. The students watch the television monitor closely as the camera pans the mesas and canyons while following a car into Chaco Canyon, New Mexico.

In the canyon, the familiar voice of Robert Redford introduces Anna Sofaer, a photographer and artist. In 1978 she discovered and photographed the shaft of sunlight piercing the large spiral pecked in the rock face behind three large vertical slabs of sandstone near the top of Fajada Butte in Chaco Culture National Historical Park. This so-called Sun Dagger is a high-noon marker left a thousand years ago by the ancient Anasazi people. It documents with a dagger of sunlight the vernal and autumnal equinoxes, the winter and summer solstices, and the maximal and minimal phases of the moon in its nineteen-year cycle.

The stop button is pushed, and the lights come up; the students groan their dissatisfaction at the interruption, but the archaeological context has been established.

Rationale

Using the videotape clip from *The Sun Dagger* (Sofaer 1983)—with its music, the familiar Southwestern terrain, and the novelty of the subject—to establish the context of a mathematics lesson captures students' interest. The pedagogically sound practice of turning off the videotape after seven minutes, when interest is very high and the stage has been set, avoids the ennui and lethargy that usually accompany the dim lights and the television screen in the classroom.

Traditionally, the culture of the Anasazi has been difficult to interpret because they were thought to have left "no written record." With the discovery of the Sun Dagger, students become aware that pictures and symbols pecked in stone are a form of documentation that can eventually be decoded.

Although the prehistoric Pueblo Indians known as the Anasazi built monumental stone structures, great kivas for ritual worship, and an extensive network of roads to distant outlying communities more than a thousand years ago, archaeologists, archaeoastronomers, archaeomathematicians, and archaeoarchitects are not the only ones to discover and uncover new findings on the art, architecture, outliers and roads, rock art, astronomy, and environment of Chaco Canyon. New finds are continually being discovered and interpreted by amateurs in the field—including students.

Theory

Most mathematical context derives from the seventeenth-century Eurocentric mathematics that is published in standard textbooks. Few of these textbooks reflect any of the rich archaeomathematics from Asia, South America, Africa, India, or the indigenous people of North America. Consequently, few teachers, and even fewer minority students, are aware of their own rich, broad mathematical heritage.

James Banks (1991) suggests that concepts related to mathematics can be incorporated into a multicultural curriculum in ways related to content: perspectives, paradigms, concepts, and equity issues.

In introducing Anasazi mathematics and astronomy, we also introduce four different perspectives on mathematics teaching and learning that can and should be recognized and used in classrooms: archaeomathematics (Sun Dagger), ethnomathematics (childhood games based on a spiral), folk mathematics (map measurement and estimation), and academic mathematics (equations using parametric and polar mode).

PRACTICE 2

From the basket of supplies on each table, students take a highlighting pen and a tourism road map of New Mexico and begin looking for Chaco Culture National Historical Park. Students highlight the location of the park (this information is quickly shared with all the tables) and then mark the roads from their own home to the park. They calculate the mileages (with or without calculators) by adding the distances given on the map. The cost of gasoline is calculated accordingly. Suddenly, the noise level rises and animated discussion takes place. Students cannot agree on the time it would take to cover the miles indicated. Eventually, a consensus is reached at one table: the students would assign the speed limits of 55 miles per hour for all paved roads, 30 miles per hour for all gravel roads, and 20 miles per hour for all unimproved roads. The final calculations are compared and then challenged or confirmed.

Rationale

As grounded theory evolves from the data gathered with qualitative methods, so grounded practice evolves from the culture of the multicultural classroom. Pedagogy and content are developed and refined as teachers become more attuned to the culture, interests, background, and skills of their students.

Few of the students described in this article traveled very far from their own homes or owned many printed resources. Because the free road maps supplied by the tourism bureau revealed familiar place names and highways, the students' interest was sustained while they learned to use the legend, read the mileage charts, and orient their homes to the rest of the state. In the process, they discussed authentic estimation problems, learned where one another lived, and acquired a state map of their own.

Theory

Measurement activities can and should require dynamic interaction between students and their environment. Map reading is one way to illustrate the usefulness and practical applications of mathematics. The students' need to discuss various measurements of time and distance highlights the importance of standardizing units and measurement systems.

PRACTICE 3

From the basket of supplies on each table, students take an 8.5" by 11" piece of paper, a pair of scissors, a piece of string, and a small ball of clay. Students begin constructing spirals of their own design by cutting spiral shapes, molding spirals with clay, or twisting string into a spiral shape. Most are two dimensional and curved or circular, but a few students construct three-dimensional shapes and explore the possibility of angles. As the experimenting progresses, the table with the most spirals completed is given a long string with chalk attached to the end to take outside.

The remaining students are encouraged to walk around to view the various spirals and to look for commonalities. The teacher then invites them to leave the room to examine the sidewalk outside the classroom. There, the students who had been sent outside have drawn a large spiral on the concrete with chalk. Students begin to guess how the construction has been done. After noisy debate, the designers explain their process. Several students are reminded of hopping games based on a spiral that they had played as children. Two of the students draw a rough sketch of the hopping-game spiral. Someone else suggests that we join hands to make a human spiral. Amid a great deal of laughter, a human spiral winds around the tallest person in the class.

Rationale

Working in small groups or individually to creatively construct a variety of spirals allows students to use multiple intelligences in the mathematics classroom: bodily-kinesthetic, spatial, and intrapersonal as well as logical-mathematical (Gardner 1983). Moving outside to construct larger spirals and then to take advantage of the fun inherent in the students' suggestions is memorable for students because they are learning in multiple ways.

Actually making the spirals leads students naturally into identifying the attributes of spirals in both mathematical and nonmathematical language.

Theory

Active student participation in learning through individual and small-group explorations provides multiple opportunities for discussion, questioning, listening, and summarizing. By using these techniques, teachers can direct instruction away from a traditional classroom focus on the recall of terminology and the routine manipulation of symbols and procedures toward a student-constructed conceptual understanding of mathematics.

PRACTICE 4

Back in the classroom, the whole class begins calling out the various attributes of spirals so that they can be recorded on the lines emanating from the Zia sun shown on the overhead transparency (see fig. 19.1). Point of origin, direction, dimension, width of spaces, thickness of line, and infiniteness are attributes that come rapidly. Then there is a lull. A few students start whispering. Someone mentions that they still have nine lines to fill. A brave student mentions proportionality; another begins to question the attribute but then remembers that all suggestions are accepted when we are brainstorming. Finally, all sixteen lines forming the Zia sun are filled.

Fig. 19.1. Zia sun diagram shown in class on an overhead transparency

Rationale

In good brainstorming style, all suggestions are written down without criticism or judgment. Although ideally it would be helpful if the class could identify mathematically important attributes (origin, number of dimensions, clockwise or counterclockwise rotation, finiteness or infiniteness, thickness of line, width of space), doing so is not essential at this stage because students will discover and discuss additional attributes as they become important later. Different classes come up with a variety of attributes, and all students are intellectually stretched, but not overwhelmed, to come up with sixteen different attributes corresponding to the sixteen rays on the Zia sun symbol.

The Zia sun symbol has been used in my classroom for years whenever we brainstorm. Before I started using this device, students became too frustrated with the infinite possibilities of a blank transparency. They have observed that the "right side up" lines are pretty easy. The final eight lines of the Zia sun symbol are much harder to fill.

Many students would prefer to have a working definition of a spiral. According to Davis (1993), mathematicians do not yet have clear and distinct ideas about spirals. In the spiral exploration for this lesson, a formal definition seems not only unimportant but perhaps counterproductive and confining.

Theory

In the literature about the history of spirals there are both many definitions and no definition of what a spiral is. No one definition can fit the multitudinous spirals found in nature, myth, and mathematics: the golden spiral, Pythagorean spirals, dynamical spirals, random spirals, discrete spirals, fractal spirals, sinusoidal spirals, the Cotes spiral, the spiral of Cornu, spiral galaxies, spiral-based self-similar sets, spiral structures in Julia sets, spiral patterns in fluids, spirals in chemical systems, and spiral symmetry in polymers, to name just a few. More are being discovered all the time.

Teachers emphasize the development of language and symbolism to communicate mathematical ideas so that all students can formulate mathematical definitions and express generalizations discovered through investigations and so that all students can relate procedures in one representation to procedures in an equivalent representation.

PRACTICE 5

Students take the TI-82 calculators out of the baskets on the table and help one another rediscover how they operate:

1. Enter a function (press $\boxed{Y=}$, then press $\boxed{X,T,\theta}$ for your independent variable).
2. Use $\boxed{MODE}$ to change from FUNCtion to PARametric or POLar.
3. Graph a function (press $\boxed{GRAPH}$).
4. Look at the table (press $\boxed{2nd}$, $\boxed{GRAPH}$).
5. Explore $\boxed{TRACE}$.
6. Set a "friendly window" (press $\boxed{WINDOW}$, then enter Xmin= −47, Xmax=47, Ymin= −47, Ymax=47).

Rationale

The TI-82 calculator review reminds all students of the basic keys, allows them to take notes about functions they may have forgotten, and lets students share with and help one another and explore the graphing calculator in small groups.

My experience has been very similar to that of Dan Kennedy (1995) who writes the following in "Climbing Around on the Tree of Mathematics" (p. 463):

> The graphing calculator changed my entire approach to teaching. The first thing I did was let them use it—all the time. I could then focus on how I would get the students to use it, which in turn encouraged me to focus on students' learning rather than on my own teaching. I saw how well they worked with each other with the calculators, so I began to develop ways to make them work together to discover the mathematics. I now start each class by having them work together on a problem, often the type of problem that I formerly used in a lecture to involve student interest in the lesson of the day—only now I wait for them to discover the lesson of the day. Once I saw that they could actually make that discovery, I realized how useless my crisp set of lecture notes had been all those years. Now there is no turning back.

Theory

As we reflect on the evolution of teaching practice in a technological age, we observe that new technologies have made calculations and graphing easier to teach and to learn, but the very nature of the problems and the methods used by mathematicians has changed.

PRACTICE 6

The problem: replicate the Sun Dagger spiral in the parametric mode on the TI-82 Graphing Calculator by adapting the instructions for graphing the spiral of Archimedes given in figure 19.2.

With the Sun Dagger handout (fig. 19.3) taken from the basket on the table, each student looks at the reproductions of the Sun Dagger spiral and draws the Cartesian quadrants over the right-hand spiral in order to define the origin, to determine whether the spiral turns clockwise or counterclockwise, to determine in which quadrant the Sun Dagger spiral ends, and to count the nineteen turns of the spiral from left to right along the x-axis.

Extension: Replicate the Sun Dagger spiral in polar mode on the TI-82 Graphing Calculator.

Rationale

The students who have just identified the attributes of the spirals they made with paper and scissors, clay, string, and chalk now translate those

The spiral of Archimedes can be defined by the polar equation $r = a\theta$.

The spiral of Archimedes can also be defined parametrically (when $a = 0.5$) by the following values:
$$x = 0.5\theta \ \cos\theta$$
$$y = 0.5\theta \ \sin\theta$$

1. Start with the standard default settings.
2. Press [MODE]. Arrow down to select Par (parametric mode). Press [ENTER].
3. Press [Y=]. Enter the expressions to define the parametric equation in terms of T:
$$X_{1T}=.5T\cos T$$
$$Y_{1T}=.5T\sin T$$
4. Press [GRAPH]. The graph shows only the first loop of the spiral because the standard default values for the [WINDOW] variables define Tmax as 2π.
5. Press [ZOOM]. Select ZSquare to graph the equation on a square grid.
6. To explore the behavior of the graph further, press [WINDOW], set increased values for Tmax and alternative values for Tstep, and explore options for Xmin, Xmax, Ymin, and Ymax until you can reproduce the Sun Dagger spiral.

Fig. 19.2. Instructions for graphing the parametric equations that define the spiral of Archimedes

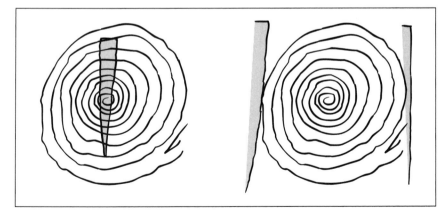

Fig. 19.3. A student handout showing redrawings of light "daggers" on the Sun Dagger spiral petroglyph at summer (left) and winter (right) solstices, Fajada Butte, Chaco Culture National Historical Park, New Mexico

attributes into the parameters on the graphing calculator that will produce a simulation of the Sun Dagger spiral. This discovery approach combines students' personal observations with the printed documentation for the graphing calculator but forces them to really think about the calculator buttons that they push. Recognizing that the Tmax default setting on the calculator (6.2831853) is the same as 2π is a predictable "aha" experience for most students.

Theory

> Spiral forms are ubiquitous in the natural world. Primitive people, in close contact with the natural order, understood the importance of the spiral as an expression of nature. Projective geometry and the mathematics of the spiral may help to bridge the enormous chasm between ancient systems of thought and the modern world of science (Hargittai and Pickover 1992, p. 46).

Ideally, students will begin to "bridge the enormous chasm" to the mathematics of ideas, leaving behind for a time the more mundane mathematics of computation.

PRACTICE 7

One at a time, a designated student at each table, with support and encouragement from their group, demonstrates graphing the Sun Dagger spiral in either parametric or polar mode on the TI-82 Overhead Unit. The students are reminded to talk while they demonstrate so that all students in the class have a chance to follow the procedures on their own calculator.

Rationale

Demonstrating the graphing process and their understanding of spirals and parametric and polar modes allows students to practice speaking in front of their peers; encourages alternative, creative processes; and builds a sense of group ownership in a solution. Students have already performed the operations successfully but are free to ask their group members for help when memory fails.

Theory

The student performance with the TI-82 Graphing Calculator Overhead Unit allows individual and group self-assessment of facility with the concepts of the spiral and facility with the graphing calculator. Demonstrating how to graph the spiral is a good assessment task; it meets the criteria for performance tasks that Stenmark (1991, p. 16) adapted from a list developed by Steven J. Leinwand and Grant Wiggins: essential, authentic, rich, engaging, active, feasible, equitable, and open.

Other students observe and practice alternative methods of solving a problem or refine their original problem-solving process. Confidence in problem solving and performing are both greatly enhanced by the process.

CONCLUSIONS

The exploratory nature of the mathematics of the Anasazi of Chaco Canyon leads to many multicultural experiences in and out of the classroom. Some possibilities follow:

1. Take a field trip to an archaeological site.
2. Collect spirals from nature, from art, and from advertisements.
3. Research stories and myths about spirals in other cultures.
4. Research one of the many historic spirals mentioned in this article.
5. Study polar coordinates.
6. Research other sun markers.
7. Research and build sundials.
8. Study or design ancient algebraic and technological iconography.

Similar cross-curricular projects are possible and probable whenever teachers and students listen to one another, share their interests, and form a community of learners. Technology, manipulatives, authentic mathematical explorations, and assessments that extend beyond the textbook and the classroom bring new life and excitement to the mathematics class and extend the applications of mathematics. Such practice is grounded in the culture of the classroom and backed by rationale and theory.

REFERENCES

Banks, James A. *Teaching Strategies for Ethnic Studies.* Boston: Allyn & Bacon, 1991.

Davis, Philip J. *Spirals: From Theodorus to Chaos.* Wellesley, Mass.: A. K. Peters, 1993.

Gardner, Howard. *Frames of Mind: The Theory of Multiple Intelligences.* New York: Basic Books, 1983.

Hargittai, István, and Clifford A. Pickover, eds. *Spiral Symmetry.* Singapore: World Scientific, 1992.

Kennedy, Dan. "Climbing Around on the Tree of Mathematics." *Mathematics Teacher* 88 (September 1995): 460–65.

Sofaer, Anna. *The Sun Dagger.* Bethesda, Md.: Atlas Video, 1993. Videotape by Bullfrog Films.

Stenmark, Jean Kerr, ed. *Mathematics Assessment: Myths, Models, Good Questions, and Practical Suggestions.* Reston, Va.: National Council of Teachers of Mathematics, 1991.

20

Know Thyself
The Evolution of an Intervention Gender-Equity Program

Trish Koontz

THE AAUW Report: How Schools Shortchange Girls (1992) summarized research that focused on many of the components of today's classrooms that overtly—but usually unintentionally—discourage females from participating fully in learning mathematics. These components include, among others, language, curriculum, teacher behaviors, assessment, physical environment, administrative policies, and student support. Before conducting professional development training on gender-inclusive teaching, I field-tested units I designed that address many of these issues in a gender-inclusive mathematics, science, and technology curriculum.

This article will focus on two projects using this gender-inclusive curriculum. The first was a successful intervention program designed to encourage middle school girls to continue mathematics, science, and computer courses throughout high school. The second project was a staff development project that helped disseminate the intervention program.

The most difficult part of professional development is getting beyond the awareness stage of gender bias and encouraging teachers to change their belief systems and therefore their classroom behaviors. Gender bias is so subtle that we barely recognize it. It is so ingrained in how we define ourselves that it is essentially invisible. If we are to create gender-inclusive learning environments, we must first recognize our own biases.

INTERVENTION PROGRAM:
ERG (ENRICHMENT READINESS FOR GIRLS)

The middle school intervention program was named ERG after a unit of potential energy. It was felt that each girl enrolled in the volunteer program brought with her untapped potential energy to be used to understand how mathematics and technology are tools for understanding the physical world.

The ERG program was conducted in a midwest suburban middle school whose "graduating" class numbered approximately 175 students. Fewer than 5 percent of the *female* graduating class went on to enroll in physics, calculus, or computer programming in high school, whereas approximately 20 percent of the *male* graduating class later completed these courses. The majority of parents in this community expected their children to receive a college education. The twenty girls in the program (ten in sixth grade and ten in seventh grade) met twice a week, forty-two minutes a session, for the entire academic year. The goals of this program were to—

- provide nonthreatening, hands- and minds-on, integrated, nontraditional physical science and mathematics units;
- encourage group problem-solving projects;
- increase career awareness in technical fields;
- research and discuss openly gender biases in our society.

At the end of the year each girl considered the six units we studied worthwhile and identified their favorites. A description of each unit is listed below in the order in which the girls ranked them, from most to least understandable and motivating.

RANKING OF ERG UNITS

1. Rockets Away

In this unit the girls built rockets from kits, changing one characteristic of each rocket to examine its effects on the rocket's stability. Using software by Estes Rockets, Stabcalc-1 (now called ASTROCAD), they entered data into the computer to determine their rocket's stability and projected altitude during flight. This program required accurate metric measuring skills and the application of geometric knowledge. Several mathematically gifted girls confused area and circumference, showing a lack of experience with these concepts. Building and using a clinometer to determine maximum altitude introduced the students to applications of ratio, proportion, and trigonometry.

2. Spatial Puzzles and Logic Games

Throughout the year logic puzzles and spatial activities were included to increase motivation and appreciation for the beauty of mathematics. I made it a point never to give answers. The girls were encouraged to work in groups at school, to continue working at home with siblings and parents, and to try new approaches to solve the problems. Early in the year it became obvious that some girls were more proficient at solving logic and spatial puzzles than others. Journal entries contained quotes like "Wendi is so much better at puzzles. She had to give me the answer." Even though I wanted the girls to discuss how they got the answers, this approach simply reinforced a feeling of inability for those girls who didn't "see" the answers. In late October we discussed how mathematicians often take years to solve a problem. A unit on famous female mathematicians and scientists was studied to reinforce the notion that all problems aren't solved instantly. After a discussion about this unit and how it felt to discover something on one's own, the girls decided to take a pledge: "I promise not to spoil someone else's *eureka* by giving her the answer unless we discover it together." They added a thumbs-up sign. This proved to be an excellent solution. The girls worked in groups, but rather than giving answers to other groups, they would show the thumbs-up sign to mean, "I don't want to spoil your feelings of success. Keep trying." Some girls were still frustrated in February, but by May most expressed journal entries similar to this one: "I can't believe I solved that puzzle; I'm proud of myself. I didn't know I could be good at puzzles." After most groups solved a puzzle, we discussed the varied approaches and added new approaches to our "puzzle board."

3. It's a Chilling Life

In January we studied heat, temperature, and insulating materials. Each group devised a plan to keep an insulated ice cube "alive" for as long as possible under a heat lamp. Planning for "Melt-Off Day," they carefully experimented with many materials, varying the shape, weight, and thickness. Several times they collected data about the "life span" of a standard ice cube, using inexpensive temperature probes interfaced to a computer. Each trial generated a temperature-and-time graph. During preparation for the "Melt Off," two teams were competing against each other but couldn't figure out which team was winning, since one computer was graphing the temperature in Celsius and the other in Fahrenheit. As teacher, I continued the "I won't tell" attitude but encouraged the girls to look for relationships between the two scales. After a lengthy discussion they derived the formula for converting Fahrenheit to Celsius.

I wanted to introduce the use of a database focusing on insulating materials; the girls, however, decided the best use for a database was a dating service. After selecting topics for fields, each girl surveyed twenty friends. Through their research, they discovered how one deals with numbers and equalities in a database. They also found that a database could sort simultaneously for more than one variable and that a new field may need to be added later. Creating and using their own database proved a more thorough way to teach the unit than using an already created database.

4. Gender Studies

Throughout the year we discussed equity issues. Female scientists and mathematicians were invited to speak to the group. I asked the girls to think of some serious questions they might ask the role model. As they were leaving class, one girl said, "She's probably some fat, ugly, Russian woman!" Most laughed as they agreed with the statement. Their negative stereotyping of women mathematicians and ethnic insinuation saddened me. The role model visits, however, helped dispel some of the stereotypical notions.

The girls also examined magazines for examples of how men and women were depicted in advertisements. They graphed the number of females and males shown as active or passive participants. The girls were amazed at how often women were pictured in evening gowns standing passively around to sell products.

In another activity, a discussion comparing the toys the girls received for holiday gifts with those gifts they would have requested from relatives revealed many discrepancies. Often the girls spoke of wanting Legos and Transformers but receiving dolls. The girls encountered another inequity during our study of electronics. One father told his daughter how electricians learn the numerical values of the color bands on resistors: the traditional mnemonic to remember black = 0 and so forth through brown, red, orange, yellow, green, blue, violet, gray, and finally white = 9 is "Bad Boys Rob Our Young Girls But Violet Gives Willingly." The girls were embarrassed and thought that this perpetuated disrespect for females. These activities promoted worthwhile discussions on gender bias. The girls became sensitive to gender bias against boys, too. One noted how her brother was teased by others for playing the flute.

5. "Leggo My Legos"

Legos gave many rich opportunities to think spatially and use mathematics. Using Legos enabled us to study simple and complex machines and build toy models of machines like hand-held egg beaters. We studied the slope of a line through inclined planes and screws, as well as ratio and proportion through gear applications. The Lego Corporation has an extensive Lego Educational Curriculum with task cards and comments available for teachers. I did not, however, directly use these cards, since I wanted to avoid any materials that might lead to a "cookbook" type of activity.

6. Bit by Bit I Count

This unit began with a study of the binary number system using straws and cups. It included the study of parallel and series circuits to discuss how a computer works. Many of the girls had used patterns for sewing, but none had ever read the electronic equivalent of a sewing pattern, a schematic. Using an analogy to water, pipes, and water pressure, we studied the concept of current, voltage, and resistance. We then began to build from scratch an electronic board that would interface with the computer. The function of the board was to turn on appropriate light-emitting diodes each time a number was keyed into the computer. The girls learned to strip their own wires, solder, read codes and schematics, and "stuff" breadboards. Many of their journal entries stated, "This is much easier than I thought it would be. I was afraid of anything electrical."

Longitudinal Findings of the ERG Intervention Program

The twenty ERG girls were compared for cognitive ability and attitudes with a control group of twenty girls who participated in more traditional mathematics and science classes. The Ross Test of Higher Cognitive Skills and the Group Assessment of Logical Thinking (GALT), a Piagetian task test, were administered to validate the comparison. Neither test showed any significant difference between the means of the two groups. A survey of twenty-five questions was also administered to all forty girls prior to the start of the intervention program. The informal survey examined feelings and perceptions about mathematics, science, and computers in general; future careers; and classes in school. The girls' perceptions of parental expectations about grades, along with their perceptions of how knowledgeable their parents were in mathematics, science, and computers, were queried. Again, no significant difference was found between the attitudinal means of the ERG and control group at the beginning of the project (Koontz 1989). The means of the attitude survey, two cognitive ability tests, and previous mathematics and science grades indicated that the ERG and control group were initially similar in motivation and achievement.

At the end of the year-long intervention program and after all forty girls had graduated from high school (more that five years after the intervention), they were again asked to respond to the attitude survey. The school counselor also supplied a list of high school mathematics and science courses completed by the forty girls. Mathematics courses taken were placed in a hierarchy giving a value of 1 for the successful completion of algebra 1 through 7 for AP calculus. A similar numbering was completed for science courses. At the .01 significance level there was a significant difference in both attitude and number of courses taken in mathematics and science between the ERG group and the control group. In mathematics the ERG group tended to become slightly more positive about mathematics and mathematics classes. The control group, too, remained slightly positive about mathematics, but they became significantly less positive toward the mathematics classes. Only the control group became significantly more convinced over time that boys do better in mathematics than girls. Another correlation investigated the relationships, if any, among mathematics, science, and computer courses taken and the attitudes toward these three areas. The attitudes about the subjects correlated highly with the number of courses taken in that area. Two ERG students commented on the survey that the more high school mathematics courses they took, the more they liked mathematics.

The results clearly support the proposition that middle-grade intervention programs that give hands-on experiences, role-model contacts, and encouragement to girls positively influence girls' attitudes and course selection dealing with mathematics and science. Many of these girls reported that their love for mathematics and science started with the ERG program: "It was different from *book* math and science." Several ERG girls also stated that until being selected for the ERG program, they never thought of themselves as "liking or being good in math or science. It really built my self-esteem." Although this particular study only qualitatively hints at self-esteem as a major factor, I suspect the self-esteem issue was of greatest importance. Once the ERG girls were "given permission" to feel comfortable as students of mathematics and science, they then continued with advanced courses. However, the control group, with equal initial ability and attitudes, did not receive that encouragement. The survey indicated that the control group bought deeper over time into the myth that boys are smarter than girls in mathematics and science. In summary, a list of instructional strategies learned during the ERG program follows:

- Encourage work in cooperative groups.
- Ignore girls' "small talk" during group work; conversations seem to be off target, but groups do complete projects successfully on time.
- Connect mathematical concepts to applications to increase participation.
- Invite female mathematicians and scientists to class as role models.
- Study famous female mathematicians and scientists to provide a more gender-inclusive curriculum.
- Provide spatial activities on a regular basis *over time* to increase positive attitudes and self-image about spatial ability.
- Encourage girls to become more proactive about equity issues for *all* as appropriate situations occur.
- Encourage girls to try nontraditional, male-domain activities.
- Provide hands-on activities, especially in areas that are unfamiliar to them, such as gears and electronics.
- Keep high expectations. It's hard to ignore constant complaints such as, "I don't care. Just tell me the answer." The frequency of complaints, however, will decrease over time.
- Expect that, given sufficient wait time, girls will be able to answer higher-level mathematics and science questions.
- Encourage computer use whenever possible.
- Encourage discussion *among* students. Avoid the "teacher as expert" role.
- Promote problem-solving activities that are hard to complete in short periods of time.
- Discuss how most real-life problems take long periods to solve and often have more than one solution.

DESCRIPTION OF ERG DISSEMINATION PROGRAMS

In order to disseminate the ERG findings, I applied for an Eisenhower grant to update twenty middle school teachers. The primary goals of the professional development intervention program were to—

1. increase these teachers' knowledge of mathematics and physical science;
2. increase their knowledge of the appropriate use of manipulatives;
3. increase their knowledge about integrating computers into mathematics and science curricula;
4. increase their positive attitudes toward a gender-inclusive curriculum by exploring instructional strategies.

PROFESSIONAL DEVELOPMENT MODEL

Using a model of effective change, the fifteen-month professional development project conducted weekly meetings throughout the academic year and continued for twenty-five days in the summer. The grant provided materials for classroom use (Legos, Science Tool Kit [distributed by Broderbund Software], rocketry kits, electronic supplies, and resource books). A list of female role models from local industry willing to visit classrooms was also provided. During the fifteen months, three graduate-level courses were offered: Computers in Middle School Mathematics and Science, Physical Science for Middle School Teachers, and Gender-Equity Issues. After the courses were completed, university faculty visited each classroom several times to offer technical and instructional support and to exchange ideas.

Faculty and participants felt extremely positive about the experience. Both groups expected to see major changes in teachers' classroom practices on the videotapes taken at the end of the program. There was a substantial positive change in the use of integrated units, cooperative learning, computer use, and hands-on activities. Comparing preprogram and postprogram videotapes, however, revealed little success in changing teachers' behaviors concerning gender equity. For example, higher-level questions were still asked more frequently of boys than girls. During cooperative lessons boys monopolized manipulatives while girls recorded information. Seventeen of the twenty teachers selected two students, one boy and one girl, to help in a demonstration. Unconsciously, however, all these teachers assigned the most technical job to the boy and the least technical job to the girl (Koontz 1993). Unfortunately, the group of twenty participants were furnished everything but perhaps the most critical component in teacher reform—*opportunities for self-reflection*. I discovered that the invisibility of gender bias makes it difficult to recognize even in oneself.

I received two subsequent Eisenhower grants that followed the same format as the first, with two exceptions. First, participants kept reflective journals, and second, participants critiqued a videotape of their own teaching once a month during the academic year. At the beginning of the year we analyzed tapes from participants in the previous grant to learn how to identify gender inequities and gender-inclusive teaching strategies. Each critique analyzed only a few selected behaviors. Additional behaviors were slowly added to each session while incorporating previously critiqued behaviors. The behaviors studied were adapted from "Self-Reflection on Your Teaching: A Checklist" by John Barell and "Classroom Observation Checklist" by S. Lee Winocur. Both appear in *Developing Minds: A Resource Book for Teaching Thinking* (Costa 1985). Our adapted list follows.

CLASSROOM OBSERVATION CHECKLIST

In creating a gender-fair program, the teacher—

1. fosters a climate of openness by
   • calling students by name, and
   • moving around the classroom;
2. encourages student interaction and cooperation by having students
   • work in small groups using varied roles (reporter, recorder),
   • respond to other students,
   • explore others' points of view,
   • listen to explanations by many students, and
   • use manipulatives cooperatively;
3. demonstrates an attitude of acceptance by
   • accepting all valid student responses,
   • giving supportive comments to incorrect answers, and
   • probing further the "I don't know" responses;
4. encourages students to gather and organize information by
   • having students classify and categorize data,
   • having reference materials readily available, and
   • having students record data in journals;
5. provides visual cues to develop cognitive strategies by using appropriate charts, pictures, mathematics manipulatives, and models;
6. makes connections to past concepts and applications;
7. elicits the verbalization of students' reasoning by
   • posing "if … then" and "what if …" questions,
   • posing questions at different levels of Bloom's taxonomy, and
   • calling on both sexes equitably at each question level;
8. promotes silent reflection by
   • giving appropriate wait time,

- withholding a "correct" response, and
- requesting more responses even after a "correct" response is given;
9. encourages equity by
   - referring to women and minority scientists and mathematicians,
   - reflecting on her or his own teaching to ensure equitable instruction,
   - encouraging females to perform traditional male tasks (load computers, move desks),
   - using gender-fair language (scientist, ... she; doctor, ... she), and
   - holding high expectations for females and minorities.

The success of the subsequent two grants is attributed to the addition of the self-reflection process that all the teachers conducted using videotapes of their own teaching. After critiquing their own tapes, many participants were embarrassed to discover their instructional biases. All forty teachers in the last two grants said that self-reflection helped make them better teachers for *all* their students.

ERG proved to be an appropriate title for the middle school intervention program for girls; Know Thyself might be just as appropriate a title for an equity intervention program for teachers. In order to change, teachers must investigate their own beliefs. Professional development programs should be an ideal place to give teachers the opportunity to learn a process of self-inquiry along with upgrading subject matter. If professional development merely offers an awareness of equitable practices, it is soon forgotten. It seems that only through thoughtful self-observation and self-reflection can one begin to unravel belief systems so ingrained in us that we consciously don't recognize or admit to them.

REFERENCES

American Association of University Women Educational Foundation. *The AAUW Report: How Schools Shortchange Girls.* Washington, D.C.: American Association of University Women and National Education Association, 1992.

Costa, Arthur L., ed. *Developing Minds: A Resource Book for Teaching Thinking.* Alexandria, Va.: Association for Supervision and Curriculum Development, 1985.

Koontz, Trish. "Longitudinal Study of an Integrated Middle School Physical Science Intervention Program." In *Transforming Science and Technology: Our Future Depends on It,* vol. 1, edited by Sharon Haggerty and Ann Holmes, pp. 187–94. Waterloo, Ont.: University of Waterloo, 1993.

———. "Technology in Middle School Physical Science: Gender Equity." In *Gender and Science and Technology,* vol. 1, edited by Yael Rom and Israela Ravina, pp. 109–16. Haifa, Israel: Technion-Israel Institute of Technology, 1989.

21

Assessment and Equity

Terri Belcher

Grace Dávila Coates

José Franco

Karen Mayfield-Ingram

We often hear that mathematics should be a pump that keeps students moving forward, not a filter that screens them out. Historically, girls, language-minority students, students from low socioeconomic levels, and students of color have been sifted out of mathematics and related fields in disproportionate numbers. Recently, new curricula and classroom strategies have helped increase students' access to mathematics. But how do they fare when assessed? Past experience tells us that assessment itself can just as easily act as a filter. What can we change to make assessment a positive factor? The answers, of course, are complex, but the following ideas may contribute to the discussion.

Make Assessment Goals Clear from the Beginning

Bring assessment to the beginning of the planning process. Let everybody know the expectations and understand how success will be evaluated before instructional materials are chosen and lesson plans made. Better yet, have teachers, students, parents, administrators, and community members take part in deciding on and clarifying expectations and evaluation standards at every level.

Assessment should relate directly to what students will be learning. Knowing how work will be judged can clarify what we want students to do and learn. It helps all of us (students, teachers, parents, ...) know where we're going and how to get there. It gives students chances to study appropriate material and practice appropriate techniques. If, for instance, students are asked to explain their thinking, they need time, practice, discussion, and feedback. When teachers know, they can design lessons and units that give students chances to learn valued mathematics. When parents understand, they can help provide support at school or home.

PROVIDE OPPORTUNITIES TO LEARN

Knowing what work will be judged and how it will be assessed can give students an opportunity to learn what is valued enough to be assessed. The opportunity to learn requires having high-quality instructional materials available to all, accommodating the variety of student learning styles through both teaching materials and methods, and allowing students to investigate their own interests and develop effective ways to communicate their understanding. Assessment can be a catalyst to help promote these attributes.

As changes involving assessment take place in many states, we have a unique opportunity to open doors to new ways of thinking about mathematics and how it is learned. Many people feel that some of the changes have already modified mathematics itself. Students are learning from a new perspective as they respond to open-ended questions, explain ideas, create portfolios, and take charge of their own progress. They see a richness to which they have previously had little access. Mathematics is no longer a matter of grinding out an answer and moving on to the next problem.

The goals of the classroom and those of assessment have to match. If students spend a large part of their time on rote drill but are tested on problem solving, not only will their scores drop but their confidence will dwindle. Conversely, if students experience a strong problem-solving program but are tested on low-level skills, they have no chance to show what they can do. Their motivation to meet challenges will wither.

The opportunity to learn happens only if we all know how learning is defined. We might say that anything worth being assessed is worth "teaching to"!

USE EQUITABLE INSTRUMENTS

Is it enough to let people know ahead of time what's on the test? What about the assessment instruments themselves? Can they be made more equitable? Some suggestions follow.

Language

The goal of assessment should be to determine what each student knows about mathematics. Therefore, directions, instructions, problems, or questions should be in plain, simple language easily understood by all. Make clear the expectations of what is to be done for tasks, without limiting students' thinking. Give students questions or problems that prompt thoughtful responses, and then give them ample opportunity to respond.

There's enough complexity in mathematical language itself. Analyzing the grade-level readability of books and tests doesn't make good sense, because mathematics vocabulary has so many multiple-syllable words. The vocabulary is important, however, and not to be neglected. The words used in assessments should be appropriate to the topic and to the levels of students, not watered down. If we do use words that are specific to particular contexts or are not common to all students, we can "shelter" the vocabulary or context and define vocabulary, provide fuller descriptions of contexts, and include diagrams, graphics, or models. By eliminating potential barriers, we increase students' access.

Special efforts need to be made to clarify language for students whose home language is not English. Allow students to respond as much as possible in their own languages (a wonderful use for portfolios), including nonstandard English. This poses a challenge, but several strategies can be useful. Maintain a list of words that students use. Encourage them to create and use diagrams and pictures to explain their work. Give students models and examples. Consider videotaping students as they demonstrate solutions—taping provides the opportunity to "reread" work. Bilingual colleagues, school staff members, students, neighbors, community members, or parents may provide additional support. Focus grades and scores for mathematics work on conceptual understanding, not grammar, spelling, and punctuation.

Design

The questions themselves should not be complex but should elicit thoughtful and interesting responses. When students are asked to explain how they solved a problem, why they chose certain strategies, or how they know their responses make sense, the variation we see is amazing. Three examples of simple questions that can generate rich responses follow.

- I am thinking of a number. When I divide it by 2, the answer is an odd whole number that is greater than 50. Write at least three statements that must be true of the original number. Explain why each statement is true.

- Take 12 blocks. Arrange them into a structure that is square on just one side. The other sides may be irregular, nonrectangular shapes, but where blocks touch each other, full faces must be together.

  You will have to make some decisions about how to build your structure. If you are not satisfied with your first structure, you may start again on another.

  Draw diagrams of your structure from the top and from each side.

  Then decide where you could add more blocks to the structure without changing its appearance (as shown in your diagram) from the top or any side.

  Explain what you found or observed.

- You have been asked to make a survey to find out what kind of activities your school should have on School Fair Day. Describe how you would organize your survey. What steps would you take?

Contexts

An often overlooked aspect of curriculum and assessment has been the issue of contexts appropriate to students. Much of what we do in school is based on the environments of middle-class white cultures, particularly that of males. It has been okay to have a question on baseball statistics, but what about street games? We need to provide a panorama of contexts that relate to the great variety of students' ages, cultures, and experiences.

Another part of context is presentation—conditions, tone, and format. Students should take on assessment tasks in environments that are familiar or friendly. Often the tone and appearance of assessments are considerably more formal than students are used to seeing in their daily work. Format, fonts, graphics, and spacing can be critical to understanding. Illustrations or other graphics need to be related to a task and mathematically correct, not misleading. If assessments are authentic and accessible, they will seem familiar enough to students and won't inhibit thinking. Thoughtful presentation leaves room for students to bring their own sense of reality to the task along with their mathematical thinking, using different ways of working through the task.

If the response is supposed to address a particular audience, make the audience one that helps students focus on the purpose of the task and the kind of response that is appropriate. Contexts should be realistic, encouraging the use of mathematics as it might be used by competent adults. Students who are familiar with a given situation may be distracted by oversimplification or misinformation.

No single group should always be the one left out, just as no single group should always reap the benefit of having the majority of questions fit their particular lives. Give all students chances to share the uniqueness of their own cultures. Include questions and tasks that allow for a great variety of personal backgrounds.

Link Instruction to Assessment

Teacher Support

Teacher support is critical. It's probably not necessary to call in experts from outside so much as to give teachers plenty of chances to sit down together, discuss what they see in their students' work, and jointly clarify the goals of their instruction. Each teacher needs to be well informed about current trends in curriculum and assessment, but what they need most of all is to know that they can determine what their students understand and what more needs to be addressed. Teachers become guides and facilitators, helping students understand where they are and what to do next.

Grades

The assessments that have been introduced in the last ten years allow for far more information for both teachers and students than grades or "percent correct." Grades usually assign a rank or position in a group. Grades have often been considered to be the motivation for students to work hard. This might be true for students who are doing well in a particular situation, but for others who are not doing well, it can have the opposite effect. Can you imagine going through twelve or thirteen years of school and never being considered good at anything? Why try?

Different systems of assessment and reports allow us to look at the quality of a student's thinking. Once we look at thinking, we can do a better job of helping students learn. We are accustomed to looking for objective criteria in a quest for reliable and valid tests. Tests based on this kind of criteria often focus on skill-based tasks and cannot give us a clear picture of high-level thinking. They usually limit the ways students can show what they understand about mathematics. At best, they are one-dimensional measures that fall short of reflecting the rich mathematics we want students to learn. Assessment instruments that allow students the opportunity to show connections and understanding require us to recognize evidence of sound mathematical thinking no matter what its form or source.

Discussion and Writing

Discussion is a powerful key to learning. Talking about ideas is the preliminary step, but students will still need a lot of help in learning to write things down. They can identify the important ideas in paragraphs and emphasize these. They can reorder sentences or paragraphs to trace the development of an idea. What comes first? Then what?

They can identify the relative importance of information and how it is presented. Is there a repetition of ideas? Can some words be eliminated? What did you really want to say? Would a poster, diagram, or chart illustrate that point and help make your idea clear? We can encourage the use of not only clear writing but also diagrams, charts, graphs, and other important ways to represent mathematical situations.

The Organization of Materials

Assessment, just like other parts of learning, requires a lot of organization. Teachers should be enabled to work together to find ways of keeping students' portfolios without having huge mounds of paper and file cabinets full of file folders that are never reviewed. They can help one another decide what has enough importance and meaning to be worth keeping.

Manipulative materials and calculators need to be organized so that students can take care of their distribution and storage and so that materials will be readily available during assessment. Students themselves need to be full participants in organization. Choosing appropriate tools is part of the learning process and should be assessed. This is important not only for teachers' sanity but also for the development of students' clarity of thinking.

INCLUDE SELF-ASSESSMENT

Being able to assess one's own work is essential to success in most future careers. Artists decide when they have completed a piece of art. Defense lawyers determine when their case is strong enough to prove their client's innocence. Each of us faces assessing our work, our position, and our progress daily. Sometimes we use external standards. Sometimes we impose our own.

Having papers evaluated by a teacher can be effective, but even more effective is a student's own understanding of what makes success—what it takes, for instance, to get into college. Students can be given opportunities to give one another feedback in small groups, to present their strategies to the class for discussion, and to revise their work after it has been reviewed by peers and adults. They can learn to interpret standards for good work and should have a chance to see samples of top-level student work. They can learn about rubrics, develop their own, and apply these criteria to their own work. Some teachers make individual agreements with their students for their learning goals and the assessment criteria to be used.

Many educators agree that student self-assessment is the most worthwhile feature of all our efforts to change assessment. If that were the only change made, we'd still have progress; and if we haven't given students this tool, the rest may not get us where we want to go. In the end, the student who takes responsibility will become the most successful.

A LAST COMMENT

In no way is the discussion of equity in assessment meant to suggest "dumbing down the test." Rather, it is an effort to provide opportunity for excellence for all. Competence is not to be sacrificed in striving for inclusion. What we really want is to make it possible for every student to have a fair chance at as much high-quality education as possible. Standards should be exactly as high for one group of students as for another. The way to get there may be different and the pace may be faster or slower, but the end result should be equally supportive for all.

We talk, in national documents, at school board meetings, and in teacher in-service sessions, about the need for success for every student. Personal and group expectations should be rising as all those involved understand how it can be achieved. As time passes, we should see more and more superb results from all students. If we can create that level playing field, we'll still have hard work ahead, but wouldn't it be great if assessment didn't have to mean that half of our students were failures?

22

Reshaping Perspectives on Teaching Mathematics in Diverse Urban Schools

Paulette C. Walker

Michaele F. Chappell

IN DECADES past, we have witnessed increased attention given to education in urban school settings—an environment that includes students who are from low socioeconomic families and exhibit diverse learning styles. The authors recognize that not all students in these settings are African Americans and, conversely, that not all African American students are urban students. Urban students vary in ethnicity; African American urban students, however, will be the focus of this article.

Urban education is defined to be the process that enables students attending schools in urban areas to receive their education. The key word is *process;* it infers a set of actions or changes occurring in some special order. Given this interpretation and the need to create an opportunity for all students to learn mathematics, we will address three fundamental questions: (1) What are current perspectives on teaching in diverse urban schools? (2) What kinds of actions and changes should occur in order to enhance mathematics instruction in urban school settings? and (3) What existing exemplars will help reshape and advance our thinking of teaching mathematics in diverse urban school settings?

CURRENT PERSPECTIVES ON TEACHING IN URBAN SCHOOLS

Description of Schools and Students

It is known that urban schools are often affected by the same forces affecting the areas in which the schools are located—high rates of crime, infant mortality, teenage pregnancy, and substance abuse. As a consequence of these forces, urban schools tend to operate in a different climate from other schools.

Students attending urban schools are frequently labeled "at risk of failure," "economically disadvantaged," or "unteachable/unreachable." Such labels lead one to believe that students attending urban schools *cannot* achieve the same academic levels as other students. If teachers in particular embrace this attitude about teaching in an urban setting, then the learning environment becomes very restrictive and limiting. Conversely, if teachers embrace the notion that urban school students can achieve and learn, then the focus of schooling becomes the *means* of instruction, instead of instructional *outcomes.*

Means and Outcomes

The question is not whether urban school students can or cannot achieve mathematical skills; rather, it is which *means* will elicit maximum success in mathematics. Gilbert and Gay (1985, p. 133) assert that "the key to improving success in school for poor black students is modifying the means used to achieve learning outcomes, not changing the intended outcomes themselves." Thus, mathematics teachers in urban classrooms should develop and implement teaching strategies that will enhance their students' learning capabilities, dispelling the myth that urban school students are at risk of failure.

There is a tendency to avoid instructional methods requiring urban students to use higher-order and critical-thinking skills. Literature indicates that urban students often receive "less instruction in higher-order skills than other students, and are given a curriculum that is less challenging and more repetitive. Teachers in those classes are more directive, breaking each task down into smaller pieces, walking them [the students] through step-by-step, and so leaving students little opportunity to exercise higher-order thinking skills" (McGrath 1994, p. 26). We often find urban students in mathematics classrooms that focus primarily on recall and comprehension; they are seldom given opportunities to advance to synthesis and evaluation (Bloom 1956).

Summary

Varied perceptions exist about students attending urban schools and about teaching in an urban school. Certain perceptions have detrimental effects on all stakeholders in the schooling process—students, parents, teachers, and administrators alike. Mathematics is a discipline in which urban school students historically have exhibited lowered performance (Mullis et al. 1993). The authors contend that it is essential for those urban school mathematics teachers who hold limiting perspectives to examine their perceptions and then create classroom environments that will enhance mathematics instruction.

ENHANCING MATHEMATICS INSTRUCTION IN URBAN SCHOOL SETTINGS

Instructional Process

Instructional delivery is the result of a process that begins with examining one's own value system. According to Nel (1992, pp. 38–40), "teachers' thinking, knowledge, perceptions, and beliefs could be a major contributing factor in the empowerment or the disabling of minority students.... Research literature shows a high correlation between successful academic performance of minority students and educators' sensitivity (attitudes and beliefs), knowledge of cultures, and application of cultural information." The results of her study indicate that cultural sensitivity plays an integral role in the learning process. Teachers with a heightened level of cultural sensitivity realized a need to promote instruction that would actively involve minority students.

In earlier years, Gilbert and Gay (1985, p. 134) recognized that instruction is a behavioral process and noted that "teaching and learning are sociocultural processes that take place within given social systems." Generally speaking, however, teaching and learning are two interdependent processes. That is, as the literature on social learning theory suggests (Bandura 1975), the social context of learning may affect the academic success (i.e., the learning) of students in urban schools. Because children learn behavior patterns from adult models, the presence of teachers and administrators who have special preparation in urban education could provide assistance in eliminating certain difficulties urban school students often experience.

Instructional Strategies

The means for teaching students in urban schools may differ from the means for teaching other students (Gilbert and Gay 1985). Callahan (1994, p. 124) suggests that cooperative learning groups, the use of technology, supervised practice, and good questioning techniques are among the teaching strategies that may be implemented to help urban students "bridge the gaps of cultural and mathematical difference." Strategies that de-emphasize the traditional lecture and emphasize hands-on mathematics exercises and activities have been found effective for urban students (Beckum, Zimny, and Fox 1989), and furthermore, "flexibility and experimentation were [and are] viewed as superior to reliance upon formulaic and static instructional strategies" (p. 438).

Let us examine more closely two components: supervised practice and good questioning techniques. Collins (1992) submits that the purpose of practice is for students to reinforce their mental constructions. Supervised practice extends this purpose by encompassing individual assistance and allowing for expressions of praise and encouragement (Callahan 1994). The following scenario depicts a demonstration of supervised practice in an urban mathematics classroom (all names are pseudonyms):

A teacher and two or three students, all sitting close together, are reviewing the process for dividing whole numbers using base-ten models. After one student successfully completes a problem, the teacher remarks, "Good work, LaTonya! I want you to share your solution with the others." The other two students appear to have some difficulty with the process. Recognizing this, the teacher says to them, "It looks like you're off to a good start. What is your next step?" If constructive criticism is needed, then the teacher could say, "Reggie, I'm not sure how you arrived at your answer. Could you please explain to me what you did?" This interaction allows the students to communicate their mathematical thinking to one another and to the teacher.

Similarly, good questioning techniques should be applied to "advance the lesson, diagnose, or to help students explore new mathematical concepts" (Callahan 1994, p. 124). Johnson (1982, pp. 9–13) proposes a variety of episodes using the art-of-questioning instructional strategy. Each episode highlights questions phrased to involve students actively in the mathematics learning process. His guideline, although not exhaustive, is appropriate for urban students in all grade levels.

The Issue of Curriculum and Instruction

We view a curriculum as those specific constructs and skills that students are expected to comprehend and apply. The development of appropriate curricula for urban youth should be guided by the culture of the stakeholders involved in the educational process (Akbar 1985).

In the process of enhancing mathematics instruction in urban schools, one must examine the curricular framework on which that instruction is built. Tate (1994) argues that mathematics instruction for African American students should build on their thinking and experiences. This implies that the urban school mathematics curriculum—that is, *what* concepts are learned and *why* they are learned—should be constantly reevaluated to assure that each student has the opportunity for meaningful mathematics learning.

The mathematics curriculum for urban students should be the same as the curriculum for suburban and rural students. There are several ways of contextualizing the mathematics so that it becomes meaningful and useful for urban school students, however (Ladson-Billings 1995). The process for contextualizing mathematics depends on instruction, and instruction depends on the learning styles of the student participants. Similar to Tate (1994), Rowser and Koontz (1995) acknowledge that instruction should reflect the experiences and interests of African American students. These experiences and interests necessitate an evaluation and affirmation of the students' learning styles.

The Issue of Learning Styles

"Mathematics ... content and skills instruction are easily adaptable to instructional strategies which allow students to develop as self-confident problem solvers, form appropriate conceptual schemes, and engage in instruction based on diagnosed learning styles and needs" (Midkiff, Towery, and Roark 1991, p. 5). A learning style is a mode through which one effectively processes information from knowledge and recall to synthesis and evaluation. Similar to Midkiff, Towery, and Roark's idea, the authors believe that teachers' sensitivity to learning styles plays a significant role in enhancing mathematical outcomes for urban school students. According to Anderson (1988), learning styles such as field-dependent/relational/affective or field-independent/analytic/nonaffective operate along a continuum of neutral value. Neither a positive nor a negative value is associated with any particular learning style. To this end, the authors profess that learning styles require assessment, not judgment.

The implication for mathematics instruction in urban schools is that the discipline itself is amenable to all learning styles; therefore, instructional presentation must embrace the perspective that problem solvers are cultivated from both field-dependent/relational learners and field-independent/analytic learners. Failure to accommodate learning style in mathematics teaching could lead to academically unsuccessful mathematics students.

EXEMPLARY PROGRAMS FOR TEACHING MATHEMATICS IN URBAN SETTINGS

The future of urban school students as successful and productive citizens in society depends on the process and progress of the education they receive in their urban setting. Urban education should continue to be the focus of inquiry for those who hold firm the belief that "education's goal must be to train all children so that they can live full lives, adapt to change, and contribute to productive work and the service of others" (Gill 1991, p. 14). Given this, it is worthwhile to reflect on a model of the larger urban school structure and, ultimately, understand how mathematics instruction can be enhanced within this structure.

Inasmuch as schools do not operate in isolation, they should be viewed as microcosms of the larger society. This view is central to Walker's (1994) conceptual model for examining issues that relate to urban schools (see fig. 22.1).

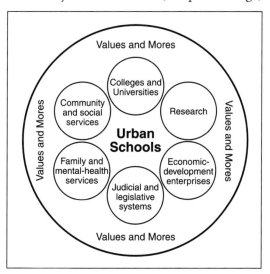

Fig. 22.1. A conceptual model of an urban education program

Although the model addresses organizational development and structure, behavior, and curricular issues, the scope of this discussion is limited solely to curricular issues. The larger circle in the model represents the context for the values and mores of the communities in which urban schools are located. The values and mores influence the experiences and interests of the students. The smaller circles within the model are those six community entities that the authors contend affect urban schools; these entities interconnect and exist within the preestablished values and mores.

The conceptual model evolved from the social learning theory (Bandura 1975) that suggests behavior may be modified if an *awareness,* an *acceptance,* and an *affirmation* of the desired behavior is explored by the behavior-modification participants. Altering the perspectives of teaching mathematics in urban schools may require a change in teacher behavior.

In recent years, numerous innovations to increase the mathematics achievement of urban students have emerged. Such innovations have ranged from small-scale projects to larger, more complex programs. One innovation is Project IMPACT (Increasing the Mathematical Power of All Children and Teachers). See chapter 6 for detailed information about this project. Another, designed to study overall mathematics education reform as well as influence the philosophy of teaching in urban settings, is the QUASAR (Quantitative Understanding: Amplifying Student Achievement and Reasoning) Project (Sullivan 1993). QUASAR's fundamental goal is to "demonstrate that disadvantaged, underachieving students can learn mathematics through a system of instruction that integrates higher-order conceptual reasoning with the learning of basic computation skills" (Sullivan 1993, p. 4). The project emphasizes increased access to high-quality mathematics instruction, improved quality of instruction, and enhanced relevance of school mathematics (Silver, Smith, and Nelson 1995).

In keeping with Gill's (1991) idea of education's goal, other exemplary programs focus on enhancing mathematics instruction for urban school students in order to increase their interest in the mathematics- and science-based professions. One such program, the Academic Year Program, is a major mission of the PRIME organization (PRIME 1994, p. 2). In designated PRIME classes, "led by teachers who are enthusiastic and creative in their teaching styles," the Academic Year Program offers motivational, enrichment, and developmental activities that illustrate mathematical applications and real-world problem solving. Other PRIME programs, like PUP (Prime Universities Program), STEP (Saturday Tutorial and Enrichment Program), PACT (Providing Activities for Careers in Technology), and Collaboration 2004, are committed to preparing African American, Latino, and Native American urban school students to succeed in mathematics and the sciences.

Lastly, Ventures in Education (Widmeyer Group 1995), an educational organization based in New York City, implements a more multifaceted approach to enhancing mathematics and science achievement for students in urban school settings and preparing them for college. Ventures in Education helps schools and districts appraise their curriculum and instruction and improve conditions for effective educational reform. The organization prepares teachers to use student-centered instructional techniques that are research-based and designed to increase students' performance and expand their growth as lifelong learners.

Elements embedded in projects—like Project IMPACT and QUASAR—and programs—such as PRIME and Ventures in Education—challenge mathematics teachers in urban settings to understand and respect the values of their students. Teachers must recognize that the values students establish before entering school affect how they initially perceive mathematics *and* how they respond to mathematics instruction throughout their school years. The authors propose that the elements embodied in these and other exemplars should become the norm and not the exception for teaching mathematics in diverse urban school settings.

CONCLUSION

Reshaping teaching perspectives involves self-reflection, which at times might cause some discomfort. Self-reflection requires an examination of one's own value system; the image could be either pleasing or displeasing. The process, although highly productive, can be demanding and exhausting. Since the concept of "process" implies longevity, desired results are not always immediate. Long-range results are composed of varied small daily differences that ultimately add up to *big* differences. Marian Wright Edelman has stated that "we must not, in trying to think about how we can make a big difference, ignore the small daily differences we can make which, over time, add up to the *big* differences that we often cannot foresee" (Copage 1993). For mathematics classrooms in diverse urban schools, these differences constitute a powerful force that could propel mathematics teaching in these settings in a new and promising direction.

REFERENCES

Akbar, Na'im. *The Community of Self.* Tallahassee, Fla.: Mind Productions and Associates, 1985.

Anderson, James A. "Cognitive Styles and Multicultural Populations." *Journal of Teacher Education* 39 (1988):2–9.

Bandura, Albert. *Social Learning Theory.* Englewood Cliffs, N.J.: Prentice Hall, 1975.

Beckum, Leonard C., Arlene Zimny, and Amy E. Fox. "The Urban Landscape: Educating for the Twenty-first Century." *Journal of Negro Education* 58 (1989):430–41.

Bloom, Benjamin S. *Taxonomy of Educational Objectives: Cognitive Domain.* New York: David McKay, 1956.

Callahan, Walter. "Teaching Middle School Students with Diverse Cultural

Backgrounds." *Mathematics Teacher* 87 (February 1994):122–26.

Collins, David. "Practice." Unpublished manuscript. Duplicated. 1992.

Copage, Eric V. *Black Pearls.* New York: William Morrow & Co., 1993.

Gilbert, Shirl, and Geneva Gay. "Improving the Success in School of Poor Black Children." *Phi Delta Kappan* 67 (1985):133–37.

Gill, Walter. *Issues in African-American Education.* Nashville, Tenn.: Winston-Derek, 1991.

Johnson, David R. *Every Minute Counts: Making Your Math Class Work.* Palo Alto, Calif.: Dale Seymour Publications, 1982.

Ladson-Billings, Gloria. "Making Mathematics Meaningful in a Multicultural Context." In *New Directions for Equity in Mathematics Education,* edited by Walter G. Secada, Elizabeth Fennema, and Lisa B. Adajian, pp. 126–45. New York: Cambridge University Press, 1995.

McGrath, Dennis. Review of *Teaching Advanced Skills to At-Risk Students: Views from Research and Practice,* by Barbara Means, Carol Chelemer, and Michael Knapp. *Alliance* 2 (Fall 1994):26–27.

Midkiff, Ruby Bostick, Ron Towery, and Susan Roark. "Accommodating Learning Style Needs of At-Risk Students in the Library/Media Center." *Ohio Media Spectrum* 43, no. 2 (1991). (ERIC Document Reproduction no. ED 331632)

Mullis, Ina V. S., John A. Dossey, Eugene H. Owen, and Gary W. Phillips. *NAEP 1992: Mathematics Report Card for the Nation and the States.* Princeton, N.J.: Educational Testing Service, 1993.

Nel, Johanna. "The Empowerment of Minority Students: Implications of Cummins' Model for Teacher Education." *Action in Teacher Education* 14 (1992):38–45.

PRIME. "The Prime Directive: Annual Report." Philadelphia: PRIME, 1994.

Rowser, Jacqueline F., and Trish Y. Koontz. "Inclusion of African American Students in Mathematics Classrooms: Issues of Style, Curriculum, and Expectations." *Mathematics Teacher* 88 (September 1995):448–53.

Silver, Edward A., Margaret S. Smith, and Barbara S. Nelson. "The QUASAR Project: Equity Concerns Meet Mathematics Education Reform in the Middle School." In *New Directions for Equity in Mathematics Education,* edited by Walter G. Secada, Elizabeth Fennema, and Lisa B. Adajian, pp. 9–56. New York: Cambridge University Press, 1995.

Sullivan, Oona. "QUASAR Work in Progress: Math for the Thinking Student." *Ford Foundation Report* 24 (1993):3–7.

Tate, William F. "Race, Retrenchment, and the Reform of School Mathematics." *Phi Delta Kappan* 75 (February 1994):477–84.

Walker, Paulette C. "A Proposed Urban Education Program." Working Paper. Tampa: University of South Florida, 1994.

Widmeyer Group. *Ventures in Education.* New York: Ventures in Education, 1995.

23

Microinequity Skits
Generating Conversation
about Gender Issues

Catherine Anne Wick

Patricia Clark Kenschaft

How can teachers and administrators begin to look at the gender inequities that occur with alarming frequency in schools? How can equity
issues attract large audiences at professional conferences? Can equity programs be fun as well as challenging?

Encouraging answers to these questions arose at Joint Mathematics Meetings of the American Mathematical Society and the Mathematical Association of America (MAA) and have spread to the National Council of Teachers of Mathematics (NCTM) and the K–12 mathematics teaching
community through skits. Collecting and dramatizing actual incidents that
portray the relationship between the sexes provide an outlet for frustration,
a method for connecting with other people, and a powerful learning experience for all concerned. This article discusses the various contexts in
which skits have been used to explore gender issues and promote communication. It is an innovative approach that has met with great success.

Small incidents that do not in themselves have much significance, called
"microinequities," constitute a significant portion of discrimination.
Noticing them can seem petty, and even the victims can find them hu-
morous in retrospect. But cumulatively, they render us invisible, require us
to work harder, and steal time and energy as we contemplate whether to
fight back, laugh, or pretend not to notice. They generally divert us from
functioning as competent professionals. In classrooms, inequities in the interactions between teacher and students or among students themselves
send subtle messages about who can do mathematics. Microinequities
wear away at our strength, bit by bit, like drops of water on a rock. Moreover, they create a climate in which outrageous acts are accepted.

A first step in addressing inequities is recognizing their existence. Skits can help an audience consider the issue of inequity in a nonthreatening way, removed from the individual. At a recent conference of an NCTM state affiliate, Cathy Wick presented a session advertised as addressing gender equity. The first few attendees who entered the room were given scripts for the skit "Voices" (see fig. 23.1), which they performed after the presenter's opening remarks. The audience of twenty-four middle school and high school teachers then used the discussion questions at the end of the skit to relate their own work to the depicted scene. Because

---

Voices

Scene: The teacher in a ninth-grade algebra class is developing procedures for solving systems of equations. The thirty students are
seated at desks, and the teacher is working at the overhead projector in the front of the room.

Teacher: I need some points that will lie on the line described by equation number 1.

(*Responses are called out, almost at the same time.*)

Boy A: Zero, eight!

Boy B: Four, zero!

Boy C: Two, three!

(*A brief pause occurs.*)

Boy D: That's wrong. It's two, *four.*

Teacher: (*Records the answers given.*) Does everyone agree? (*There is no response.*)

Teacher: Give me some coordinates to plot for equation number 2.

(Girls A, B, and C and boys E and F raise their hands.)

Boy B: (*Loudly.*) Two, one!

Boy A: Zero, zero doesn't work!

Boy C: One, zero!

Boy A: Four, three!

Teacher: Good! That should be enough. (*The raised hands are lowered.*)

(*The teacher plots the points and continues the lesson.*)

Afterward, the teacher comments to an observer that the girls never
seem to answer questions in class.

Discussion

What is familiar in this classroom scene?

What would you advise this teacher to do to increase the participation
of the girls in class?

Fig. 23.1. "Voices." This skit was modeled on the work of the Woodrow Wilson Gender Equity in Mathematics and Science Congress.

the participants discussed what was performed rather that what any individual was doing or not doing, the tone of the session remained positive and productive.

The idea of using skits to address equity issues arose at a meeting of the MAA Committee on Participation of Women at the 1989 summer Joint Meetings. The committee members were disappointed at the meager attendance at its panel discussions and began relating irritating incidents that had occurred at that very meeting. "These would make good skits," joked Gloria Gilmer. Her joke has since grown into a movement.

The first set of skits, performed at the MAA meeting the following January, was planned too late for official publicity, but two hundred people crowded into the room, standing around the sides and back. The next year, with a better room and adequate publicity, there were four hundred in attendance, and the following year, six hundred. Each year a new script, based on true incidents reported to the committee the previous year, depicted the interactions between men and women within the mathematics community. Several of these skits are included in the MAA publication *Winning Women into Mathematics* (Kenschaft and Keith 1991). Some are available from the MAA in the form of kits for leaders (Geller and Kenschaft 1992). Recent skits are available online through the MAA home page on Gopher (http://www.maa.org).

At the 1991 national Joint Mathematics Meetings, the Committee on Participation of Women began following the skits with discussion groups, led by mathematicians trained by a professional discussion leader. In 1992, they interspersed the skits with intentional breaks during which groups of audience members could discuss the skit they had just seen and report their reactions to the entire audience.

The skits are good fodder for conversation. After skit sessions at the Joint Mathematics Meetings, publishers in the exhibit hall reported overhearing much informal talk about the skits in and around the display booths. Since the session at the NCTM affiliate's conference reported earlier in this article, participants continue to suggest to the presenter new ideas for skits from their own experiences. The interactions stimulated by skits can comfortably balance personal and impersonal reports.

In the summer of 1993, the Woodrow Wilson National Fellowship Foundation sponsored the Congress on Gender Equity in Mathematics and Science. Twenty-five secondary school master teachers devoted ten days to studying research, talking with scholars, reading, and sharing personal experiences, with the goal of developing action plans for increasing gender equity in mathematics and science classrooms. Cathy Wick, director of the congress, brought the idea of microinequity skits to the attention of the congress participants. A small group of the teachers decided to dramatize some of their stories. Using the work of the MAA committee as a model, these teachers wrote skits to portray microinequities in their world of work, the secondary school.

The activity of writing the skits provided a forum for the skits' authors to discuss the many situations in which inequity can rear its ugly head in the school setting. "Whose Schedule Is It?" in figure 23.2 dramatizes one example. Once written, the skits were performed by their authors for a sympathetic audience, the other congress participants. Some editorial privilege, broad direction, and minimal props helped make the performances a light look at a rather heavy topic. A published report of the

---

Whose Schedule Is It?

Scene: At a K–12 open school, a female staff member is welcoming a new female student and her parent to the fall scheduling conference. The three players greet each other, mumble pleasantries, and sit down around a table.

Advisor: Let's talk about your class schedule. It would be good to have some English on your schedule. There is a letter-writing class. (*The advisor pauses and looks at the student for a response. Seeing none, she continues.*)

Advisor: Some of my advisees have enjoyed the mythology class. (*Pause. Student shrugs noncommittally.*)

Advisor: How about poetry?

Student: (*Brightens visibly.*) That sounds good!

(*Parent nods approvingly.*)

Advisor: Good! Now let's see what else we can find for you. If you like poetry, you won't want to take math.

Student: (*Interrupts.*) Oh, math is my favorite.

Advisor: (*Undaunted, ignoring the girl's comment.*) Even if you're not very good at it, it would probably be a good idea for you to have some math on your schedule.

Student: Sure. I like math.

Parent: She did very well in math at her previous school.

Advisor: (*Still not hearing.*) Let's see, you just finished seventh grade. Well, a poet wouldn't want to take algebra.

Narrator: We'll leave this scene, as parent and daughter try to get the advisor's attention. With some effort, the student and her parent persuade the advisor to include algebra in her schedule.

Discussion

What are the stated and unstated messages in this scene?

How can you determine if such scenes occur in your school?

What can you do about the similar situations in your school?

Fig. 23.2. "Whose Schedule Is It?" This skit was developed as part of the Woodrow Wilson Gender Equity in Mathematics and Science Congress, 1993. The skit's writers are Kathie Anderson, Mary Gromko, Paul Jones, Linda Padwa, Loretta Rector, Teddy Reynolds, John Roeder, Jackie Simms, and Cathy Wick.

congress (Woodrow Wilson National Fellowship Foundation 1993) includes all the skits developed by the participants.

It is impressive to note how much the leaders learn each time they are involved in skit presentations. Watching our own experiences come alive again sheds a whole new light on them. As we see them from the outside, we feel them again inside. Both minds and emotions respond.

The writing of skits can be used to help teachers, counselors, administrators, and other school professionals share their stories and their concerns in a way that doesn't accuse or blame. In a workshop setting, the participants have time to work in groups, to tell of their individual experiences, and to develop a script for one or more of the stories in their group. This approach was used by Cathy Wick in a workshop at a recent NCTM annual meeting. The participants were teachers, teacher educators, and mathematics supervisors. They performed a prewritten skit, then worked in groups to select a story from some member's personal experience and to dramatize it for the other participants. Although the writing task was not completed in the allotted time, the participants agreed that they were well on their way to using skits in their teaching and in their work with colleagues. What was accomplished in the groups, when presented to all in attendance, allowed them to recognize the many faces of inequity and the ways in which it is perceived by different people. The workshop participants departed with ideas about where to look within their own settings to find and correct inequities, as well as how to use skits in the process.

We encourage other groups to use skits as a vehicle for promoting awareness and discussion about equity issues, either by producing some already written skits, by writing and producing new ones, or by helping others generate their own. The demand for acting ability is minimal; enthusiasm and willingness are the only requirements. No audience objects to actors who read scripts; serious memorization is not necessary.

Whether we are involved as writers, performers, or observers, it is in sharing our responses to the drama of microinequity skits with others that we realize how much we are part of a web interdependent with other people. Our decisions and actions depend on theirs, and theirs on ours. None of us is completely innocent, and we can help one another become more nearly the people we want to be. The skits help us listen to one another kindly and cheerfully.

REFERENCES

Geller, Susan, and Patricia Clark Kenschaft. *Skit Kits.* Washington, D.C.: Mathematical Association of America, 1992.

Kenschaft, Patricia Clark, and Sandra Zaroodny Keith, eds. *Winning Women into Mathematics.* Washington, D.C.: Mathematical Association of America, 1991.

Woodrow Wilson National Fellowship Foundation. *Woodrow Wilson Gender Equity in Mathematics and Science Congress (WW-GEMS).* Princeton, N.J.: Woodrow Wilson National Fellowship Foundation, 1993.

24

Communication Strategies to Support Preservice Mathematics Teachers from Diverse Backgrounds

Rheta N. Rubenstein

MANY educators agree that schools in a diverse culture are strengthened by a diverse teaching force (Orlikow and Young 1993; Gollnick 1992; Grant and Secada 1990). Yet data show that the teaching force of the next century is expected to be homogeneous—in fact, increasingly white and female (Grant and Secada 1990). If this prediction is to be altered, teacher education programs need to identify ways to recruit and support candidates from a variety of backgrounds. (See Gollnick [1992] for promising recruitment practices.) Nelson-Barber and Mitchell (1992) reviewed five programs that address these concerns and found that they shared several important elements:

- Practical field experience in multicultural communities (not just in schools)
- Guided reflection about those experiences done with professors, veteran teachers, and cohorts of varying backgrounds
- Attention to, and support of, the personal as well as professional growth of student teachers
- Learning experiences related to communication

The last, communication, is the focus of this article.

There is strong agreement that effective teaching is a human-relations and communicative activity (Irvine 1992). Current thinking about effective learning and teaching, including attention to varied intelligences (Gardner 1983), the roles of contextualization and applications, constructivist views of learning (Davis, Maher, and Noddings 1991), and the recommendations of the National Council of Teachers of Mathematics (1989, 1991), recognizes the central role of communication in the teaching-learning process. This insight is of particular importance for student-teachers for whom English is not the first language. Often these teacher-candidates have chosen to teach mathematics because they perceive it as less language based than other subjects. Moreover, their university coursework in mathematics typically requires less writing and speaking than many other majors, which further limits their opportunities to use language in their own learning.

CONTEXT

At the University of Windsor in Windsor, Ontario, I have had the opportunity to work with student-teachers from eastern Europe, the Middle East, south Asia, the Far East, and Africa, all of whom spoke first languages other than English. These students were in a one-year postbaccalaureate preservice program that included nine practice-teaching weeks spread over the year in four two- or three-week placements. In addition, during most non–practice-teaching weeks, the students spent two days in one school, observing and doing teaching-related field activities. My students were preparing to teach youngsters from grades 4 through 10. Even though their area of specialization was mathematics, their most probable future job would be as a seventh- or eighth-grade teacher in a general classroom because many Ontario elementary schools encompass grades K–8 in self-contained classrooms. They were all Canadian citizens, had lived and worked in Canada for a number of years, and were generally fluent in English.

TWO STORIES AND FIRST SUGGESTIONS

Let me begin with experiences with my first international student-teachers—experiences that stirred my interest in identifying supportive strategies. The first experience took place in my office very early in the term in a conversation with Sal. (Pseudonyms are used throughout.) As his advisor for student teaching, I asked one of my typical questions, "What do you feel most confident about?" He responded, as many students do, that he was interested in youngsters, mathematics, and helping people learn. Then I asked what he was most concerned about. He said, "I will pronounce words wrong and the students will laugh at me." I suggested that Sal consider one of my favorites of life's remedies, "If you can't fix it, feature it." I suggested that he consider telling the students that he and they were both learning, but learning different things. He would appreciate their helping him with his pronunciation while he helped them with their mathematics. He was relieved and pleased by this idea.

The second story involves Mel, whom I first observed teaching in a fourth-grade classroom early in his October placement. He was going through the motions of teaching, but in a totally perfunctory way. For example, he read the children a story but was nearly inaudible and used no expression or introduction. He followed the story with questions that I was amazed to hear the students answer. I learned later that the story was a movie they had all seen! He seemed like a stranger in the room, giving directions that students followed, but only because they knew the routines and their "real" teacher was watching. He made little eye contact with the students, spoke very timidly, and seemed to be in a daze about what was happening.

In November, when I observed Mel in an eighth-grade class, he greeted the students warmly at the door before class, chatted with several informally, and seemed generally relaxed. I was amazed by the difference and very pleased. I spoke to the associate (cooperating teacher) and learned, among other things, that the school had a tradition of holding class lunches on Fridays. When she learned of Mel's background, she invited him the week before his student teaching began to share Middle Eastern foods with the students at their Friday lunch. The students liked the hummus, baba ghanoush, and pita bread, and Mel had an opportunity to talk with them about his heritage. I remarked to the associate about the tremendous difference I saw in Mel. She told me that she herself had immigrated to Canada from Sweden when she was a school-aged child. She remembered the wonderful things people had done for her, and she enjoyed doing the same for others.

One can glean many lessons from these two stories. Here are two things I learned: pronunciation, although certainly a concern, is not the most important issue in working with international student-teachers. Getting to know people and building human relationships is.

As a result, my first suggestion for everyone involved in preservice programs—university professors, student teachers, associates, pupils—is to build human relationships, to get to know one another and appreciate one another's uniqueness. Of course, this is a long-term goal, but it must be actively worked toward. This concept is confirmed by Nelson-Barber and Mitchell (1992), who note the value of professor-student relationships and heterogeneous student cohorts in effective programs for student-teachers from diverse cultures.

The second suggestion is to recognize that students not native to North America may be unfamiliar with North American schools and their structures, organization, and culture. As future teachers, students need to visit schools, observe, and reflect on their observations in a guided way (Nelson-Barber and Mitchell 1992). Professors, associates, and majority-culture teacher-candidates benefit when they reflect together on what was observed, what is expected, and how these observations and expectations compare with students' personal experiences and expectations. Such conversations promote cultural understanding in more than one direction and provide further opportunities for personal and professional growth and communication.

PERSPECTIVES ON SUGGESTIONS

Since I was operating at a naive level of language concerns when I first met Sal, my initial suggestions (fig. 24.1) were simplistic. When I visited Mel in the second school and I realized the value of sharing oneself with others, I decided that this strategy needed to be communicated to the other student-teachers, so I began to identify suggestions based on relationships (fig. 24.2).

TEACHING SUGGESTIONS

As I continued coaching all my student-teachers and reflecting on good teaching, I also thought about the changing paradigms in teaching. Irvine (1992) noted that although all effective teachers structure learning activities to promote meaningful learning, effective teachers of minority students more often use interactive rather than didactic methods. They give frequent feedback and use demonstrations, questions, and rephrasings. In

---

General Suggestions for Teachers Teaching in a Nonnative Language

1. Socialize with native speakers.
2. Work together with language majors. They may have suggestions for language support and resources for you.
3. Ask friends to identify and assist you with pronunciation, idioms, and unfamiliar expressions.
4. Continue to use all the strategies you've developed for learning a second language.
5. Use the local language as much as possible each day .
6. Read literature, magazines, comics, and other sources your pupils read.
7. Keep a journal with new words and expressions. Underline one or two language structures that you want to learn and talk about them with a "buddy."
8. Get and use a good dictionary of the local language.
9. Make a list for yourself of essential teaching and content words, phrases, and expressions and practice pronouncing them, for example, *assignment, example, ratio, angle, decimal, geometry, please give me your attention*. Rehearse these with a native speaker. Keep a card file of important phrases and sentences. Record the pronunciation in the way that works best for you.
10. Check the way mathematics symbols are read. It may vary in different parts of the world or in different parts of mathematics.
11. Speak clearly and slowly. Project your voice. Maintain eye contact with students.

Fig. 24.1. A list of general suggestions for teachers teaching in a language other than their native one

Suggestions for Building Rapport with Pupils

Get to know your students.

1. Talk to several students individually at recess or before or after school.
2. Learn your students' names.
   a. When they are sitting quietly, study the seating plan and their faces.
   b. Have each one tell you something special about her or him and note what is said.
   c. Take photographs or make sketches or descriptions of the students.
   d. Quiz yourself daily on students' names when they enter the classroom.
   e. After a few days, identify pupils whose names you still don't know. Look closely at them and learn their names.
3. Talk with associates, other teachers in the school, and teaching partners to learn what students are interested in and to share your observations about them.
4. If possible, get involved in some out-of-school activity with youth.
5. Share with students your enthusiasm about knowing them better.

Help your students get to know you.

1. Share things about yourself, your culture, your heritage, your language; use your international experience to increase your pupils' global awareness.
2. Find ways to share food, art, writing, photographs, and other cultural materials.
3. Build into the mathematics instruction opportunities to learn about your culture and others. For example, use international data as sources for statistics work; use jewelry, flags, architecture, or other significant items as sources for geometry work; use maps and scale drawings related to your background as sources for work in ratio and proportion. (See Rubenstein [1993] and other chapters in this yearbook for more suggestions.)

Build an environment in which everyone is learning together.

Remind students that they are all learning together and that you expect them to assist one another in class. Tell students that you will help them learn mathematics and other subjects but they can help you with English. If they hear you say something that sounds funny, ask them to help you instead of laughing at you. Thank them when they help you and invite them to thank one another for assistance with their studies.

Fig. 24.2. A list of suggestions for building a rapport with pupils

mathematics education in particular, these strategies have been translated into an emphasis on tasks and discourse in classrooms (NCTM 1991) and include group work, the use of manipulatives, multiple modes of representation, and open-ended questions. I realized that although these changes, with their focus on communication, may create increased challenges for those for whom English is not the first language, they may also present increased opportunities. Indeed, many of the reform suggestions for effective classroom interactions need only slight modification and more emphasis for teachers who are second-language speakers. Figure 24.3 identifies several of these strategies.

When I coach student-teachers, rather than "tell" them what to do, as these lists might suggest, I try to keep suggestions in mind, and I pose questions to get the students to reflect, self-evaluate, and figure out strategies for themselves. In the course of debriefing after a teaching episode, for example, I ask questions like "What strategies did you use today that promoted successful communication?" "What other strategies might you use?" "How can you help the students help one another to learn?" With all student-teachers, the goal is to self-evaluate and find effective strategies for their own teaching.

Textbooks and curriculum guides, too, present challenges. For example, the day I observed Mel in the eighth-grade class, I learned that he assigned problems from the textbook without carefully reading the directions. Consequently, he was confused when students asked how to do the work. This and related observations led to ideas for working with textbooks and other teaching materials (fig. 24.4).

COMMUNICATING WITH ASSOCIATES

Associates, pupils, and student-teachers need to put a priority on getting to know one another. Student-teachers are given many directions and suggestions by associates. Sometimes misunderstandings occur. One method I try to use and encourage others to try is paraphrasing. Listeners repeat what they understand the speaker to have said: "Let me see if I understand you. You want me to help the fifth graders understand what fractions mean by using pictures, bars, and circle models. By the end of the week they should be able to draw and explain when fractions are equivalent for halves, thirds, fourths, sixths, and eighths. Is that correct?"

When associates give comments or an evaluation in writing, it helps for the associate and student-teacher to read the notes together. I found that one student-teacher was tucking away all his associate's comments and saving them to read at home. This preempted his opportunity to clarify them and risked his misunderstanding what was intended.

CONCLUSION

If we are to celebrate diversity in our communities and schools, we must celebrate it, too, in our teacher-preparation institutions. This article has offered several ideas for supporting such efforts in the area of communication. Foremost is building human relationships among everyone involved in the teaching and teacher-education processes. As with other

Suggestions for Classroom Interactions

1. Use tools to help you communicate with students.
   a) Use manipulatives, pictures, contexts, stories, and drama.
   b) Write directions, key questions, terms, or ideas on chart paper, the chalkboard, or the overhead projector.
   c) Demonstrate (show, don't just tell) what you want students to do.
   d) If you use handouts, have students read the directions. Have them repeat them in their own words before following them. Check for understanding.

2. Listen to students. Don't assume you know what they will say.

3. Watch for clues that students are understanding.
   a) Use eye contact.
   b) Watch their facial expressions and other body language.
   c) Notice if they are asking one another to explain what you are saying.
   d) Ask them to say back to you what you have explained (directions, new ideas, etc.).

4. When students respond and you don't understand, try one of the following:
   a) Ask them to speak slower or use different words.
   b) Ask another student to explain what the first student said.
   c) Ask them to show what they mean by coming to the chalkboard, drawing a diagram, or using concrete materials.
   d) If appropriate, promise to speak personally with them later, then do so.
   e) Identify what you think you *do* understand and say it back to the student: "What I heard you say was that you have another method you'd like to use. But I'm not following your method. Please explain it again slower or show us at the board."

5. Use lesson openings and closings to your advantage (and your students'!).
   a) Begin by asking them where you left off yesterday or ask key questions to review what they should have learned. Ask more than one student to say what was learned in a different way. Listen to how they phrase things. Ask other students for corrections or modifications.
   b) Include a summary at the end of your lesson. Have students tell what they have learned. Listen to how they say it. As above, ask for other ways to express the new ideas.

6. Use guided practice in your lessons, as appropriate, for example, for skill development. "We'll do number 1 together." Then develop it with them. "Now, you do number 2." Give them an item just like the first, monitor them, and see how they do. In this way you get evidence of their learning, and you see which students understand and can be resources for explaining to others. Continue alternating between examples done together and those done by students individually or in pairs.

Fig. 24.3. A list of suggestions for classroom interactions

Suggestions for Working with Textbooks

1. Be sure to read the directions in front of problems. Don't assume from the format of the page that you know what students are being asked to do.

2. Look back to see how the authors developed earlier concepts and skills. Doing so may give you words or visuals to help refresh (or reteach) students on prerequisites.

3. Look ahead to see where the authors are going. You may find that you can teach less because more will be done later with a new idea.

4. Read student textbooks and other learning materials to become more familiar with language constructions.

Fig. 24.4. A list of suggestions for working with textbooks

educational endeavors, individual instructors and institutions need to examine their goals, needs, and resources to design what is appropriate for their own program.

References

Davis, Robert B., Carolyn A. Maher, and Nel Noddings. *Constructivist Views on the Teaching and Learning of Mathematics.* Reston, Va.: National Council of Teachers of Mathematics, 1991.

Gardner, Howard. *Frames of Mind: The Theory of Multiple Intelligences.* New York: Basic Books, 1983.

Gollnick, Donna A. "Understanding the Dynamics of Race, Class, and Gender." In *Diversity in Teacher Education: New Expectations,* edited by Mary E. Dilworth, pp. 63–78. San Francisco: Jossey-Bass Publishers, 1992.

Grant, Carl A., and Walter G. Secada. "Preparing Teachers for Diversity." In *Handbook of Research on Teacher Education,* edited by Robert W. Houston, pp. 403–22. New York: Macmillan Publishing Co., 1990.

Irvine, Jacqueline Jordan. "Making Teacher Education Culturally Responsive." In *Diversity in Teacher Education: New Expectations,* edited by Mary E. Dilworth, pp. 79–92. San Francisco: Jossey-Bass Publishers, 1992.

National Council of Teachers of Mathematics. *Curriculum and Evaluation Standards for School Mathematics.* Reston, Va.: National Council of Teachers of Mathematics, 1989.

————. *Professional Standards for Teaching Mathematics.* Reston, Va.: National Council of Teachers of Mathematics, 1991.

Nelson-Barber, Sharon S., and Jean Mitchell. "Restructuring for Diversity: Five Regional Portraits." In *Diversity in Teacher Education: New Expectations,* edited by Mary E. Dilworth, pp. 229–62. San Francisco: Jossey-Bass Publishers, 1992.

Orlikow, Lionel, and Jon Young. "The Struggle for Change: Teacher Education in Canada." In *Inequality and Teacher Education: An International Perspective,* edited by Gajendra K. Verma, pp. 70–88. London: Falmer Press, 1993.

Rubenstein, Rheta. "A Mathematical World Matrix." *Australian Mathematics Teacher* 49 (August 1993): 28–31.

25

Building Bridges between Diverse Families and the Classroom
Involving Parents in School Mathematics

Dominic Peressini

RECENT reform recommendations for education emphasize the importance of developing partnerships with parents, families, and the community (U.S. Department of Education 1994). Parental involvement assists
teachers and parents in recognizing and capitalizing on the diverse cultures that compose a typical mathematics classroom. This article describes
parent involvement that recognizes and uses the varied backgrounds of
families, numerous types of parent involvement applicable to the mathematics classroom, and examples of strategies and materials that mathematics teachers employ in order to involve parents actively in their children's mathematics education. (I use the terms *parents* and *parent
involvement* throughout this paper; I recognize, however, that other
adults—guardians, stepparents, aunts, uncles, grandparents, siblings, and
cousins—may carry the primary responsibility for a child's health, development, and education. Therefore, all references to "parents" and "parent
involvement" are meant to include any adults who play an important role
in a child's home life.)

THE INVOLVEMENT OF CULTURALLY DIVERSE PARENTS

Students of color have traditionally not performed as well in school as
their nonminority peers (Chavkin 1993). This is especially true in mathematics (Secada 1992). These lower levels of achievement result, in part,
from differences in what the child experiences at home and what is experienced and expected at school (Comer 1980). As America becomes increasingly multicultural and multilingual, the discontinuities between home and
school demand increased attention. Because of differences in culture and
ethnicity, children from minority families may have different preparation

222

from what schools expect. Lightfoot (1978) refers to this as "worlds apart" and describes the dilemma of this situation (quoted in Liontos 1992, p. 11):

> Children cannot be expected to bridge the gaps and overcome the confusion of who to learn from. The predictable consequence in such situations is that children usually embrace the familiar home culture and reject the unfamiliar school culture, including its academic components and goals.

Swap (1993), extending Ogbu's (1990) work, describes how bridges between schools and culturally diverse homes can be constructed through parent involvement. She describes parents as resources who, by their involvement, enhance the culture of the school and the educational activities that take place there. Parent involvement can help mold the school and its curriculum so that it reflects the values, beliefs, and cultural backgrounds of the student population in the school. Including parents' personal and professional expertise, as well as their cultural backgrounds, further enriches schools by encouraging the participation of all parents. In addition, emphasizing parent involvement at home as well as at the school and including activities that inform parents about their children's education further diminish the gap between school and home. This approach necessitates that parents and educators maintain two-way communication and mutual respect and support, viewing one another as experts.

PARENTS AND MATHEMATICS EDUCATION

Parent involvement in mathematics education includes a variety of activities. Epstein (1994) lists a useful set of six parent-involvement categories that can guide educators. These categories—*parenting, communicating, volunteering, learning at home, decision making,* and *community collaboration*—describe various ways to involve parents in their children's mathematics education.

Parenting

Parenting refers to the support that families give their children: ensuring their children's health and safety, developing child-rearing approaches that prepare children for school and maintain healthy child development across grades, and building positive home conditions that support learning and behavior throughout the school years. Since this type of involvement is most often outside of the classroom teacher's realm, it may not normally be a consideration for mathematics teachers' parent-involvement strategies.

Communicating

Communicating refers to establishing a clear school-to-home and home-to-school flow of information about school programs and children's progress. Communication from mathematics teachers to parents is essential as the ideas outlined in the NCTM *Standards* documents—ideas very different from what most parents experienced as learners of mathematics—are implemented (NCTM 1989, 1991, 1995).

One of the more effective avenues for mathematics teachers to communicate with their students' parents is through mathematics newsletters. Newsletters often contain updates on what is occurring in mathematics classrooms, descriptions and explanations of curricular content and teaching pedagogy, samples of student work, student-written articles, sections for parent questions, and invitations to parents to visit the mathematics classroom.

Sensitivity to the cultural diversity of student populations can be achieved by offering multiple translations of mathematics newsletters, including in them a broad mix of students' work that reflects their cultural backgrounds, and giving parents a means to inquire about, and respond to, the newletter's contents. In addition, newsletters allow mathematics teachers to communicate with parents who may not be able to talk with the teacher at the school for a variety of socioeconomic or cultural reasons.

Communication between the mathematics classroom and families can also be accomplished through a number of other strategies: establishing networks of families who keep each other informed about what is occurring in their children's mathematics classrooms; organizing back-to-school nights at which families can hear about the mathematics program and instruction; offering formal and informal parent-teacher conferences; writing comments on individual student's grade reports; sending home portfolios of students' work; and establishing an open-door policy for visits so that parents know they are welcome to approach their child's mathematics teacher for any information they desire.

It is essential, however, that communication not be limited to teachers' informing parents. Parents must have an opportunity to respond and ask questions when necessary. Two-way communication ensures that parents are aware of what their children are experiencing in the mathematics classroom, have a variety of avenues for voicing their concerns, are able to express their cultural values, and remain in contact with their children's mathematics teachers.

Volunteering

Volunteering refers to parents' and families' volunteering and observing at the school or in other locations to support students, teachers, school programs, and the school. Encouraging parents to become active in the classroom is a powerful way of helping them understand the changes taking place in their children's mathematics education. It not only garners support for the classroom teacher's efforts to implement reformed mathematics instruction but also is the most effective means for shaping the school culture so that it more accurately reflects the diverse cultures of its student population.

Mathematics teachers can engage in a variety of activities that focus on parent involvement at the classroom and school level. Some of these include creating "parent rooms" at the school, emphasizing an open mathematics classroom in which parents feel comfortable to drop in and observe a mathematics lesson, and using parent volunteers in classrooms. Parent volunteers can help students with their mathematics assignments, create mathematics bulletin boards, help correct and record students' mathematics assignments and quizzes, and participate in the daily mathematics lesson. Parents can also direct lessons that incorporate their unique cultural backgrounds, lead field trips to their working environments, and develop and implement integrated curricular activities that reflect some of the variety in the students' cultural backgrounds.

One powerful method for including students' cultural backgrounds in mathematics classrooms is the use of literature. A variety of books are written with a multicultural perspective. (See, for example, *Ashanti to Zulu* [Musgrove 1976] and *Pueblo Storyteller* [Hoyt-Goldsmith 1991].) Families can help mathematics teachers identify these books and participate in reading them to students in the mathematics classroom. These stories can then furnish a multicultural context for a variety of mathematics problems. (For an example of these types of problems, see *Good Books/Good Math* [Jenkins et al. 1991].)

Learning at Home

Learning at home refers to parents' monitoring and assisting their children in learning activities at home, including homework and other curricular-linked activities and decisions. As the ideas of the NCTM *Standards* are implemented in mathematics classrooms, it is essential that parents be involved in their children's mathematics education at home. This is especially true of parents who may not be able to involve themselves in other types of activities because of socioeconomic factors or cultural beliefs and norms.

Helping with their children's home assignments is perhaps the most common way that parents are involved in mathematics education. As changes in mathematical content and teaching pedagogy continue to develop, however, and because of reform recommendations and students' progression through the schools, parents may find themselves on unfamiliar ground when they attempt to work with their children on mathematics. Mathematics teachers can assist parents by organizing and offering activities that are meant to be completed by both the parent and the student, thus making parents' efforts more guided and, therefore, more productive. Examples of these types of activities are presented in figure 25.1. This approach offers guidance for parents who become involved in their students' mathematics assignments and allows parents and students to learn from one another as they progress through the activities.

HOMEWORK IDEAS

What is mathematical about my family?

Have the children generate with their parents the following types of activities and record them in a family math journal (spiral notebook):

- Question your family members and relatives about how they use numbers in their lives.
  Make a list.
  Write a book.

- List as many ways as you can think of to make a number using other numbers (e.g., 12 = 5 + 7; 12 = 6 + 6; 12 = 3 + 3 + 3 + 3).

- Write word problems about something that happened at your home today.

- Figure out how many days until your birthday. How many days until your mom's or dad's birthday?

- Go on a walk in your neighborhood.
  Look for numbers.
  Look for shapes.
  Count the number of a chosen item.
  Estimate the distance walked or the amount of time to cover a set distance.

- When you go to the store with your child, ask the child questions like these:
  Which item would be a better buy?
  How much change should we get back?
  How much money will we save if we use our coupons?

- Talk about the mail that comes:
  How much postage is there on the mail that came today? This week?
  Graph the kinds of mail that come to our house for a week or a month.

- When reading the newspaper, ask or do the following:
  How many different numbers can we find in 5 minutes?
  Let's cut out graphs and see what we can learn together.
  If we used all the coupons in the paper today, how much money could we save?

- Involve your child in the process of buying, especially those things that he or she may need or want, such as clothing, books, snacks, school supplies.

- When you read a book together, ask the child questions that relate to numbers, shapes, and so on.

- Counting:
  There are always things to count. Even if your child knows how to count, she or he continues to learn new things about the relationship between numbers. So keep counting and count more than 10 or 50 or even 100 items.

Source: These activities were developed as part of the Cognitively Guided Instruction (CGI) project (Carpenter and Fennema 1992) and were adapted from *Cognitively Guided Instruction, Communication with Parents: A Compilation of Ideas* (Jenkins and Keith 1991). Used with permission.

Fig. 25.1. Mathematics activities that promote parent involvement

Often when parents help their children with their mathematics assignments, they do it in a fashion that does not support what the mathematics teacher is trying to accomplish in the classroom. For example, instead of letting the child struggle with the mathematics needed to solve a problem and come up with her or his own solution, parents may simply provide the answer. Mathematics teachers can overcome this problem by offering parents suggestions and techniques. The program in *Family Math* (Stenmark, Thompson, and Cossey 1986) is a well-organized project that focuses on parents and children learning mathematics together.

Decision Making

Decision making refers to parents' participating in school decisions, governance, and advocacy activities through the PTA, committees, councils, and other parent organizations. Many educators and parents view decision making as the most empowering and productive type of parent involvement. It is also considered the most difficult and challenging type to organize and implement.

As teachers, administrators, and parents become comfortable with parent involvement in mathematics education, the role of parents in the schooling process can increase to include more central decision-making activities. This includes giving parents a voice in decisions regarding the mathematics curriculum, textbooks, forms of assessment, general policy, personnel, governance, and global reform issues. Comer (1980, p. 70) emphasizes the importance of creating this type of shared responsibility and decision making among educators and parents:

> Parents are more likely to support a school program in which they are partners in decision-making and welcome at times other than when their children are in trouble. Parent interest and support for the school and its staff makes it easier for youngsters to relate to and identify themselves with the goals, values, and personnel of the school, a powerful motivation to tune in and turn on to education. At the same time, parental involvement insures that their cultural values and interests are respected.

Community Collaboration

Community collaboration refers to coordinating the work and resources of community businesses, agencies, colleges or universities, and other groups to strengthen school programs, family practices, and student learning and development. This includes holding community meetings that not only inform the community about the mathematics programs in their schools but also allow mathematics educators to hear the needs of the community. Schools may also organize mathematics "carnivals" in which their students demonstrate mathematics projects and activities.

Businesses can offer their expertise and financial or material support. Local businesses may establish partnerships with schools so that students can spend a day at the particular business and observe how mathematics is applied in the real world. The employees of the business may volunteer to spend an hour a week at the school tutoring students in mathematics or offering career counseling to interested students. Local universities can offer professional development opportunities for mathematics teachers. In addition, universities can organize campus orientation events that include parent and student visits to mathematics and science departments, seminar and laboratory observations, and informal discussions with university faculty. These activities—some of the many that support community collaboration—foster a reservoir of goodwill between schools and the community and, as a result, enhance mathematics education for students.

CONCLUSION

Certainly, all parents want the best education for their children and are interested in involving themselves in their child's mathematics education. It is important to realize, however, that implementing parent-involvement activities is at times difficult. Parents may hesitate to become involved in their children's mathematics education for a number of reasons: they may not have the time or means to involve themselves; they may have had prior negative experiences with schools and mathematics; they may believe that it is not proper to question educators; they may be suspicious of schools and teachers; or they may have feelings of low self-esteem and inadequacy (Liontos 1992; Swap 1993). Mathematics teachers can overcome these challenges with patience, respect, understanding, and a well-planned system for parent involvement incorporating a variety of activities and strategies.

Parent involvement offers much hope for enriching mathematics programs by making them more culturally diverse and by increasing the mathematical power of those students who come from a variety of cultural and ethnic backgrounds. Parent involvement in the mathematics classroom builds a bridge from the classroom to the outside world. This bridge allows for communication between schools and families, so that parents can be informed and understand the changes in their children's mathematics education. In turn, this bridge allows teachers to hear the voices of their students' families and to better recognize the cultural diversity of their students' backgrounds. As both mathematics educators and parents become more comfortable crossing these bridges and experiencing a variety of perspectives, mathematics education will become more reflective of the diverse population that it serves.

REFERENCES

Carpenter, Thomas P., and Elizabeth Fennema. "Cognitively Guided Instruction: Building on the Knowledge of Students and Teachers." In *International Journal of Educational Research,* vol. 17, special issue edited by Walter G. Secada, pp. 457–70. Oxford: Pergamon Press, 1992.

Chavkin, Nancy F., ed. *Families and Schools in a Pluralistic Society.* Albany, N.Y.: State University of New York Press, 1993.

Comer, James P. *School Power: Implications of an Intervention Project.* New York: Free Press, 1980.

Epstein, Joyce L. "Theory to Practice: School and Family Partnerships Lead to School Improvement." In *School, Family and Community Interaction: A View from the Firing Lines,* edited by Cheryl L. Fagnano and Beverly Z. Werber, pp. 39–52. Boulder, Colo.: Westview Press, 1994.

Hoyt-Goldsmith, Diane. *Pueblo Storyteller.* New York: Holiday House, 1991.

Jenkins, Mazie, and Annie Keith. *Cognitively Guided Instruction—Communication with Parents: A Compilation of Ideas.* Madison, Wis.: Wisconsin Center for Education Research, 1991.

Jenkins, Mazie, Lois Lehmann, Jeff Maas, Barbara Marten, Kent Wells, and Pat Wood. *Good Books/Good Math.* Madison, Wis.: Wisconsin Center for Education Research, 1991.

Lightfoot, Sara L. *Worlds Apart: Relationships between Families and Schools.* New York: Basic Books, 1978.

Liontos, Lynn L. *At-Risk Families and Schools: Becoming Partners.* Eugene, Oreg.: ERIC Clearinghouse on Educational Management, 1992.

Musgrove, Margaret. *Ashanti to Zulu: African Traditions.* New York: Dial Press, 1976.

National Council of Teachers of Mathematics. *Assessment Standards for School Mathematics.* Reston, Va.: National Council of Teachers of Mathematics, 1995.

———. *Curriculum and Evaluation Standards for School Mathematics.* Reston, Va.: National Council of Teachers of Mathematics, 1989.

———. *Professional Standards for Teaching Mathematics.* Reston, Va.: National Council of Teachers of Mathematics, 1991.

Ogbu, John U. "Overcoming Racial Barriers to Equal Access." In *Access to Knowledge,* edited by John I. Goodlad, pp. 59–90. New York: College Entrance Examination Board, 1990.

Secada, Walter G. "Race, Ethnicity, Social Class, Language, and Achievement in Mathematics." In *Handbook of Research on Mathematics Teaching and Learning,* edited by Douglas A. Grouws, pp. 623–60. New York: Macmillan Publishing Co., 1992.

Stenmark, Jean K., Virginia Thompson, and Ruth Cossey. *Family Math.* Berkeley, Calif.: EQUALS, Lawrence Hall of Science, University of California, Berkeley, 1986.

Swap, Susan M. *Developing Home-School Partnerships.* New York: Teachers College Press, 1993.

U.S. Department of Education. *Goals 2000: A World-Class Education for Every Child.* Washington, D.C.: U.S. Government Printing Office, 1994.

26

Mathematically Empowering Urban African American Students through Family Involvement

Marilyn Strutchens

Debbie Thomas

Fran Davis Perkins

ALL too often, systemic educational change is attempted without considering the parents of school-aged children. This disregard has led to misunderstanding the changes occurring in schools and why they are needed. Moreover, valuable resources are left untapped or are not used in ways that lead to students' success in schools. To make educational change profitable for all students, parents and community leaders must have an informed and educated view of the changes and how they can help students adapt to new methods of teaching and learning. Furthermore, schools and change agents must try to ensure that proper forums and programs are in place to achieve these ends. This paper will (1) discuss barriers between the homes and communities of urban African American students and their respective schools, (2) describe intervention programs that have successfully bridged the gaps between the mathematics taught in school and that emphasized in urban African American students' homes and communities, and (3) suggest ways that schools can form more productive alliances with urban African American students' families.

Throughout this article we will use the word *parents* to represent all primary caregivers of school-aged children. Primary caregivers include natural parents, foster parents, legal guardians, and others who have full parenting responsibilities.

BARRIERS TO PARENTAL AND COMMUNITY SUPPORT IN URBAN SETTINGS

Interactions between urban African American students' parents and their teachers are directly influenced by teachers' beliefs and expectations. In a study investigating elementary school teachers' attributions for students' school failure in a large metropolitan area, Irvine and York (1993) found that teachers attributed African American students' academic failure to lack of parental support. Such beliefs about African American students' parents often serve as barriers to teacher-parent contact. Furthermore, many teachers make assumptions on the basis of students' social or economic status as well as their ethnicity. These teachers believe that parents of low socioeconomic status are often lazy and unconcerned, and therefore do not make any contact with the students' parents.

Parents are usually called on only for reasons of discipline or other problems. They are hardly ever contacted to be praised. Furthermore, parents are often not encouraged to take an active role in their children's education. Jackson and Cooper (1989) assert that low-income parents quickly realize that their concerns are not welcomed during parent-teacher-organization meetings.

Some parents report that more contact with schools and teachers is desirable. Several factors, however, inhibit more-intensive participation. In particular, many urban African American students' parents often work during school hours and have difficulty getting time off to participate in school functions. Some parents do not have adequate transportation to reach schools when their children have been bused out of their neighborhoods. Other obstacles include parents' feeling unable to help their children with mathematics or other subjects that were particularly difficult for them in school, being unaware of the importance of parental involvement at all levels of their children's education, and not knowing how to facilitate learning at home.

SUCCESSFUL MATHEMATICS AND SCIENCE PROGRAMS INVOLVING FAMILIES

Several programs have been designed specifically to empower parents and help parents facilitate effective mathematics learning, with the ultimate goal of increasing the number of people qualified for quantitative fields. One program is the Governor's Minority College Awareness Program (MCAP) at the University of Kentucky in Lexington, Kentucky. The program is designed to prepare students in grades 4–12 for college mathematics and science.

The goals of the program are threefold. First, MCAP is designed to give students experiences that would help improve their mathematical, problem-solving, and written and verbal communication skills. Second, the program offers professional development for teachers so that they will feel better prepared to work with students from diverse backgrounds and equipped to teach lessons and use instructional strategies that are innovative and adaptable to different grade levels. The third goal is to develop workshops for parents so that they can be role models for their children, increase their involvement in their children's education, and become more knowledgeable about the mathematics and science curriculum.

The MCAP curriculum is designed to be adaptable to each level. Each lesson consists of problem-solving situations, concept explorations, evaluations of students' learning, and home-connection problems. To stimulate students' interest in a lesson on ratios and proportions, MCAP teachers gave students a chart comparing the lengths of body parts that have been found to be proportional. Students were given a measuring tape to explore some of the proportional body relationships.

Later, students participated in other activities designed to help them develop a conceptual understanding of ratios and proportions. In each one, students constructed a table of data based on the situation, generalized a rule to describe the data, and then plotted the data on coordinate axes. By comparing number patterns and graphs, students could see the difference between proportional and nonproportional situations. At the end of class, students were given home-connection problems similar to some of the problems worked in class. At home, students and their parents worked together to solve the problems. Students were told to explain to their parents how to solve the problems. They were encouraged to use objects at home to help make their explanations clearer.

As a result of the home-connection problems, parents requested tutorial sessions to help improve their own mathematics skills. The sessions enabled parents to become role models in that they too had actually become learners of mathematics.

What makes MCAP a successful intervention program? Cognizant of the barriers to parental involvement mentioned earlier, the designers of MCAP sought parental support by sending home-connection problems to parents so they could work with their children. In the partnership between MCAP directors and parents, the parents were not reluctant to ask for mathematics tutoring for themselves in order to help their children. Parents could converse with the school superintendent and other educators, who gladly apprised them of their parental rights to ensure their children's education.

Another program is Family Math, from the University of California at Berkeley. Family Math is designed to bring children and their parents together to learn and enjoy mathematics in a pleasant environment (Stenmark, Thompson, and Cossey 1986). During a Family Math class, "parents and their children learn strategies for solving problems and how mathematics is connected to everyday life and to different careers"

(Kreinberg 1989, p. 134). Parents and their children use hands-on materials to help them understand mathematics concepts. Family Math is usually taught by a teacher-parent team in a school, church, or community center over a period of several weeks. Parents receive overviews of the mathematics topics covered at their children's grade levels and explanations of how the Family Math activities relate to these topics. Family Math has been successful because it is community based; the mathematics is taught in a manner that is practical and useful to the parents and their children; and it has helped the parents become more aware of the mathematics their children are learning and how that mathematics will affect their children's present and future (Kreinberg 1989).

The Algebra Project is another successful program for bridging the gap between schools and minority parents. The Algebra Project was founded by Robert Moses, an African American parent concerned with the mathematics education of his children. Moses, a former secondary school mathematics teacher, was invited to assist his daughter's teacher in teaching eighth-grade algebra at a middle school in Cambridge, Massachusetts (Silva et al. 1990). A political activist, Moses transformed the assistance into a program that has enabled students who normally would not have been successful in algebra to become successful.

The Algebra Project has three major objectives (Silva et al. 1990). First, the project helps middle school learners become mathematically literate, competent, and motivated to master the college preparatory high school mathematics and science curriculum and the mathematics necessary for mathematics- and science-related careers. Next, it helps mathematics teachers construct learning environments in which mathematics is grounded in real-life experiences and in which students' social construction of mathematics is supported. Finally, the project brings together parents, community volunteers, and school administrators to build a broader community that understands that it takes the collective efforts of many to ensure students' learning.

The Algebra Project uses a five-step process to help students and parents understand algebra: (1) a physical event familiar to everyone in a particular setting, giving a relevant context for the mathematics, (2) a picture or model of the event, (3) a description of the event in intuitive (idiomatic) language, (4) a description of this event in regimented English, and (5) a symbolic representation of the event (Moses et al. 1989).

The Algebra Project raises parents' expectations about their children's abilities to do algebra, teaches algebra to parents so that they are able to help their children with their homework, and educates parents about school policies so that parents can have a greater voice in their children's education.

The Winburn Family Project is an academic-intervention collaboration between a small, local community and the University of Kentucky. This project was designed to develop mathematics skills while introducing parents and their children to a variety of cultures through multicultural literature.

For eight weeks, three African American families met weekly to read, discuss, and collaboratively solve mathematical problems embedded in culturally diverse texts.

The students ranged from age seven to age twelve (grades 2 through 6) and were accompanied by one or both parents. *The Hundred Penny Box*, written by Sharon B. Mathis (1986), was one of the stories used in the project. In this story a young African American male, Michael, has a special relationship with his great-great-aunt Dew, who lives with him. She has a box with one hundred pennies, each penny representing a special memory. Michael loves to sit and share in her memories. Mathematical situations are naturally present in *The Hundred Penny Box*. Most of the problem situations that we created were related to Aunt Dew, who is one hundred years old and has a penny dated for each year of her life.

The literature discussions provided a rich context for self-affirmation of the families' cultures in addition to serving as a viable means for constructing knowledge about other cultures. Parents showed an increase in their ability to ask meaningful questions when assisting their children and expanded their use of, and competence in, physical models as a means of helping their children and themselves to understand mathematical concepts better. During the weekly seminars, parents and children gained problem-solving skills as they interacted to create multiple solutions to a variety of situations in the stories.

These four effective programs have several characteristics in common: educating parents and their children, allowing parents to take an active role in their children's education, and bringing together a community of people to achieve a common goal. Therefore, these programs have shown that acknowledging parents and treating them as partners in their children's education can help ensure that students reach their full mathematics potential.

IMPLICATIONS AND CONCLUSIONS

It is important that educators provide parents with opportunities to be involved in their children's mathematics education. We have highlighted four programs that have successfully involved parents and given them an opportunity to play important roles in their children's mathematics education. Here, we offer suggestions for positive, active family involvement in mathematics education.

How can teachers encourage and support parental involvement in their mathematics classroom? First, they must **R**ealize and acknowledge that parents desire to become valued participants rather than merely tolerated observers in their children's education. Second, parental involvement needs to be **E**xperiential to facilitate the creation of learning communities of students and their parents. Teachers and administrators should provide opportunities for parents and their children to work together to learn mathematics on a regular basis. During these sessions, teachers can serve as facilitators and role models. As a facilitator, the teacher provides the problems and the materials to solve them. As a role model, the teacher demonstrates what types of questions and actions on objects should occur to effect learning.

Further, parental involvement needs to be Socially relevant so that both parents and children can recognize the connections between their involvement in the microsociety of the school and the larger macrosociety. Parents as Partners is the key to facilitating academic success. Throughout each of the programs highlighted here, it is evident that the parents and the educators became partners in pursuit of academic excellence for the students. Mutual Empowerment of parents and educators must be evident in this partnership to ensure success. When parents feel empowered to effect positive change in their children's academic performance, they no longer feel like unwelcomed onlookers who are merely tolerated but rather like valued members of the team whose mission is to ensure success for their children. Collaborative Communities of learners should evolve from this active participation. Such a community is likely to ensure that the educational processes undertaken are not confined to the classroom but instead extended to include real-life situations and circumstances. Finally, it is imperative that parental involvement be Timely. Parental involvement needs to be proactive rather than reactive and should be incorporated throughout the educational process. Implementing the suggestions above will result in a working environment that epitomizes **RESPECT** for parents and teachers.

REFERENCES

Irvine, Jacqueline, and Darlene E. York. "Differences in Teacher Attributions of School Failure for African-American, Hispanic, and Vietnamese Students." Paper presented at the annual meeting of the American Education Research Association, Emory University, Atlanta, Ga.,12–17 April 1993.

Jackson, Barbara L., and Bruce S. Cooper. "Parent Choice and Empowerment: New Roles for Parents." *Urban Education* 24 (October 1989): 263–86.

Kreinberg, Nancy. "The Practice of Equity." *Peabody Journal of Education* 66 (1989): 127–46.

Mathis, Sharon B. *The Hundred Penny Box*. New York: Puffin Books, 1986.

Moses, Robert P., Mieko Kamii, Susan M. Swap, and Jeffrey Howard. "The Algebra Project: Organizing in the Spirit of Ella." *Harvard Educational Review* 59 (November 1989): 423–43.

Silva, Cynthia M., Robert P. Moses, Jacqueline Rivers, and Parker Johnson. "The Algebra Project: Making Middle School Mathematics Count." *The Journal of Negro Education* 59 (1990): 375–91.

Stenmark, Jean Kerr, Virginia Thompson, and Ruth Cossey. *Family Math*. Berkeley, Calif.: EQUALS, 1986.

27

The Complexity of Teaching for Gender Equity

Rebecca Ambrose

Linda Levi

Elizabeth Fennema

Throughout our careers we have been concerned with gender equity in mathematics education. Our collective experience includes many years of learning, teaching, and researching in classrooms. We have seen shifts both in society and in the mathematics education community. With these shifts and experiences our visions of ideal classrooms for girls have evolved.

In the past, we were concerned with girls' lack of participation in upper-level mathematics classes. We believed that if we could only get girls to enroll in advanced mathematics classes, things would change. This goal has been achieved and, on the average, girls and boys are taking the same number of secondary school courses in mathematics and science. Although we are encouraged by this statistic, we continue to be concerned that boys still have an advantage over girls on achievement test scores in mathematics and science (Hoffer et al. 1995). We are also concerned that women continue to be underrepresented in science and engineering occupations, constituting only 22 percent of all science and engineering workers and 9 percent of all engineers (National Science Foundation 1994).

We thought that gender equity could be achieved by gender-blind practices in the classroom. This belief grew out of what appeared to be preferential treatment of boys in classrooms, with teachers paying more attention to boys than to girls. We thought that if only teachers would treat students as individuals, treating all students equally, then gender equity would be achieved. We have come to believe that this is not enough. We now believe that in order for gender equity to be attained, teachers will have to attend to it directly in their classrooms. Teaching mathematics in a manner consistent with the ideas in the NCTM *Standards* (1989) without this specific attention to gender equity will not necessarily ensure that gender equity will be attained.

We are totally committed to gender equity and believe that it needs to be a central concern for teachers, but we are still uncertain about how it will be achieved. When we try to envision a gender-equitable classroom, our vision is blurred—blurred because we are torn between an idealistic stance and a pragmatic stance. Our idealist stance grows out of a conviction that the world should value women's ways of knowing and doing as much as men's and that feminine approaches to knowledge and social interactions should be nurtured in schools. Our pragmatic stance grows out of a realization that the world today values masculine approaches to knowledge and social interactions and that if a female is to succeed in a traditionally male-dominated field, her school experience should give her access to masculine approaches to knowledge and social interactions.

We propose a scheme to help teachers reflect on the decisions they make about solving problems of gender inequities that exist in their classrooms. This scheme is a continuum that parallels our pragmatic and idealistic stances. At one end of the continuum, teachers make decisions to address gender inequities by changing the mathematics classroom for girls. At the other end of the continuum, teachers make decisions to change girls by helping them acquire skills or beliefs that will enable them to communicate and compete in the society as it is. In short, at one end the teaching changes, and at the other end the girls are encouraged to change.

Several examples might serve to explain this scheme further. On the one hand, a teacher might say,

> I disagree with the use of competitive games to teach mathematics. Many of my girls don't like to compete with their friends; they don't feel good when they appear smart at the expense of making one of their friends appear stupid. I value these girls' feelings, so I never use competitive games to teach mathematics.

This teacher wants to change the mathematics situation (competitive games) rather than change the girls (to make them more willing to compete). This statement tends to fall toward the idealistic side of the continuum. On the other hand, let's suppose a teacher said,

> Many of the girls I teach don't believe that mathematics will be a large part of their professional futures. They tell me that their mothers and other women they know say they do not use much mathematics in their jobs. Since I know that women are underrepresented in mathematics-related fields, I understand where these girls get their ideas from. However, I believe that women should participate in these fields that are currently male dominated. There is nothing about these fields that makes them unsuitable for women. It is my job as a teacher to convince girls that they will be happy and fulfilled if they pursue mathematics-related careers.

This statement tends to fall toward the pragmatic end of the continuum. The teacher sees her or his role as that of helping girls to change (to see that mathematics-related careers are for them) and not changing the mathematics situation (there is nothing about these fields that makes them unsuitable for women).

The two examples presented above fall toward one end of the continuum or the other. We realize that teachers often make decisions that fall in the middle of the continuum. We also realize that the same teacher might make a decision about one situation that falls toward one end of the continuum while making a decision about a different situation that falls toward the other end of the continuum.

Whichever stance teachers might take, we advocate that they pay particular attention to gender equity in their teaching. This attention involves looking for patterns, monitoring interactions, recognizing differences in achievement or beliefs, and correlating interest and activity. Once patterns are discerned, the teacher must become a problem solver and determine what to do. Because of the uniqueness of each classroom, it is impossible for an outsider to prescribe teaching that will ensure gender equity. We believe that equity can be attained only if each teacher generates solutions for the specific pattern of inequities that exist in her or his classroom.

We mentioned before that our vision of a gender-equitable classroom is blurred because we are torn between an idealistic and a pragmatic stance. It is further blurred because mathematics teaching is currently in a state of flux. Teachers are changing their practice in response to the NCTM *Standards*. As teachers change their practice, some gender-equity issues will be diminished at the same time that new gender-equity issues will arise. Some of the new approaches suggested by the *Standards* documents will entail new gender-equity dilemmas for teachers. We will present some of the dilemmas and then use our scheme to suggest alternative strategies for addressing these dilemmas.

DISCOURSE AND DEBATE

The kinds of classroom discussions envisioned in the *Standards* involve students in arguing, questioning, and disagreeing—in other words, debating. Students present ideas and endeavor to convince their peers of their claims. The peers are expected to listen critically and to refute claims they deduce are faulty. Below, we outline some dilemmas that arise out of using discussion as an instructional tool in the classroom and suggest responses that fall along the continuum from changing the student (pragmatic) to changing class structures (idealistic) in order to accommodate different students' orientations.

Dilemma 1: Participation

We do not doubt that students who engage in this sort of debate will learn from the experience, even though there is little research to support it. We wonder, however, if all students will readily engage in debate. Some students, often female, are uncomfortable with disagreement. They might decline to contest friends' claims because they do not want to have their friends' weaknesses exposed or to jeopardize relationships. Other students might not participate because they are not confident enough about their understandings to feel comfortable explaining their ideas. Some may lack the self-esteem required to speak publicly about anything (American Association of University Women 1992). Several teachers have told us that when they promote debate in their classroom, boys are more likely to participate than girls (Levi 1995). If learning depends on participating in discussions, then the nonparticipants would be at a disadvantage.

A teacher faced with the challenge of having students who do not participate in discussion might try a strategy somewhere along the continuum illustrated below. This continuum maps onto the pragmatic-idealistic continuum discussed earlier.

Help all participants gain the skills they need to participate.	Make discourse less confrontational.

Supporting the participation of all students reflects a pragmatic stance and would mean that the teacher focuses on helping students get beyond the discomfort they feel with public debate. For example, a teacher might work individually with a student outside mathematics class so that the student could practice explaining her or his point of view. During class time, the teacher might call on students in some systematic way so that all students would participate. Each student might know in advance that she or he was expected to make an argument or present a solution. This orientation reflects a belief that framing arguments and publicly defending them are important skills for all students.

An alternative response that reflects an idealistic stance to this challenge involves creating alternative forums for discussions—forums that are less confrontational or more private. Students might present their arguments in writing rather than orally. They might discuss problems in small groups rather than in the whole group. The teacher might explore ways to reorient whole-group discussion so it is less of a debate and more of a sharing of emergent ideas. The discussion period could be a time when incomplete understandings and partial knowledge are expressed and then built upon. Students would not need to be definite or certain and could express doubts about their knowledge. Rather than change the students to make them more comfortable with public argument, the debate is changed into a conversation.

Dilemma 2: Peer Affiliation

Another dilemma that a teacher might face is having students who participate but base their agreement or disagreement with an argument not on the mathematics involved but rather on their peer affiliation. We can imagine a student saying, "I think Chris is right because Chris is always right." A teacher's strategy might fall somewhere along this continuum:

Encourage autonomy and independence.	Take advantage of peer affiliation.

Encouraging autonomy and independence is a pragmatic response to this dilemma and includes some of the strategies mentioned for encouraging participation. In addition, the teacher could directly address some students' reluctance to disagree with their friends by doing some activities with the students that demonstrate people's natural tendencies to want to agree with their friends. The class could then discuss these activities and talk about the importance of having one's own ideas rather than just agreeing with friends. The teacher could then remind students of this activity when they seem to agree with an argument on the basis of friendship.

The alternative strategy of taking advantage of peer affiliation is an idealistic response and might involve having students solve problems and frame arguments as groups rather than as individuals. These groups may even be student-selected to capitalize on existing peer affiliations, since capitalizing on peer affiliation would reflect a belief that cooperation is as important if not more important than independence and autonomy.

Dilemma 3: Listening

In order to learn from group discussion, students must listen to one another. Girls are often perceived as better listeners than boys (Levi 1995). Although boys tend to dominate the discussions, girls are often better able to summarize what has been said and to learn from other students. One teacher observed,

> I would prefer it if my boys were more passive—and not so aggressive and so argumentative—because they close their ears to listening to other opinions. So now, when I'm working with these groups, it's the boys that are having the hard time because their minds are closed. They're thinking, "My way is right." ... So I want to open up the boys' channels to other possibilities of thinking.

In regard to our pragmatic and idealistic stances, valuing listening reflects our idealistic stance and passively accepting the lack of listening by boys reflects our pragmatic stance. This is an instance where a teacher might encourage the boys to change rather than the girls.

To remedy this gender difference, strategies would fall along this continuum:

Summarize and repeat students' comments.	Help students develop listening skills.

A teacher who takes a pragmatic stance acknowledges that not all students listen well and does not require students to become better listeners. This teacher might reiterate students' statements, giving other students a second opportunity to hear the argument. Another alternative would be to ask the student to repeat the argument until it is clear or to ask another student to reframe the argument.

A teacher who takes an idealistic stance would want to promote listening in all students. This teacher might choose never to reiterate students' comments so that students have to listen to one another. The listening expectation might have to be made explicit to the students, and the teacher might have to come up with mechanisms to hold students accountable for this. The teacher might occasionally stop the class and have everyone write about what has been discussed.

CONCLUSIONS

We have attempted to illuminate the challenges inherent in using discussion as a focus of instruction in mathematics classrooms. We presented strategies for overcoming the challenges and suggested the assumptions underlying those strategies. We chose to articulate these strategies because we think that it is important for teachers to reflect on their personal stances toward equity. Their stances affect their decisions, and their decisions reveal their stances. Addressing gender equity in the mathematics classroom is a complex process. Since the forces shaping mathematics education are in a constant state of change, teachers will continually be facing new gender-equity dilemmas. Analyzing their own stances toward equity will help teachers decide how to address these ever-changing dilemmas. We have faith that reflective teachers will generate effective strategies for overcoming gender-equity dilemmas in their mathematics classrooms.

As feminists interested in empowering young women, we are constantly moving back and forth along our continua—vacillating back and forth between our idealistic and pragmatic stances. We would love to see mathematics classes where all students'—girls' as well as boys'—attitudes, predilections, and ways of knowing are affirmed. We also recognize that in the world today some approaches to problems and interactions are valued over others. We don't want to see girls disadvantaged because their approaches are not valued. We are afraid that if we simply reorient our classes to accommodate their styles, then girls will not develop the skills required to operate in the real world. So we often find ourselves trying strategies on both ends of the continua we outlined. We envision classrooms where all students have forums for comfortable participation and where all students are challenged to work in situations that are less familiar.

REFERENCES

American Association of University Women. *The AAUW Report: How Schools Shortchange Girls.* Washington, D.C.: American Association of University Women/National Education Association, 1992.

Hoffer, Thomas B., Kenneth A. Rasinski, Whitney Moore, and NORC. *Statistics in Brief.* NCES 95-206. Washington, D.C.: National Center for Education Statistics, U.S. Department of Education, Office of Educational Research and Improvement, 1995.

Levi, Linda. "Teachers' Beliefs about Gender Equity in Mathematics." Paper presented at the annual meeting of the American Educational Research Association, San Francisco, April 1995.

National Council of Teachers of Mathematics. *Curriculum and Evaluation Standards for School Mathematics.* Reston, Va.: National Council of Teachers of Mathematics, 1989.

National Science Foundation. *Women, Minorities and Persons with Disabilities in Science and Engineering.* Arlington, Va.: National Science Foundation, 1994.

28

Diversity, Equity, and Peace
From Dream to Reality

Ubiratan D'Ambrosio

Some people say that violence and war cannot be ended because they are part of our natural biology. We say that is not true. People used to say that slavery and domination by race and sex were part of our biology. Some people even claimed they could prove these things scientifically. We know they are wrong. Slavery has been ended and now the world is working to end domination by race and sex.

—United Nations Educational, Scientific, and Cultural Organization,
The Seville Statement on Violence

THE QUOTATION above is taken from the introduction to *The Seville Statement on Violence,* a proposal for a better world, written in 1986 for the International Year of Peace and sponsored by several scientists from all over the world. In the booklet introducing and discussing the published version of *The Seville Statement* (Adams 1991, p. 41), we read the following:

> As a teacher you can be a role model by taking action yourself and telling your students about what you have done [to attain these goals]. You can also tell your students about actions for peace by other role models [who influenced *The Seville Statement,* such as Martin Luther King, Jr., Margaret Mead, Mahatma Gandhi, and Albert Einstein].

To end domination by race and sex and to achieve peace in all its dimensions is the essence of my dream. I consider my role as a mathematics educator absolutely compatible with my dream. Otherwise, I would rather spend my energy in another professional practice.

No one will disclaim that as mathematics educators we must teach mathematics. But we must also join the forces of those who are struggling to end domination by race and sex and consequently to end violence and war. Peace in all its dimensions, that is, not only military peace but also interior peace, social peace, and environmental peace, is intrinsically associated with nondiscrimination by sex, race, and culture. To achieve peace means to live with dignity, which implies an atmosphere of diversity and equity.

I invite all mathematics teachers to work for a more essential goal than merely to transmit mathematical knowledge: the survival of the human species and full dignity for all. Discrimination by race, sex, and culture negates dignity.

Some critics will say that these issues have nothing to do with our practice as mathematics educators. It is easy to recognize in their arguments the underlying claim that mathematics is not related to culture. They say that we should teach well and see that our students learn good mathematics but that to develop values is a matter for another discipline.

A look into modern theories of cognition and into history offers an alternative perspective. Multicultural mathematics education is one response to these issues. Ethnomathematics grew out of these concerns.

MATHEMATICS IN THE EDUCATIONAL SYSTEMS

Mathematics is taught to every child in all the school systems of the world. Unlike language, reading, and writing—which are taught differently in different nations—dress—since different cultures dress differently—and even nourishment—because different cultures have different cuisines—the same mathematics is taught to everyone all over the world. Mathematics has become the only cultural manifestation that is unquestionably universal. Of course, some cultures—that in a deprecating tone are labeled primitive—have different styles of counting, measuring, sorting, and inferring. But these styles, when recognized and even when incorporated into the school systems, are regarded as traditional practices and put in the category of folklore, not mathematics. At best they serve as bridges to the teaching of "school mathematics," that is, Western mathematics. For a school to be "real," "real" mathematics must be part of the program.

The important World Conference on Education for All, which took place in Jomtien, Thailand, in 1990, addressed three main goals for education:

1. The acquisition of knowledge, attitudes, and values that allow every human being to survive and engage in society and to attain full citizenship

2. Equity in gender, ethnicity, age, religion, and belief. Equity must be made a priority beginning in early childhood. Schooling should include such broad issues as health, nutrition, and peace, understood in its several dimensions: internal peace, social peace, environmental peace, and military peace.

3. The development of effective strategies to realize these goals in school systems and to generate human and financial resources for change

The results and recommendations of the Jomtien conference have been published by the United Nations Educational, Scientific, and Cultural Organization and constitute a basic book on equity (Haggis, Fordham, and Windham 1991).

MATHEMATICS AND ETHICS

We live in a global world. The economy is global, production is becoming increasingly global, communications systems are interconnected, and major political decisions are not taken unilaterally. But people continue to speak different languages, eat and dress differently, and adhere to different religions. Such diversity is normally seen as indicating that schools respect different cultures, but schools expect students to learn the same mathematics, arguing that otherwise students can hardly operate in the modern world. This practice may lead to the conclusion that language, dress, food, and religion are culturally influenced behaviors but mathematics is not! This distorted view, supported by many current histories and philosophies of mathematics, leads us to look into the concept of ethnomathematics and its pedagogical implications.

The entire modern world has been plagued by inequities involving race, gender, culture, economics, and religion. All these inequities play a role in suggesting that some people are more evolved, some are more intelligent, some are more civilized, some have more and are entitled to more material comforts, and that some are favored by their gods. In short, some people feel they are better and deserve more than others. This attitude has been an intrinsic feature of modern occidental philosophy and has been the tenor of the development of modern science. The turning point of modern thought, and hence of the modern world, is easily traced to the mathematization of culture.

Little has been done by historians to relate these issues. Particularly among historians of mathematics, these issues are usually disregarded—or avoided.

Mathematics education leaves no room for a critical look at the origin, rise, and expansion of the current domination of other modes of thought by mathematics. Similarly, no one questions whether mathematics has anything to do with inequities or with the accepted practice of aggression against the different.

ETHNOMATHEMATICS AND MULTICULTURAL MATHEMATICS

Multicultural education can be successful and give more than lip service to equity and diversity if it recognizes that the practices and perceptions of learners are the substratum on which new knowledge is built. Thus it has to be constructed on the individual and cultural history of the learner and has to recognize the diversity of extant cultures that are present in specific communities. At the same time, a new historical attitude is needed that recognizes the contribution of past cultures in building up the modern world and modern thought. We are making progress toward another approach to languages, to history and geography, and to the arts. But scientists, and particularly mathematicians, are resisting.

Encounters with other peoples and other cultures all over the planet after the great navigations of the sixteenth century led us to identify mathematical practices and mathematical ideas—mainly those relating to measurement, counting, classifications, and modeling—in every culture. In many instances—for example, in ancient India and the Mediterranean civilizations—mutual influences are noticeable and have been well known since antiquity. In other instances, no mutual influences are discernible, but there is a remarkable coincidence of practices, results, and even ideas. In all these instances, however, equally remarkable differences are noticeable, which leads us to consider many different "mathematics."

We are increasingly recognizing different "forms of doing mathematics" or different "practices of a mathematical nature" or, even better, "mathematical practices of a different form" or "mathematics of a different style." But we must also recognize different theoretical frameworks or philosophical systems that support these practices and into which they fit.

In the daily practice of a school teacher, opportunities for experiencing multiculturalism abound. Observe the way children count and perform the very elementary operations (e.g., 3 + 4): most of them will use fingers, but others will draw tally marks.

What can the teacher do in this situation? From the multicultural standpoint, the teacher can learn from the student. The important point is to create a learning environment in the classroom in which the teacher recognizes that the student has preexisting knowledge, mainly knowledge based on cultural practices. The classroom is a place for the teacher also to acquire knowledge.

Some topics can be treated by using examples from other cultures. For instance, in dealing with numbers, the study of number systems from African and Chinese traditions and from pre-Columbian cultures may be very attractive to students of African, Chinese, and Latin American descent. Such approaches, however, risk limiting multiculturalism to non-European cultures, which is subtly discriminatory behavior. Equally attractive multicultural examples can be drawn from cultural differences among Europeans. People of various European cultures differ from one another, just as Africans and Chinese do.

Language and mathematics are closely associated. As an example, in the French language "twenty" plays an important role: eighty is "quatre-vingt," that is, 4×20. Why? And in English, eleven and twelve are also interesting cases. Why don't we say, "oneteen" and "twoteen"? The teacher does not have to know the answer to present a rewarding educational experience using these facts.

In fact, in multicultural education the teacher can answer only a few questions. But it is important to raise issues and to let the students explore their cultural past and present. A very important result of multicultural education is a change in teachers' attitudes toward knowledge. It is absolutely necessary that teachers adopt a posture of learning from their students.

Ethnographic methods must be part of both preservice and in-service teacher education. Everyday occurrences can be excellent subjects for research. For example, the activities of nearby stores in a community and family discussions about grocery costs can suggest excellent themes for ethnographic research. A number of examples, with a focus on equality and justice, are given by Shan and Bailey (1991). Although literature on this subject is growing, it is regrettably not well known to mathematics educators.

ACTION IN THE CLASSROOM

It is a mistake to believe that the only resources available for introducing cultural issues into the mathematics classroom are practices and objects related to popular culture. Indeed, teachers should not see themselves as folklore animators. Of course, no possible motivation should be overlooked. Students' major motivation nowadays is high technology. Is it possible to integrate cultures with technology? Multicultural education can be instrumental in meeting this major challenge for the mathematics educator. Teacher educators will have to pay more attention to preparing teachers to assume their role as facilitator of a learning environment in which the teacher is no longer the main provider of knowledge. Authentic learning environments, using networks, CD-ROMs, and future technologies, are necessarily multicultural.

In a very interesting paper, Graf (1995) presents the history of numbers in several cultures as examples of attempts to develop information processing. He emphasizes the algorithms of coding and decoding instead of treating number systems from different cultures as mere curiosities, as frequently seen in classrooms. Teague and Clarke (1995), who have done considerable work in gender-based factors in computer science, have summarized that work in the article "The Failure of the Education System to Attract Girls to Formal Informatics Studies."

How can we bring the considerations above to our classroom practice? This question is at the same time essential and tricky. By giving a number of examples, we risk teachers' reproducing and using examples out of context in their classes. The most important feature of multicultural mathematics is to let students' motivation to do mathematics grow out of the natural cultural environment. Mathematical explorations should be generated by discussions among the students. Also, the sophistication of the mathematical concepts and skills—what we might call the contents—necessary to deal with the problems depends entirely on the overall aspirations of the students and the difficulty of the problems posed by the group.

Whereas the teacher's usual working strategy focuses on objectives, contents, and methodology in developing a topic in the mathematics program, my proposal for a new concept of curriculum is based on motivation, contents, and execution. This concept lends itself naturally to an interdisciplinary approach. Changes of paradigms are affecting all sectors of human activity, including mathematics education. Interdisciplinarity is a modest change of paradigms, absolutely within the reach of mathematics educators. For a good introduction, with a copious bibliography, see Klein (1990).

The application of mathematics to environmental issues in elementary and high school gives a good example of the need for an interdisciplinary approach (D'Ambrosio 1994). This need arises because many of the initiatives to create new mathematics involving new, real-world problems come from people who are neither mathematicians nor mathematics educators. Thus, interdisciplinarity results naturally when we deal with environmental issues. The social component, always involved in important discussions of environmental issues, is probably one of the most important components in reorganizing school mathematics for greater diversity, equity, and peace.

REFERENCES

Adams, David, ed. *The Seville Statement on Violence: Preparing the Ground for the Constructing of Peace.* Paris: United Nations Educational, Scientific, and Cultural Organization, 1991.

D'Ambrosio, Ubiratan. "On Environmental Mathematics Education." *Zentralblatt für Didaktik der Mathematik* 94 (1994): 171–74.

Graf, Klaus. "Promoting Interdisciplinary and Intercultural Intentions through the History of Informatics." In *Integrating Information Technology into Education,* edited by Deryn Watson and David Tinsley, pp. 139–50. London: IFIP/Chapman Hall, 1995.

Haggis, Sheila M., Paul Fordham, and Douglas M. Windham, eds. *Education for All.* Paris: United Nations Educational, Scientific, and Cultural Organization, 1991.

Klein, Julie Thompson. *Interdisciplinarity: History, Theory, and Practice.* Detroit, Mich.: Wayne State University Press, 1990.

Shan, Sharan-Jeet, and Peter Bailey. *Multiple Factors: Classroom Mathematics for Equality and Justice.* Staffordshire: Trentham Books, 1991.

Teague, Joy, and Valerie Clarke. "The Failure of the Education System to Attract Girls to Formal Informatics Studies." In *Integrating Information Technology into Education,* edited by Deryn Watson and David Tinsley. London: IFIP/Chapman Hall, 1995.